C000173764

Doing Theology in Alt

Also by Kenneth Leech:

Drugs and Pastoral Care
Soul Friend
The Eye of the Storm
The Sky Is Red
Through Our Long Exile
We Preach Christ Crucified

Doing Theology in Altab Ali Park

A project in Whitechapel, East London
1990–2004

KENNETH LEECH

DARTON · LONGMAN + TODD

First published in 2006 by
Darton, Longman and Todd Ltd
1 Spencer Court
140–142 Wandsworth High Street
London SW18 4JJ

ISBN–10: 0–232–52571–4
ISBN–13: 978–0–232–52571–7

A catalogue record for this book is available from the British Library.

Typeset by YHT Ltd, London
Printed and bound in Great Britain by Page Bros, Norwich, Norfolk

London feels different today. It is quieter. Those who have a choice have left the city. The East London Mosque is deserted, between prayers. Two women pass within a couple of feet of each other in Altab Ali Park: one in a black burqa, carrying a shopping bag; the other in shorts and a T-shirt, sitting in the dusty grass, drinking cider from a can while she waits for a bus. The 205, when it comes, is busy downstairs, but there is a not a soul in the upper deck. We pass Aldgate station, where bloody, blackened victims staggered out two weeks ago. They left eight dead behind. The iron gates are open just a little, and in the gloom an Underground worker sits by a makeshift desk, waiting for stray passengers to ask for travel advice. That looks like a lonely job.

COLE MORETON, 'Attacks on London',
Independent on Sunday, 24th July 2005

Spitalfields and the City of London outwardly symbolise the huge contrasts between poverty and wealth existing in Britain at the end of the twentieth century.

EVE GREGORY AND ANN WILLIAMS,
*City Literacies: learning to read across generations
and cultures,* Routledge 2000, p. xv

Contents

Introduction

This book is an account of ministry from 1990 to 2004 when I worked as a community-based theologian in Whitechapel in the East End of London. I was closely involved with the East End for over forty-six years, and most of my adult life and ministry was spent there. I have written and published a good deal already about the area and about work within it. The present study differs from earlier works (although there is some inevitable overlap) in that I have tried to reflect on this particular experiment in 'local theology', both year by year and thematically, though dates and themes are all mixed up together. I have done my best not to repeat material from earlier books except where it is essential in order for the reader to make sense of what I am saying. Some of the chapters are very short: Chapters 3 (on liturgy), 6 (on prayer), 7 (on secularisation and religion), 9 (on the Cross) and 12 (on darkness) in particular. This is *emphatically not* because I regard these themes as less important, but because I have tried to focus mainly on the urban work as it developed, and because I have written extensively on the above themes elsewhere. However, I felt that I needed to attend to them within these pages, and to have omitted them would have left a seriously diminished and misleading picture.[1]

'Whatever happens, you must not leave East London,' wrote Lesley Barlow, then Head Teacher of Bonner Primary School in Bethnal Green on 15th October 1990. I didn't then, but I have done so now. This book, in fact, began to be written as I left East London, and as the project which I and others had created ended. As I look back over these years, I find it is a record of failure and disappointment, of uncertainty, confusion and frustration, of darkness and perplexity, as well as of joy, fulfilment and creativity, excitement, stimulation, solidarity in struggle, and, I think and trust, growth for many of us in the knowledge and love of God and the people. I left happily, open to the possibilities of a new phase in my life, but also with a sense that so much of what I had, perhaps naïvely, hoped to achieve had not been achieved, and with a feeling of incompleteness. Yet to be part of the organism which is the Body of Christ and of the movement which is the Kingdom of God is to share in collective work, and I am confident that others will carry on and develop theological work in these neighbourhoods and beyond them.

My geographical base for the work was of the greatest importance. The building, No 2 Whitechurch Lane, which provided my home and working base from 1993 to 2004, was once the clergy house of St Mary's Whitechapel (the original 'white chapel' of St Mary Matfelon from the fourteenth century) and stands at the point where two busy main roads – Whitechapel Road and Commercial Road – move towards convergence. Six major bus routes are within minutes of the building, while Aldgate East underground station is so close as to have been in effect our neighbour. I know of no other building owned by the church in East London which is so strategically placed for pastoral work. It would be difficult to imagine a site more convenient for gathering people from all parts of the area, and it is hardly surprising that a former Mayor of Tower Hamlets, Arthur Downes, was heard to comment that it was far more accessible than the Town Hall.

My impression has been that the officials – bishops and other bureaucrats – of the Diocese of London, who own the property, have never had the imagination, and, almost certainly, the necessary local knowledge, to use it to its maximum pastoral effect. At various points since the 1940s, it has housed the Children's Department of the London County Council, a firm of solicitors, the Design and Artists' Copyright Society, a Post Office, and, most recently, the now defunct St Botolph's Project, a leading group in the field of homelessness. (The scandal of its demise, as far as I am aware, still awaits a proper, public and independent investigation and report.) Yet there is no building in the whole of East London which is so accessible by train and bus. So while I am immensely grateful to the former and present Bishop of London for allowing me to use part of it for my work, I am sad that the Diocese has never, of its own initiative, realised the potential of this building and acted on it. Nor, however, has there, to my knowledge, been much, if any, pressure from Christians in the East End to do so. Since I left – and at the time of writing I still have the key! – the building stands abandoned and unused. My guess is that, after some lapse of time, the Diocese will ignore its pastoral potential and simply lease it to the highest commercial bidder. I hope I am wrong, but suspect I am right. The story could be repeated all over London and no doubt elsewhere: it reflects structurally a massive failure of imaginative vision at the heart of the Church's life.

The original church of St Mary Matfelon was made of white brick, and the local people named it the 'white chapel'. This later gave the name to two major roads, Whitechapel Road and Brick Lane, and one small street, Whitechurch Lane. The bricks were carried from a Roman cemetery in Spitalfields, southward to the site of the new church, and the route became known as Brick Lane. The church was burnt down in the eighteenth century and rebuilt. It was burnt down again in the nineteenth century and rebuilt, but then bombed in 1940, when the parish was dissolved and reabsorbed into the parish of St Dunstan, Stepney, out of which it had been created. For many years, probably since the early nineteenth century, the churchyard, now a park, was known locally as 'Itchy Park' because of the numbers of homeless people who slept there, and of the presence of many lice and fleas. Many older residents still use that term. However, in May 1978, a young Bengali clothing worker, Altab Ali, was murdered as he crossed the park to vote in the local elections. As a result, the park was renamed Altab Ali Park, and ornamental gates were erected in his memory. I was very honoured to be asked to take part in the dedication of these gates. I think that Sue Carlyle, then a Labour councillor, and I were the only non-Bengali people to be involved in this moving event.

Some years later a monument, Kendrio Shaheed Minar, the Martyrs' Monument, was erected in the park to commemorate the martyrs of the Bengali language movement. On 21st February 1952, seven Bengali students had been killed by the Pakistani army during a protest at the imposition of Urdu as the only national language in Pakistan. It was this imposition, and the attack on the Bengali language, which eventually led to the War of Independence and the emergence of Bangladesh as a nation in 1971. The original monument is in the University of Dhaka and has been called 'the foremost symbol of the Bengali nation'. The 21st February became a day of immense symbolic importance, referred to as *amader ekushey*, 'our 21st'. In Altab Ali Park too, on 21st February each year, Bengali Language Movement Day, flowers are placed at the monument there.

This park is a very important site for many people, not least for me, for many years its only legal resident. Many political demonstrations begin or end there, and there have been regular commemorations of

Altab Ali and vigils for the victims of racial violence. The park has on occasions been a focus for territorial conflicts among rival drug gangs. Drug deals take place there, homeless people still sleep there from time to time, and, more recently, a block of flats has been built on the south side overlooking the park. By 2004 I was no longer the park's only resident.

Very early in the theology project's life, it became clear to me how crucial is geographical position to the course of any contextual work. How we see things depends to a large extent on where we stand. For the early part of the work I was based in the crypt of St Botolph's Church, Aldgate, a location which led some to call me the 'cryptic theologian'. That base had distinct advantages in terms of co-operative work. At that time the church staff and the workers in the Crypt Project with homeless people were very much a team, working together, sharing much work and many people in common. It was wonderful to be part of this interdisciplinary team in an open-plan space. But my Bengali friends, who lived on the other side of Middlesex Street, the boundary between the City of London and the London Borough of Tower Hamlets, and other East End people, invariably got lost trying to find me, or were reluctant to make the journey at all. 'The City' was alien and unfamiliar territory, and Middlesex Street was a major dividing line, although there is a small Bengali community in the City itself. The 'divide' at Middlesex Street is even more marked today. Geographical location is a crucial part, though only a part, of what we mean by contextual and local theology. It is significant that, in recent years, 'psychogeography' (a term first used around 1953 by some early Situationists) has become an important influence on artists, town planners, and students of urban space.

One building of great importance, which closed after 113 years in July 2005, was Whitechapel Library, located a few yards from me on the opposite side of Whitechapel High Street. This building, now absorbed into the adjacent Whitechapel Art Gallery, played a key educational role, particularly for the Jewish population. Many Jewish students have testified to the crucial place of Whitechapel Library in inspiring them and setting them on a life of study and creative writing. The whole area of 'informal education' figured largely in my work during these years, and I have said more about it in Chapter 10.

What follows is a record of work in a very small urban, inner-city area, yet an area which is profoundly global, housing both the financial centre of the City, and the largest Bengali community in the world outside of Bangladesh and the Indian subcontinent. I have tried at least to identify, if not always develop, many of the challenges which confronted a Christian theologian in this place. I hope it will be of use to others both in the inner cities and elsewhere.

As I left the East End, St Botolph's Project — the charity which was based at the church for many years, and in the Altab Ali Park building for several years, and worked with homeless people — had collapsed and gone into liquidation. As I began to write these words, the liquidators were at work in the rooms below me. It was all desperately sad. The Project grew out of work which began with volunteers in the late 1950s when I first came here. The first paid worker was Terry Drummond in 1976. By 1990, when my work began, the staff of the Project was about 13, and by the time Malcolm Johnson left in 1992, it was over 30. By the time of the collapse I guess it was around 75. It was this work, begun by George Appleton in 1957, and massively developed by Malcolm Johnson (1974–92), which made St Botolph's known throughout the country. There was a close and co-operative relationship between the congregation, the homeless people (some of whom were members of the congregation) and, later, the paid workers. Over the last decade the links between the church and the Project became much weaker, though the continued use of the name of St Botolph's confused many people into thinking that there was an explicitly Christian dimension, and even some theological input, to the work. That had not been true for a while. Like many projects which had grown out of the Christian community, it became increasingly secular, which was welcomed by some and regretted by others. Some of the Project workers wanted the name changed in order to emphasise this fact, but that never happened. The idea had also grown up, not least in theological colleges, that St Botolph's was on the 'cutting edge', a radical voice, a pioneering community, in a way which also had not been so for some time. Such is the power of mythology.

As with all my work, I am grateful to many others. My main debt here is to those who were members of my support group during the years described, friends and colleagues at St Botolph's, Aldgate, and a wider advisory panel. Their names are listed in Appendix 1. I am especially grateful for the love, help, solidarity and support of Kinsi Abdulleh, the late Caroline Adams, Dr Sadia Ahmed, the late Tassaduq Ahmed, Ayub Ali, Bodrul Alom, Sindee Bass and the children of Kobi

Nazrul Primary School, Whitechapel, Janet Batsleer, Joe Batty, Angela Broome, John Downie, Terry Drummond, Andria Efthimiou-Mordaunt, Liz Ellis, Mary Everingham, Mavis Fernandes, Professor Bill Fishman, the Revd Alan Green, Savi Hensman, the Revd Professor Leslie Houlden, the Revd Dr Jenny King, Mary Kneafsey, the Revd Brian Lee, Sara Maitland, Trisha Mata, Tim Mills, Marybel Moore, the late Sarah Mussington, the late Revd Dr David Nicholls, Bill Risebero, John Rowe, Shiraj Salekin, Petra Salva, the Revd William Taylor and Julie Wood.

During visits to the USA, over thirty years, I was greatly helped, inspired and supported by so many comrades, including Claude-Marie Barbour, Han van den Blink, George Brandt, Sarah Buxton-Smith, Richard Downing, Sara Fischer, Tim Hall, Emmett Jarrett, Gail and Jim Keeney-Mulligan, John Kevern, John and Elizabeth Orens, Virginia Peacock, Sam Portaro, Linda Powell, Janice Robinson, Anne Scheibner, Jacqueline Schmitt, Bob Schreiter, Charles Witke, the late Richard Young, and many others.

All of these people, in both countries, have helped me, nourished me and challenged me, in ways of which they may not always have been aware.

1

Steppin' out of Babylon, Marching to Zion: theology as movement

We're steppin' out of Babylon,
one by one.

We're marching to Zion,
Beautiful, beautiful Zion.
We're marching upward to Zion,
The beautiful City of God.

NINETEENTH-CENTURY REVIVALIST SONG

My situation in 1990

Immediately before this work began, I had, for several years, been Director of the Runnymede Trust, a research and educational unit, and a 'think tank', concerned with race and racism in Britain. In 1988 I moved its offices to the heart of the East End, to 11 Princelet Street, where we shared premises with Tower Hamlets Training Forum. We were located a few yards from the old Princelet Street Synagogue, then being redeveloped as a museum of the history of minorities in the area. Princelet Street was the centre of the Census Enumeration District where the early East Pakistani (later Bangladeshi) community had settled in the 1960s. By the late 1980s it felt to me and others that Runnymede, formed in 1968, was, for the first time, being 'earthed' in a real community, and this filled me with joy. Yet there was tension and uncertainty about questions which had been rumbling on for years. Could Runnymede be both a pressure group, seeking to influence the 'corridors of power' and the course of policy, and also a grass-roots organisation, as one of its precursor bodies, the Campaign Against Racial Discrimination (located at Toynbee Hall, within yards of Runnymede's offices) had tried to be? How important was it to be located at the heart of a multi-racial community? What were the priorities – influencing the power structures, 'the establishment', or combating racism and working in solidarity with those who were its victims? Were these two equally important priorities, and, if so, were they compatible with each other within the same organisation? The parallels with the Church are all too obvious, as will emerge in the following pages.

I was encouraged by the reception that Runnymede, in its new East End home, received. Abbas Uddin, later to become Leader of Tower Hamlets Council, wrote to me on 7th August 1990 to express his delight about the 'positive decision on your part to move it into the East End, into the centre of a community that has been affected adversely by whole ranges of racism and oppression'. I experienced too a real sense of collegiality and comradeship, a strong corporate commitment to racial justice, among my colleagues. When Professor Bhikhu Parekh (now Lord Parekh) wrote to my predecessor, Ann Dummett, on 2nd January 1986, about the need for 'committed friends', he was saying something of great importance, in words very similar to those used by Alasdair MacIntyre and Cornel West in their writings. I certainly found committed friends among my colleagues at Runnymede, and some remain so to this day.

In terms of the national climate, however, the years at Runnymede were tense and harsh. On 11th July 1988, Eric Hobsbawm wrote in the *Guardian:*

> Britain after Thatcher will be a scene of destruction. Those who will need to rebuild what has to be reconstructed – not necessarily in the same way as before – need a preliminary survey of the bomb damage ... Answers to particular questions are given by most reports but nobody has sketched the general picture.

Part of our work was along these lines, surveying the bomb damage, seeing what could be reclaimed, how we could begin to build again. I am sure we did not succeed, but I believe that we made a significant contribution.

Runnymede – named after the place where Magna Carta had been signed on 15th June 1215 – had been formed in October 1968, in the aftermath of Enoch Powell's 'rivers of blood' speech, and of a subsequent growth in the public manifestation of racial hatred in Britain. It has played a really important role in disseminating accurate information and in developing social policy, acting, in fact, as one of its founders, Anthony Lester, QC (now Lord Lester of Herne Hill), saw it, as an 'alternative civil service'. The first director, Dipak Nandy, in a proposal of 14th June 1968, laid great stress on influencing 'key people' in the upper levels of the media, industry, housing and education. That seemed, and seems, vital to me, yet I felt that we were in danger of losing touch with communities at the harsh end of racism.

It was a great privilege to have worked at the Runnymede Trust. However, this was a period in which the British tradition of policy-oriented social investigation had weakened. One issue which was becoming an acute problem at this time was that of the nature and discernment of 'the facts', and how this related, if it did, to political change. On 4th September 1989 Sir Geoffrey Chandler claimed, in a letter to the *Independent,* that it was necessary 'to treat with caution government figures on almost any subject'. A few months later, at a meeting of the Royal Statistical Society, the distinguished statistician Sir Claus Moser attacked changes in the gathering of the unemployment figures, warning of manipulation. When the late Brian Redhead, a leading BBC commentator and one of the sponsors for my work at St Botolph's, was attacked by the Conservative government for accusing them of 'massaging' the unemployment figures, he replied with an apology in which he acknowledged that the term 'massaged' did involve a sensitive area for some politicians, and promised that in future he would always avoid it, and would instead use the word 'fiddled'!

Comments of this kind raised the whole issue of the alleged impartiality and 'objectivity' of 'facts'. Originally the word *factum* meant a deed, an action: only later did 'fact' come to mean a reality independent of judgement. Nietzsche had said that there were no facts, only interpretations. Alasdair MacIntyre, writing in 1988, insisted that 'facts, like telescopes and wigs for gentlemen, were a seventeenth-century invention'. MacIntyre had been writing for some years about the need for the location of rational thought within committed communities of discourse. In 1988 he pointed out that 'one cannot think for oneself if one thinks entirely by oneself ... It is only by participation in rational practice-based community that one becomes rational'.[1] I think he is right, but I am still committed to the search for accurate data, for 'the facts', while recognising that they can only be grasped, interpreted, made sense of and acted upon within the framework of a tradition of inquiry and of moral, spiritual and political commitment.

The death of my dear friend and mentor Ruth Glass on 7th February 1990 strengthened this sense. Her death was expected, but it came as a kind of crisis point in my own life. More than any other single figure, Ruth had helped me to see the need to connect academic rigour with passionate moral and political commitment within the urban context. She was an atheist and a Marxist, but it seemed appropriate that I was on the point of beginning a Christian theology project which would draw on many of the insights of this 'organic intellectual', as Gramsci would have called her (and maybe did). Through the Centre for Urban Studies at University College, London, which she had established in 1954, many sociologists, architects, urban planners and others had come to a clearer understanding of the economic and political issues in urbanisation and had come to involve themselves in responses to urban needs. I still miss her greatly. One of her customary comments was 'This is not quite correct', and nobody could say it with the passion and, at times, ferocity that Ruth could and did. Ruth's insistence on the integration of intellectual work and moral commitment has been tremendously important to me and has been something which I have tried to put into practice in pastoral ministry.

There is still, in many quarters, a naïve assumption that policy change follows data collection as night follows day. For example, we already know a great deal about the position of ethnic minorities – in some ways, more than we know about the general population. Governments have gathered or received an abundance of data for many years on all kinds of matters in the field of race, yet action has not necessarily followed. Expensive research has often produced results which had already been known for some time. Books on poverty are often so expensive that only the very rich can afford them. Surely we should now know that the relationship between data and change is highly problematic: in the absence of political will, whether on race, housing, homelessness or inequality, the more we know, the more things stay the same.

By early 1990 I was feeling increasingly the burden of administration and fundraising, and worried that I was getting little time to think. The work at Runnymede was extremely important, and I was working with an excellent staff team. Yet I felt swamped beneath the volume of paperwork, while the urgency of combating racism in the immediate area, and my inability to contribute as effectively as I would wish, was causing me great distress. I was frustrated by the needs on my doorstep, and was feeling a prisoner of the desk, a position I had often criticised in others.

I was desperately concerned, for example, at the increase in, and the expansion of, drug abuse in the area. It was in the early 1960s that the first known teenage heroin addict was identified in the East End. I knew him well, and am still occasionally in touch. Having become involved with the growing addict community in those years, I had watched with alarm the persistence – and promotion – of ignorance, and of policies based on ignorance, as the number of addicts had grown from a few hundred to many thousands. During 1989 we had set up the Maze Project with a focus on education, accurate knowledge and building resources to help young people to survive and flourish in a society in which drugs were going to be around for the foreseeable future. We found a brilliant team of workers, but there was so little money available for preventive work, in spite of a superfluity of rhetoric from national and local government. I was not sure that we would survive. I agreed to chair the project, and remained as chair for almost ten years.

By May 1990 it was clear that I should resign as Director of Runnymede, and I made this public on 8th June 1990. What was not so clear was the next move. The idea of creating a post which would enable me to concentrate on a number of key issues in the East End, and reflect on them theologically, was very appealing, and I began to think about how it might work. My resignation more or less coincided with the 25th anniversary of my ordination to the priesthood – 13th June 1990. But we decided to celebrate it a few months later, to coincide with the publication of a book which was an attempt to reflect on issues raised during these years. However, through the initiative of three friends, I received a lot of letters on 13th June. One, from a retired consultant psychiatrist, said that he was 'touched to receive this reminder of those days when you did so much to help the poor buggers who had needles hanging out of their arms, and for whom no single person gave a roaring shit – with the exception of yourself and a handful'. I felt grateful. Yet so much remained the same as it was in those days, and much had got far worse.

St Botolph's, Aldgate came into my mind as a possible base for some street-based contextual theology. I had known this parish since I was 19, and had worshipped there, on and off, since 1958. I was involved with the beginnings of their work with homeless people in the late

1950s, and taught English to Somali immigrants in the crypt. In the 1970s I helped to set up the Kipper Project, working with homeless young people, also based at St Botolph's in its early years. In the same period I was involved, as an advisor, with the detached youth ministry of the late David Randall, also based at St Botolph's. It is difficult to exaggerate the crucial role which this parish played in outreach, innovative ministry and prophetic witness during the 1970s and 1980s. It shone like a bright light of hope in the midst of the surrounding culture of mammon. I felt it would be an honour to work there if they would have me.

The church is on the edge of the City, close to the East End, and in 1990 it was still heavily involved in East End issues. The advantages of it as a base would be that it would not need me, having a good staff team already, that it had a history of having odd characters on its staff, and that it had credibility in the area among Christians, Muslims, atheists and agnostics. So I went to see Malcolm Johnson, the Rector, to see if there would be interest in such a post. He was very sympathetic and invited me to meet with the staff team of the church and of the Crypt Centre for homeless people. It seemed that my own frustration as Director of Runnymede, and my worries about turning into a manager/fundraiser and neglecting all kinds of other issues, connected with a feeling at St Botolph's that reflection, theology and serious thought were being squeezed out as a result of the pressure of daily work with individuals. Putting the two together, we began to see the possible shape of a post. 'Reflection in the midst of action, theology from the East End context' . . . but it was still all rather hazy. However, I was clear that for me it would mean the end of employment in which the funding was secure, and an attempt to create a style of working which was entirely dependent on donations and on what I might earn through educational work, writing books, and so on. I felt hopeful, since it is usually through such frustration and turbulence that important pieces of work emerge.

The response from the people at St Botolph's was encouraging. The relationship between the worshipping congregation and the work with homeless people ('the crypt', as it was known, since most of the work went on in the area underneath the church) was a close one. The agreement to create my post came from the entire staff of church and crypt, Christian and non-Christian. Without such agreement, I would not have gone ahead. It was vital to base the work at a place which was sympathetic to, and in solidarity with, what I had in mind, and which was willing to have me as part of the team. There seemed to be a clear advantage also in being part of a multi-disciplinary team including priests, deacons, social workers, art and literacy tutors, people with a wide range of expertise. However, it was agreed that my work would mainly be in the East End, using St Botolph's as a sacramental and working base. It was a good decision, certainly for me, and I hope for the people at St Botolph's and the wider community.

Many important shifts and moves in life occur as a result of some personal life crisis. It was encouraging at that time to get a letter from an old friend, one of the wisest and most perceptive of my comrades and critics:

> If your choices in life are appearing too narrow, try not to be dismayed. You may be being pushed 'where you would not' but where you ought to be. I have found this to be true for myself in recent years. My faith is in constant war with dismay, but I keep struggling. It's strange that your crisis should arise just as you are commemorating the jubilee of your ordination. Perhaps it is a backhanded form of congratulation from 'I'm up there'.

A few days before my resignation from Runnymede was made public, the *Guardian,* on 5th June 1990, published a major article entitled 'Battle Cries in Banglatown'. It raised issues which concern us to this day, not least the incursion of the property developers of the City of London into the East End. The decay of Spitalfields from the nineteenth century onwards had been in part a result of a policy of drift, in part one of systemic neglect. Today the Spitalfields Ward remains the most overcrowded in Britain, As in other areas of London, gentrification has spread. Now the very wealthy are buying property to the east of Brick Lane and, combined with the movement into Docklands, what was once the cheapest borough in London has become very expensive. The fate of the poor, black and white, is not hopeful. One gets the impression that, from the developers' point of view, it does not matter. Regeneration can often mean getting rid of the ordinary people.

On 19th September the launch of my book *Care and Conflict: leaves from a pastoral notebook* was celebrated alongside the postponed celebration of my 25th anniversary of ordination.[2] Archbishop Trevor Huddleston presided and Paul Oestreicher preached. To my surprise,

Malcolm Johnson made public the fact that I might be joining the St Botolph's team. The cat was out of the bag! In retrospect, this was a good move, typical of Malcolm who always seemed to follow Archbishop Michael Ramsey's advice to 'act on your consecrated hunch'. So now it looked as if something was going to happen.

The liturgy was wonderful. However, I had (unsuccessfully) tried to stress to our organist (now deceased) the importance of speed during the gradual hymn 'We're marching to Zion'. I heard a close friend in the back row, in between verses, say to her companion, 'At this rate, we're not going to get there!' That hymn, from the revivalist tradition, had been sung with great power and jubilation at the consecration of Barbara Harris, the first female bishop in the world. It captures the sense of pilgrimage and the vision of the City of God.

> We're marching to Zion,
> Beautiful, beautiful Zion.
> We're marching upward to Zion,
> The beautiful City of God.

After the Mass, *Care and Conflict* was launched. What I tried to do in that book was to reflect theologically on 25 years of ministry. It had begun as pastoral theology lectures in the University of Durham, and during September 1991 I presented a more popular version of it in four weekly programmes, with poetry and music, on BBC Radio 4's *Seeds of Faith* series. On 26th October Eric James reviewed *Care and Conflict* in the *Church Times,* with his usual critical perceptiveness. He referred to 'the curious feeling when you lay the book down that you have not really been allowed to come all that close to Ken Leech'. This, I felt, was a criticism which I needed to take seriously. It is so easy to write in a detached way as if one were not involved in the struggles described, and I may have fallen into this danger. I really dislike book reviews which do no more than commend, flattering as they can be. The critical reviews are the most useful as long as we — I, in this case — try to learn from them and do something about what they say. I have been trying to respond to Eric's comment ever since, and I hope that part of this response may figure in these pages.

The beginnings of the theology project

The initial steering group for the new project met on 10th December 1990. We decided that a job description would be drawn up, and that a list of 'the great and the good' would be asked to lend their names in support of the post. They included Kum-Kum Bhavnani, now a professor in California, Simon Jenkins, then Editor of *The Times*, Brian Redhead of the BBC *Today* programme, Rowan Williams (now Archbishop of Canterbury), and others. It was not clear how we could raise the money. Doing theology in Whitechapel Road did not seem very 'fundogenic'. At an open meeting of friends, which formed the basis of the future Support Group, someone said that we needed to find an unusual charitable trust that would fund me to 'cause trouble'. I can still hear Sara Maitland's reply: 'It would be a damn sight easier to find one to pay him to keep quiet for five years.'

The work of the urban theologian, as outlined in 1990, was to develop thinking and action in the fields of drug abuse, homelessness and racial justice; to help to link local with global, to connect the work at St Botolph's with wider networks of thought, with the Church beyond Aldgate, and with social and political issues nationally and internationally; and to pursue theological reflection from the context of inner East London, making links with the growing numbers of people in many different places who had chosen to do their theology mainly outside the academic world. The immediate context was to be the area between Aldgate and Stepney, going north to the border of Hackney and south to Shadwell, though it was recognised that there were important connections with work elsewhere in the UK and the USA. The commitment to 'reclaiming theology for ordinary people' was central.[3] It was vital to emphasise the all but forgotten truth that 'to be a Christian at all is to be a theologian. There are no exceptions.'[4] A key idea in the work was that of 'theological reflection', a commonly used, but relatively new, term. Only in the last few years has there been serious discussion about what this might involve.[5]

At the outset of the work, we approached the Christendom Trust, which had been set up by the late Maurice Reckitt on 31st March 1971, for the promotion of Christian social thought. Reckitt had been the key figure in the Christendom Group which grew out of the volume *The Return of Christendom,* published in 1922. It was only after the Christendom Trust had withdrawn from funding the project that I realised that the establishment of the Trust in 1971 was linked with the publication of the last work edited by Reckitt, *For Christ and the People* (SPCK 1968), to which I had contributed — a pleasant and perhaps symbolic discovery! The Christendom Trust funded my work longer than they had ever funded any piece of work. Without their core grant, we could not have started or continued. Of course, there were other sizeable contributions — some of which came from donors who wished to remain anonymous — but the vast majority were small amounts from individuals, parishes and small groups. This raises important questions for other innovative projects in the future. However, the constant need to supplement the Christendom grant meant that I had to take accountability seriously, and to document regularly what I had been up to, to 'sing for my supper'. This was good for me and also for the work. So it is worth saying something more about the Christendom Trust and its place in British Christian social thought.

When Reckitt established the Trust he was emphatic that its purpose was 'the promotion of research into *the application* of Christian social thinking' (my italics), not simply the thinking as such. Reflecting on the aims soon after the Trust's creation in 1971, V. A. Demant identified two preliminary axioms.

> One, our world today needs a Christian judgment upon the structure of society, and not only upon the behaviour of men in it, for the structure largely imposes its own conflict of aims upon the purposes of citizens. Two, a Christian understanding of the nature and destiny of man is a source of guidance for the validity of secular goals, using all that the natural and social sciences make suitably available . . . In the intellectual situation of today, Christian prophecy requires a new assessment of the cohesive and divisive factors in human behaviour, and moral directives for a human social order. That may well be a field for Christendom studies.

Demant went on, in words which could have been written with East London in the late 20th and early 21st centuries in mind, to refer to poverty in the midst of affluence and to vast inequalities of power. Moreover, he noted that

> the state is no protection against the insuperable powers of large companies, big corporations, trade unions, employing monopolies, selling and advertising rackets, planners and developers, nor against

over-grown bureaucracies and expensive inquiries thriving on social dislocations. There is a growing sense that the human being is attacked and deceived by these dominant social forces.[6]

I hope that my work in the East End helped in a small way to apply Demant's axioms. It certainly exposed the truth and urgency of his warnings. The injustices which he identified in 1971 were manifested in much stronger form in the East End as the twentieth century moved towards its close.

In July 1991, within a few months of the formal beginning of the project, the Christendom Trust was involved in organising an international conference at Lancaster University on 'Religion and the Resurgence of Capitalism'. I gave a paper on 'The East End, the Urban Economy and the Churches'. This was a challenge and an opportunity to think more carefully about the problems of resurgent capitalism as it came into collision with working-class communities. I concentrated particularly on developments in Spitalfields and Docklands, two areas which were to dominate much of my theological reflection over the whole period. One of the people who attended my presentation was the neoconservative writer Michael Novak. He was very gracious, and commented that we needed to communicate better. I am not sure that he understood what I had been saying at all.

One organisation which did not fund my work directly was the Church of England itself. We made a deliberate decision not to ask 'them'. (I am never quite sure if it is 'them' or 'it' as it is never clear where the power lies, and the buck is constantly passed.) We felt, rightly or wrongly, that the Diocese of London was so busy maintaining established structures that the likelihood that it might support some innovative work was very slight. We were criticised for letting them off the hook, but we felt that we could not wait indefinitely while the questions were debated by numerous committees. By the time they had finished their discussions, I would be due to retire, or even dead! So we went ahead, leaving them to catch up later if they were so minded. (I am not sure if that happened, but I suspect that it did not.) Later I persuaded the new Bishop of London, David Hope, that, since the Diocese gave no money to my work, and got rather a lot of work out of me (for which, on occasions, they claimed the credit), they could at least provide the flat and office space, rent free, and this was done.

In fact, the period when the project began coincided with the appointment of David Hope as Bishop. He and I had been students together at St Stephen's House, Oxford, in 1962, and on 6th June 1991 I wrote to him, welcoming him to London and sharing some of my thoughts about the state of the church there. Most of this letter must remain confidential for some time, but some of it can, and should, be shared. I referred to the fact that, for as long as I could remember, bishops had been very remote figures. I had never met the bishop who ordained me, apart from the brief pre-ordination interview. He never had any idea who I was, and, after he had laid hands on me, we never met again. David was very different, a warm, loving pastor, but I warned him:

> you will have to pick up the pieces of pastoral neglect, ridiculous appointments, unanswered letters going back years, and an almost total breakdown of communication between the hierarchy and the grass roots of the diocese. You will have the task of restoring cred- ibility to the office [of bishop], and of creating some real pastoral care out of the ruins. You will have a major task in winning the confidence of the women, ordained or not. The diocese, and the church as a whole, has lost many intelligent women over the years, and I am amazed that so many stay.

I was particularly worried about the appointment of a new Bishop of Stepney, which was imminent, and I wrote:

> It would be terrible if a narrow, churchy and gynophobic person came here. Please make sure that you appoint a mature and sensible person who can relate to the different communities, and who can be an ally for those who are fighting the evils of the Docklands exploi- tation and the growing polarisation of rich and poor.

The arrival of David Hope himself as Bishop of London was refreshing in many ways – not least in the fact that he answered urgent letters by return of post, or by early morning telephone calls – and many of us were sad that he was transferred to be Archbishop of York so soon. When we met some time after his arrival, he thanked me for my letter, expressed, as he said, 'in your usual tactful way'.

The person who was appointed Bishop of Stepney (later of Lon- don), Richard Chartres, turned out to be, in his eccentric way, very effective, and he earned the respect of the Bengali community by his ability to listen and not to make utterances without thought. I recall going to a meeting at Osmani School after a vicious attack on a young Bengali in Commercial Road. It was a crowded meeting, and around 95 per cent of the people were young, and very angry, Bengalis. The meeting was addressed by 'the great and the good' who said important things, but they almost all gave what I can only call 'single transferable speeches'. They had clearly given them before. The exception was Richard Chartres, a new bishop and fairly unknown quantity. He received tremendous applause from the Bengali youth. The reason was that he had clearly spent time, in the previous week, asking advice from them and others, about what would be most helpful for him to say – and it showed.

From the start I realised that there was a delicate balance to be held between local, national and international commitments. I tried to keep national commitments to a minimum and to restrict them to areas where I felt that I had a contribution to make which perhaps could not be so effectively made by others. From time to time the criteria needed to be reviewed. I was already involved with the Drug Policy Review Group, an informal think tank looking at British and European drug policies. I became a trustee of the Searchlight Educational Trust, an offshoot of *Searchlight* magazine, which, for over thirty years, had on a monthly basis monitored the activity of fascist and racist groups. I am still a trustee of the John Mordaunt Trust, and of the David Nicholls Memorial Trust, set up after David's untimely death in 1996. Later I served for several years on the Home Affairs Committee of the General Synod Board for Social Responsibility, which involved me in work on two documents on drugs, as well as others on mental health legislation and penal policy. I acted throughout the whole period as co-ordinator of the Jubilee Group network, a loose network of socialist Christians, and was responsible for their newsletters, updates and discussion papers. But I felt that, without the working base in this small area of the East End, the wider work would have lacked roots and credibility.

Theology as movement

What had been driving me was the idea of theology on the move, theology as pilgrimage, as a movement of people, not a static entity but a reality focused in historical time. The Second Vatican Council had moved away from the view of the Church as the 'ark of salvation' towards a more dynamic view of the Church as the 'pilgrim people of God'. Gustavo Gutiérrez, the Peruvian pastor who is often credited with coining the term 'liberation theology', subtitled one of his books 'the spiritual journey of a people'.[7] In similar vein, Fr Gilbert Shaw once described spiritual direction as simply words of encouragement uttered by one pilgrim on the road to Jerusalem to others who were passing. Pilgrimage, two recent writers have said, is 'a venture which is open to unforeseen developments through the evolving partnership between pilgrim, saint and Holy Spirit'.[8] That certainly has been my experience. Theology is a movement, not a position. Consequently, it is open to change, risk, danger and the possibility of disaster.

The notion of movement, travel, pilgrimage is deeply rooted in the Jewish and Christian scriptures, from the early records of the call of Abraham onwards. Both he and his offspring were to be aliens, having no permanent abode (Gen. 15:13; 23:3; 2 Sam. 1:13), and the repeated injunctions to act justly toward the alien are rooted in the experience of being aliens in Egypt (Exod. 23:9; Lev. 19:33–4; Deut. 10:18–19, 24:17ff, etc.). Throughout this ancient literature there is an emphasis on courage in the course of movement, based on the belief that God is with us wherever we go (Josh. 1:9). There are warnings not to look backward, and the figure of Lot's wife, who did so and was turned into a pillar of salt, has a valuable and warning place in Jewish mythology (Gen. 19:26). Yet, while there is a consistent biblical tradition of warning against those who 'looked backward rather than forward' (Jer. 7:24), Jeremiah himself tells people to 'ask for the ancient paths where the good way lies' (6:16). Isaiah tells the people: 'Look to the rock from which you were hewn, and to the quarry from which you were dug' (Isa. 51:1), going on to urge them to look back to Abraham and Sarah. But there is then an abrupt switch to the future, and the word 'will' occurs twelve times (Isa. 51:3–6) and 'shall' four times (51:11). What matters most is the future and being open to the work of God. 'Do not remember the former things . . . I am about to do a new thing' (Isa. 43:18–19).

Movement involves travel on roads, and there are various roads which figure in the biblical record – the Jericho Road (Luke 10:25–37), the Jerusalem Road (Luke 19—23), the Emmaus Road (Luke 24:13–35), the road to Africa (Acts 8:26–39), and the Damascus Road (Acts 9; 26:12–24). Each of these records points to major themes in our history of movement. Roads are seen as sites of violence and compassion, of crisis and renewal, of travel beyond boundaries, of enlightenment and change. They remain so today.[9]

These ideas recur in the New Testament letters, not least in the Epistle to the Hebrews. We look forward to 'the city that has foundations whose architect and builder is God' (11:10) and to the 'kingdom that cannot be shaken' (12:28). 'For here we have no lasting city, but we are looking for the city that is to come' (13:14). Within the Christian tradition there is the sense both of being 'exiles of the dispersion' (1 Pet. 1:1), and also of being strangers and aliens no longer (Eph. 2:19) because our true home is elsewhere. This paradox, aliens and exiles, yet citizens of the City of God, runs throughout 'the great tradition'. Christians are called to be 'resident aliens' (Acts 7:6), a term which originated in the Mosaic law. The community which is to be called Church is a community of 'resident aliens' in relation to the existing order. The early Christian *Letter to Diognetus* expressed this sense of the Church as a community of resident aliens in this way:

> There is something extraordinary about their lives. They live in their own countries as though they were only passing through ... Any country can be their homeland, but for them, their homeland, wherever it be, is a foreign country.[10]

The focus on movement has led some writers, including Richard Sennett, to the view that Christianity had undermined people's idea and sense of 'placement'. Sennett argues that the Christian focus on pilgrimage has led to a sense of dislocation, and he blames Augustine for a stress on the eternal City of God over against the cities of this world.[11] I am not sure that he is right, but it is certainly true that many Christians see the world as nothing more than something through which we pass on the way to eternity.

Movement is a complex force. Some movement is slow, as is pastoral and political work, and we should not be constantly charging about. Some years ago the Sisters of the Love of God published a devotional card containing the words: 'Snails obey the holy will of God – slowly.' In my work in East London, and elsewhere, I realised the spiritual importance of loitering. One edition of *The Shorter Oxford English Dictionary* defined 'to loiter' in this way: 'to linger indolently on one's way; to hang idly about a place; to dawdle at a task. To travel indolently and with frequent pauses.' It helpfully added that the term might have been introduced into English by vagrants from the Low Countries. Yet even loitering, slow as it is, is movement. I was struck by Joseph O'Leary's comment that theological work needs 'venture, slowness and strain', but that much conventional Western theology is marked by 'safeness, haste and ease'.[12] I hope that, and certainly felt that, my work in the East End had more slowness and strain than safeness, haste and ease. I hope it had a sense of venture too.

There is, of course, a real danger here: the danger of confusing the future hope with abandonment of 'the faith once for all delivered to the saints'. This is one of the central problems of liberal theology. Even the liberal theologian Maurice Wiles reminded us that 'not back to the creeds but forward from the creeds' was a slogan of the German Christians, who accommodated themselves utterly to Nazism. Jeffrey Stout, using words which had been used by Alasdair MacIntyre many years ago, has reminded us that liberal Christians often give atheists less and less in which to disbelieve.[13]

From one perspective, my entire time at St Botolph's could be seen as a struggle between seeing the priority as the City of God, with the Church as a movement of struggling pilgrims, and the City of London, the citadel of mammon and of unrighteous wealth, with the Church as a chaplaincy to the current order. The Texan priest Wes Seeliger, in his entertaining cartoon book *Western Theology*, saw this struggle in the Christian world as a struggle between pioneers and settlers, between pioneer theology and settler theology, between the dynamism of movement and the false comfort and complacency of settlement.[14]

The concept of the 'parish' arose from ideas of exile. *Paroikia* (1 Pet. 1:17) is translated as 'exile' (Revised Standard Version) and 'living away from home' (Jerusalem Bible) or 'strangers' (New International Version). How sad that many today see the notion of 'parish' as equivalent to a place which exists only for the 'settled'.

Like most people, I am emotionally attached to comfort and settlement, and I am often not good at being disturbed, interrupted and thrown off course. Yet I believe strongly that theology is not about the provision of comfort, or the support of comfortable positions. Rather, as Elisabeth Schüssler Fiorenza has said, the theologian should be a 'troublemaker . . . a resident alien, who constantly seeks to destabilise the centres'.[15] An equally important aspect of contextual theology is that of transgressing boundaries, particularly necessary in this era when so much is compartmentalised in ways which make nonsense of reality and the common life of human beings.

This emphasis, in my view, calls into question the notion of 'systematic theology', at least insofar as it is seen as an adequate account of what theology is like. The idea of 'systematic theology' developed only in the seventeenth century, and it has tended to obscure and exclude the essentially untidy and even messy character of theological work. This does not mean that we should not be seeking clarity and as much precision as is appropriate, but it does mean that theology points toward mystery, and that there is a dimension of 'unknowing' at the heart of orthodoxy.[16]

The themes of journeying, of return home and of journeying onwards were common in the literature of ancient Greece. Homer's *Odyssey* is still read by people all over the world. The Italian Jungian analyst Luigi Zoja believes that one reason for this is that many people recognise in Ulysses' return home a symbol of their own journey in search of their true selves. However, like the biblical texts, he warns of a false backwardness.

> To look backwards – that is, to base one's knowledge primarily on trodden paths – maximises the risk of not identifying a false path *en route* to the future ... Life is frequently unpleasant, but it is not through a return to Eden that we can make it better.[17]

In an earlier book I described how Aldgate and its environs had been places of refuge, settlement and transition for many communities of people. It seemed appropriate therefore to use the symbol of exile as a governing symbol, and so I entitled that work *Through Our Long Exile*.[18] The symbol of exile is deeply rooted in the history of peoples, not least in the Jewish and Christian traditions. It is possible to see the entire Hebrew scriptural record as a response to the Babylonian exile. The oppressive symbol of Babylon stresses the importance of maintaining spiritual integrity in exile, which is the central theme of the Book of Daniel.

God is, I believe, encountered in ongoing history, ancient, modern and, if there is such a condition, postmodern. Increasingly, I feel that Christians are becoming ever more divided into those who seek simply to preserve, contain and regurgitate truths from the past, and those who seek to listen to tradition, listen to God's word in scripture, but also listen to the 'signs of the times'. As 1990 drew to its close I hoped that this new project would contribute something to overcoming this division. I hoped that it would encourage those who were 'marching to Zion, the beautiful city of God'. I hoped that it would help Christians and others to treat theology as an important contribution to human life.

The division which I perceive here cuts right through the Christian world, and through other faiths and political movements. It appears, in its Christian version, in unexpected as well as predictable places: in Anglicanism and Roman Catholicism, among Baptists and Eastern Orthodox, in the Church of God and the Church of the Nazarene. It is a division between those who see 'the faith' as fixed, closed, static, a kind of package to be handed down, and those who see faith as a movement, rooted in history, rooted in revealed truth, yet open to change, development and renewal. I believe that the former path is the path of heresy, of one-dimensional thought, leading to sterility, false certainty and spiritual death; the latter path is that of orthodoxy and dynamic tradition, leading to ongoing life, new vision and the freedom of the children of God. This division affects the practice of theology. There are people who see theology as simply a 'given', a set of propositions and dogmatic decrees which are there to be received, absorbed and repeated. They have a point, and a point which should never be forgotten: there is a received tradition. But theology is also a process of continuous reflection, questioning and rethinking. It is a movement, not a position.

This sense of turbulence in theology was evident in the 1960s, and was expressed memorably by Langdon Gilkey in 1965.

> The most significant recent theological development has been the steady dissolution of all those certainties, the washing away of the firm ground on which our generation believed we were safely standing. What we thought was solid earth has turned out to be shifting ice – and in recent years, as the weather has grown steadily warmer, some of us have, in horror, found ourselves staring down into rushing depths of dark water.[19]

In the early 1960s there was a small epidemic of British theological writing which was inspired by St Paul's turbulent travels across the Sea of Adria, recorded in Acts 27. The authors saw this moment as characteristic of the contemporary Church in its own particular turbulence. The symposium *Soundings* was followed by books with titles such as *Four Anchors from the Stern* and *Praying for Daylight,* while the inimitable Eric Mascall offered his own reflections in *Up and Down in Adria.* Stanley Evans, in the last paper he wrote, delivered to the

Federation of Catholic Priests by Fr Percy Coleman a few days after Stanley's tragic death in 1965, reflected on the issues raised by these books and the ensuing debate. He referred to the importance of movement and to the danger of seeking a false stability.

> The two theologies, old and new, both seek for an impossible stability. Both think in terms of rest; the one will sound, and the other will lie at anchor. But the only purpose of taking soundings is to aid navigation, and they have, in practice, to be taken from a vessel under way. The Pauline vessel in the Sea of Adria dropped its anchors because its navigation had failed, and it was on the verge of wrecking. Navigation is really learned only by those who sail, and this is a fundamental principle of the church. 'He that doeth the will shall know of the doctrine.' We are concerned to discuss faith as a handmaid to the living of the Christian life, as a navigational aid to those who would be in the way that leads to God's Kingdom, not as an academic exercise for members of a hydrographical department who have lost their taste for putting to sea, or as a reflective study for those who would spend their days lying quietly at anchor.[20]

Only a theology which is marked by the spirit of adventure, the urge to discovery and the practice of pilgrimage, rather than one which is static and propositional, can respond to people in transition and upheaval.

2

'Outside the Gate': theology on the margins

Jesus also suffered outside the city gate in order to sanctify the people by his own blood. Let us then go to him outside the camp and bear the abuse he endured.

HEBREWS 13:12-13

Salvation lies outside the gates of cultural, ideological, political and socio-economic walls that surround our religious compound and shape the structures of Christendom.

ORLANDO E. COSTAS, Christ Outside the Gate

From the beginning, this place outside the gate, at the crossroad, has been a place of holiness.

VICTOR STOCK, Foreword to Malcolm Johnson,
Outside the Gate: St Botolph's and Aldgate 950–1994

Outside the gate

Botolph built his monastery in East Anglia, probably at Iken in Suffolk, in the latter part of the seventh century. It was destroyed by the Danes in 870, but the memory of Botolph remained. A large town in Lincolnshire was named 'Botolph's Town', later abbreviated to 'Boston'. Botolph, a Benedictine, made his monastery a place of prayer and hospitality. Hospitality has been a central feature of the ministry at St Botolph's, Aldgate, and it is at the heart of Christian ministry at its most authentic. *Philoxena*, love of the stranger, was a central feature of early Christianity. Botolph was also concerned with the land, the environment, and developed basic principles of drainage in that very damp part of England. Both Boston, England, and Boston, USA, are named after Botolph, though most of their inhabitants remain unaware of this fact. More than 60 churches in England are dedicated to

Botolph, and four were built outside the ancient gates of the City of London – Aldersgate, Billingsgate, Bishopsgate and Aldgate (the 'old gate'). The church at Billingsgate was burnt down in the Great Fire of London: the other three remain. Only the Aldgate church is a parish church with a resident population, while the others exercise a weekday, but not a Sunday, ministry.

The song 'Oranges and Lemons' began in 1744 as 'London Bells', and is known by many for its references to London churches (St Clement Danes, St Martin-in-the-Fields, and so on). The first six lines are now unknown to, or forgotten by, most people.

> Two sticks and an apple
> Ring y bells at Whitechapel.
> Old Father Bald Pate
> Ring y bells of Aldgate.
> Maids in white aprons
> Ring y bells at St Cathrin.

In the late 1990s I found myself standing in the pulpit, singing the 'Old Father Bald Pate' lines for a children's video. (Anyone who has seen me will realise why I was deemed appropriate for this role.)

Of course, there are now no literal gates, but the City of London remains an elite zone, cut off from people who are outside, who do not belong. The 'gate' at the east is only too real. The division between the life and culture of 'the City' and that of Whitechapel constitutes a symbolic gate of enormous proportions. The correct name of St Botolph's Church is 'St Botolph *without* Aldgate', that is, the church outside the old gate, the gate which faces eastward. The fact that Jesus was crucified outside the city gate, and that the Letter to the Hebrews calls us to 'go to him outside the gate', has always seemed to me a key symbol of, and challenge to, our work as Christian ministers, here and elsewhere. Of course we have not lived up to the challenge. Ministry here and elsewhere has always been very ambiguous, compromised and imperfect. Yet I felt that my own ministry was located 'outside the gate', primarily with people for whom the church itself was a barrier, and for whom the other side of 'the gate' represented an alien world.

In recent years the theme of theology and ministry 'outside the gate' has appeared in a number of writings including those by Orlando Costas, Brian Castle and, in relation to St Botolph's, Malcolm Johnson.[1]

The theme of doing theology 'outside the gate' had been important to me for many years, though I saw the danger of romanticising it, and of self-deception. As a white male Christian priest, based in Altab Ali Park, I was, for the most part, a minority figure. Not in terms of being male, for there were — in view of the sizeable numbers of male homeless persons, gay men, male medical students based at the nearby London Hospital Medical College campus, and the general number of males in the population — probably more men than women living and working in the area. But I was certainly in a minority as a white man, a Christian and a priest, living in an area which was mainly Bengali, mainly Muslim, and mainly disconnected from the Christian community in its institutional form. So what could it mean to be a Christian theologian in this context? What form might it take?

It seemed, first, to involve being what Christian theologians have called a 'sacramental presence' within the area, in this case within, and in a lived tension with, a historic system of colonisation. For the East End of London was one of the major areas to have been colonised by both the Church and the monarchy, in the reign of Queen Anne, and later by Oxbridge, and by the Oxford Movement, in the nineteenth century. There is no question that this colonising movement did much good, as well as much harm, but those days are now over — though the consciousness and the mindset remains in much church thinking. Today the Whitechapel area is mainly Muslim, while the white working class remain fairly disconnected from the Church. So what I was envisaging was a very lowly and small-scale attempt to work in a different way and on different models. I was influenced in my approach by Dorothy Day and the Catholic Worker movement, Charles de Foucauld and the Little Sisters and Brothers of Jesus, and, later, by the new generation of Anabaptists, with their stress on prayer, presence and commitment to the local area and its people. I was also aware that much theology is actually done in the streets though it may not use theological language, or call itself that. During the struggles of the civil rights movement in the USA in the 1960s, a key location was the UCLA — not the University of California at Los Angeles, but the University at the Corner of Lennox Avenue in New York City. This corner played a crucial role in rooting radical Christian thinking at street level.[2]

There are similar street corners in London and elsewhere which have become focal points for what can be called 'street theology', places where people engage in debate and struggle about major questions of life and death. Tower Hill in East London is one of many sites where such questions were debated. The two people who drew the largest crowds were the Methodist Donald Soper and the East End Jewish Communist Solly Kaye. Altab Ali Park is one of these sites too, and many debates on burning issues have taken place on this spot, usually in the course of marches and demonstrations, for which the park has been a favoured spot.

Secondly, it seemed to involve trying to engage with the relatively new Muslim population, drawing on the areas of common ground between Muslim and Christian understandings of the role of theological reflection and action. Christians – or at least many of them – and Muslims share a common view that religion can never be 'private' but must affect the public realm. This engagement has become more important over the years, although my own role in it was fairly minor. John Webber, Joe Collela and others played a far greater role.

Thirdly, it seemed important to try to engage with the overwhelming mass of the population for whom the Church and religious institutions in general were largely irrelevant, though they often (but not always) retained a strong affection for them. This affection, where it existed in relation to Christian churches, had been built up over many years of pastoral ministry. We needed always to be aware of the enduring work of those who had gone before us, and whose influence remains.

Fourthly, it involved trying to help along, rather than begin, a process of seeing the Christian community in a new way, not as a hierarchical structure, organised by men (almost always men) from distant parts, but as a real *koinonia*, a common fellowship, locally rooted, small scale, gentle and flexible in approach, modest and humble in strategy – in fact, a rediscovery of the grass-roots Church. This was, of course, in conflict with the centralising tendencies of much Christianity, most marked within the Roman communion in the papacy of John Paul II. It had more affinity with the 'base communities' which grew up in Latin America in the 1970s and with the ecclesial vision of the Anabaptists, whose revival is much to be welcomed.

Fifthly, it was essential to deepen my involvement with, and to try to encourage and strengthen, forms of thought, reflection and critical engagement with issues, local, national and universal, in a way which was rooted in the experience of the local communities.

And, finally, it was vital to try to involve others in this process – students, people preparing for ministry, people working in similar fields of action but in different places, and so on.

These were some of the themes which were emerging in the early part of 1991. They reinforced for me the words of J. B. Metz: 'The important questions to be asked by theology are . . . who should do theology, and where, in whose interests, and for whom?'[3]

St Botolph's, Aldgate

The church of St Botolph has stood at the eastern edge of the City of London since at least 950. In the late seventeenth century there was upheaval associated with Anabaptists and Fifth Monarchists.[4] After this, the church became very 'establishment' and civic. By 1990, however, St Botolph's had a good reputation within London, and within the Christian community, as a place of welcome to people and communities 'outside the gate'. Much of this reputation was built up during the incumbency of Malcolm Johnson (1974–93), and at the centre of this was the work with homeless people. In his book *The Church of England: a portrait* (1993), Michael De-la-Noy wrote: 'The Church of England at its best can be experienced by visiting a parish like St Botolph's in the City of London, a few yards from Aldgate Underground Station.'[5]

However, once a church acquires a name for its outreach work, there is a danger of complacency and of maintaining a kind of façade and mystique of radicalism which may be seriously flawed. Over my time at St Botolph's, it was sad to see significant numbers of the most creative members of the congregation leave, for a variety of reasons, but always related to the fact that they felt their vision and creativity could not be contained within the institution. Not all of them would wish to be named, but the loss of Philip Groom had serious effects on the place of art in the congregation. One woman, in her explanation to the congregation, saw the church as too respectable, too safe and too obsessed with boundaries between 'members' and 'clients', the latter being there to be 'done good to' rather than seen as active agents, full members of the Christian community. In her final letter, she raised some questions which, with changes in the detail, could be put to any parish, though they are questions which most would rather not face. The following is an example:

What would happen (unlikely alas) if a number of users of the Project . . . started to attend Sunday Mass on a regular basis? Project staff and volunteers are supposed to observe 'boundaries' with their 'clients' eg they mustn't socialise with them, go for a drink or a meal. They are not allowed to exchange addresses or phone numbers, or be too friendly, or too 'physical'. What then would be the relationship of the Project to the church and *vice versa*, given that such 'boundaries' cannot be maintained between equal members of a congregation?

There were many more questions. This sister, whom sadly, but not surprisingly, we also lost, put her finger on some real problems which I felt were never adequately faced, but which boiled down to one: our inability to involve homeless people and others fully in the life of the Body of Christ in Aldgate on a basis of real equality. For a long time they were seen as 'clients'. When I objected to this condescending term, some of my colleagues called them 'visitors', which was even worse. At no point were they seen as equal members of the Body of Christ. Others left the church for similar reasons, and no doubt we were a kind of microcosm of the church at large, though I think it could have been different. The ending of the short-lived adult education project run by Julie Wood in 1994–95 was particularly unfortunate at a time when this was one of the most urgent needs of the parish community.

Throughout 1991, and beyond, I became more and more aware of the crucial role which St Botolph's Church might play as a church 'outside the gate'. The ministry to people who were literally or metaphorically outside the gate of the City was, by 1990, and for years before, central to the vision of the parish and to my own work as part of that. Although all this was easier to speak about than to practise, I think we were genuinely trying to be a church open to the marginalised, to the outcasts, to the rejects, to people who felt pushed out. Sadly, as the 1990s progressed, I felt that this was becoming less and less true. I spent some time, in 1991 and in subsequent years, discussing this with homeless people who sat outside the church and in other nearby locations. We agreed that this church was in danger of retreating from its former commitment to those on the margins, and was becoming more comfortable and safe. It is a familiar story, and none of us is guiltless. However, I did feel, in 1990, that there was enough humility, enough self-scrutiny, and enough serious engagement with the issues of the neighbourhood and of the wider world for this church to be a supportive and nourishing base for what I was trying to do.

The work begins

By January 1991 we had managed to get the funding from the Christendom Trust. Until this point much of the Trust's money had been put into research projects in universities. Now Christendom had moved into East London, and I became technically the 'M. B. Reckitt Urban Fellow', though the trustees, very sensibly, did not insist that I used this title all the time. It could be used to help promote the work of the Trust, and to encourage other individuals and groups to apply for help, but ignored where it was inappropriate.

The year 1991 was a good one to begin, for it was the centenary of Pope Leo XIII's encyclical *Rerum Novarum*, the first of the great 'social encyclicals', and the 50th anniversary of the Malvern Conference of 1941, initiated by Archbishop William Temple. It was thus a key moment to rethink what Christian social vision and Christian action meant in the context of the 1990s and beyond.

Throughout the whole period, I was supported, strengthened, criticised and nourished by an excellent Support Group. It was an extraordinary and wonderful group of people, an attempt to reflect the diverse constituencies in the East End and beyond. It was really important that they were not all Christians. There was an elderly Muslim, Tassaduq Ahmed, and a young Muslim, Ayub Ali, later to be replaced by Bodrul Alom, a local councillor and health professional. Although the membership changed over the years, there were some who remained from beginning to end. Terry Drummond, urban missioner in Croydon and now chaplain to the Bishop of Southwark, had worked with me for over twenty years and used to run the crypt centre at St Botolph's, more or less single-handed. He had known me from a variety of connections – combating racism, Jubilee Group, urban mission, and East London. Professor W. J. (Bill) Fishman is an expert on the history of the area, a Jewish anarchist, an atheist with a profound devotion to General Booth, Trevor Huddleston and, apparently, myself! Savi Hensman, a very astute Sri Lankan woman with considerable experience in the voluntary sector, had been linked with my work for many years. David Nicholls represented the Christendom Trust and attended the group almost without a break until his untimely death in 1996. Mavis Fernandes, who had been my colleague in the anti-racism work at the Board for Social Responsibility, and later at Runnymede, was also there, and played a key role in writing up some of the details of the work in its early stages. It was a really good group of people. The work officially began on 1st January 1991, and the initial Support Group met for the first time on 5th February 1991.

I find it difficult now to imagine that any pastor or person deeply involved in urban ministry can function well without some kind of support group. But the term 'support group' is an inadequate way of describing its role. Certainly, support, guidance, solidarity and loving friendship were crucial, but part of the task of the group was to raise questions, to cause me trouble, not to let me off the hook, and to subject me to ongoing and rigorous scrutiny. The African-American philosopher Cornel West expressed this role well in a lecture given in the University of Chicago in 1994.

> I look forward to our conversation or critical exchange, our engagement with one another. I hope that we can push one another, and unsettle one another, and unstiffen our prejudices and presuppositions, and yet, at the same time, enable and equip one another, because we are in deep crisis.[6]

How much I needed, and valued, this critical engagement, this mutual pushing, this unsettling and unstiffening, and I am enormously grateful to those who formed that group.

Throughout these years I was also strengthened and supported by regular meetings of what we called 'the Launde Abbey Group' (because it first met at Launde Abbey Retreat House in Leicestershire). This was a kind of reflective, prayerful and supportive cell, consisting of about eight people, all of them best described as 'dissident Anglo-Catholics'. We came together for mutual support, and I think, did a pretty good job at it. We met four times a year for 24 hours, and tried to use the time for sharing our lives, praying together, study and sheer enjoyment of each other's company. There was sometimes quite a bit of pain to share too. I can't say that what has been valuable for me is necessary for all, but I would strongly commend groups of this kind.

Drug abuse

I have written about drugs since the early 1960s, and do not intend to go over the same ground here. But it is necessary to say something about the issues around which the theology project was formed, and drug abuse was one of them. In the East End, in addition to the usual problems of alcoholism, there have been for many years the problems associated with 'rough drinkers', mostly homeless or semi-homeless men living in the streets, parks and derelict buildings. Altab Ali Park, Christ Church Gardens in Commercial Street, and 'Barmy Park' in Bethnal Green have been centres for vagrant alcoholics for many years, although the use of them fluctuates according to fashion, police action and other factors, recently including the presence of users of other drugs such as crack cocaine. Among these 'rough drinkers', the forms of alcohol in use have included 'rough cider', cheap wine, and methylated or crude spirits. The users of the latter are known locally as 'meths drinkers'. (Some North American readers have at times been confused by the use of the term 'meths' in relation to alcohol, and assumed that the reference is to the stimulant drug methylamphetamine hydrochloride, or Methedrine.) The 'skid row' alcoholic presented, and, although much has changed, still presents, a powerful image of one who is beyond the margins, and yet, in a sense, has no margins. In the East End, meths drinkers are often seen as 'the lowest of the low', and are despised and shunned by other alcoholics.

My main local activity in the drugs field in this period was through the Maze Project, which I had chaired from its beginnings in 1989. It got its name in the way things often happen. We were given pleasant but obscure offices in Toynbee Hall, and were involved in one of those interminable conversations about what we should call ourselves. After we had been debating the question for some time, Val Robertson, a local youth worker, burst in, and said in exasperation, 'Bloody hell, what a maze this place is!' We knew we had the name. The Maze Project was set up to work on drug prevention and education. It grew out of work done over many years by detached youth workers, particularly at Avenues Unlimited, one of the first detached youth work projects in Britain. Like Avenues, Maze was under the general auspices of the YWCA but had a high degree of autonomy, its own management committee, and so on. Over the years we developed work in primary and secondary schools, with families, youth workers, tenants' groups, with peer education, and more recently with the growing numbers of young prostitutes in the Whitechapel area. As a result of the work with prostitutes, the name was changed to the Maze Marigold Project. For many years we were the only group in the area working entirely in the field of education and prevention, though many agencies and disciplines were involved at the level of treatment, support and help for established addicts. The Project's primary concern was to help young people not to get to that point, with education and help at an early stage.

We were worried about increased heroin use among young Bangladeshis, and on 3rd April 1991 we met with imams and other Muslim leaders at the East London Mosque with a view to organising a conference to address the issues. This conference on drugs, aimed at Muslim parents, took place on Sunday 26th January 1992 at the East London Mosque. The numbers attending far exceeded our expectations. It was a co-operative effort involving the Maze Project, the Young Muslim Organisation and community workers from Dame Colet House in Stepney. The whole thing was bilingual, English and Bengali. After the noonday prayers, we collected some Somalis too: unfortunately their presence had not been anticipated and there was no interpreter – a lesson for the future. Around 400 people came. It was, I think, the first time that a Christian priest had spoken in the mosque, and I felt greatly honoured and humbled. More important, this conference led to two further conferences on 3rd June and 7th July 1992, and to the formation of the Asian Drugs Project, which sadly collapsed as a result of Health Authority funding cuts, a not uncommon experience. But in the long term it helped the progress of developing a Bengali response to the problems.

The nature of my involvement with people on the drugs scene had, of course, changed over the years. My role by the 1990s was mostly advisory, educational, supportive, and not, for the most part, face-to-face street work with users. But the danger that I might be reflecting on work without having a base was a question which bothered me. I tried to spend a fair amount of my time simply being around in the East End – in pubs, restaurants, in the streets, and with local groups such as congregations, projects, schools, and so on. I spent quite a lot of time wandering the streets and keeping in touch with local drug users.

Involvement in provision of services for drug users was taking up much of my time and energy, and I found myself increasingly frustrated by 'professionals' with a basically bureaucratic and a '9 to 5' way of looking at the field. In September 1992 I received a document entitled 'Draft Strategy for Drugs Services' which bore all the marks of having been produced from within such a bureaucratic vacuum. It was full of the current jargon – 're-habs', 'able to access', 'basic drugs awareness', 'specialist skill development', 'quality assurance' and 'integrated approach'. But it contained the claim, which was probably correct, that the largest age group attending drugs services was 25–29. This meant that, as late as 1992, most young drug users were not in touch with these services at all. Meanwhile, youth and community workers, the very people who are around in 'unsocial hours', were regarded as poor relations by many of the desk-focused people.

I tried to keep in touch with groups from my past. On 23rd September 1992 I went to Manchester to preach at a service at Whalley Range Methodist Church for the 21st anniversary of the founding of Lifeline, now one of the biggest and most respected drugs projects in the country. It had been set up by a colourful South African psychiatrist called Eugenie Cheesmond, and I had a certain amount to do with its beginnings in a disused coffee bar in Lower Mosley Street. This cheered me up. I realised that there were still many groups who had not been taken over by the bureaucratic and managerial models.

On 18th April 1991 *The Times* ran an editorial entitled 'Menace of drug wars' – a timely contribution. From the publication of the Second Brain report on drug addiction in November 1965, a number of us were pointing out, often through the columns of *The Times* itself, how precarious and dangerous the situation was. A combination of official lethargy (including the long delay in setting up treatment centres recommended by Brain) and inept legislation leading to the ending of some important medical activity, was bound to lead to an escalation of the criminal market in heroin and cocaine.[7]

On 23rd April 1994 *The Times* reported 'an overhaul of the Government's policy to control drug abuse'. The Government had recently set up the Central Drugs Co-ordination Unit, an important and overdue initiative. Yet by the time co-ordination had improved, many more young people had become hardened drug users. More seriously, the projects which were closest to, and most willing and able to help, the street addict were precisely those who were struggling to survive with inadequate funding. Here we were helped by the Mayor, Arthur Downes, who made the Maze Project his personal charity.

A number of events took place during the period of the project, in addition to the important work developed by Maze. My book *Drugs and Pastoral Care* was published in July 1998. This was based on the first book I wrote in 1969, published by SPCK in 1970 as *Pastoral Care and the Drug Scene,* and reissued in 1973 as *A Practical Guide to the Drug Scene.* The new book was not a revision, but it did follow the basic structure of the old book and attempted to do for the 1990s and beyond what the earlier book had tried to do for the 1970s. Linked with this was a smaller paper, *Drugs – the Challenge to the Church*, which appeared as a General Synod Miscellaneous Paper in 1998. I felt that this work, based around a specific area, was a valuable example of what contextual theology was supposed to be about.[8]

Marginality

Since 1991 the themes of 'marginality' and of ministry 'outside the gate' or 'outside the walls' have become more widespread. At about the same time as my work at St Botolph's was beginning, Mary Beasley was beginning her reflection on work with homeless people in Birmingham for an MPhil dissertation. Out of the dissertation came a book, *Mission on the Margins* (1997), and a loose network of people, from various parts of the country, who met together under the same title. Several conferences and local gatherings took place, and these brought together a large number of people who were involved in marginal areas of ministry. I became involved with Mary's network, which began from her own highly localised work, based in Balsall Heath, at that time the main 'red-light' district of Birmingham. I was a member of her support group throughout its life. Mary's subsequent writing has really made it clear to me how important it is that the local church should be present on the margins, alongside marginalised people and communities.[9] That is where it belongs. The record of the local church in East London in this respect is not bad. Yet the temptation to move to the centre, not as an act of resistance but as one of collusion and compromise, is powerful, and in most cases overwhelming. So the Cross is bypassed and 'Christianity' takes on again the mantle of the Emperor Constantine.

I recall vividly the first major conference of Mission on the Margins, on 14th–15th June 1994 in Birmingham. Both John Major, then the Prime Minister, and the Duke of Edinburgh had, within recent days, made foolish statements about poverty and homelessness. In my address to the conference I said:

> Recent comments by John Major and the Duke of Edinburgh, while they contain elements of truth, belong to a style of rhetoric which has three features. It lectures from afar. It oversimplifies complex issues with an arrogance and glibness which is staggering in its lack of self-scrutiny. And it colludes with, and reinforces, the present mood of complacency and of blaming victims for social evils. Mr Major has less excuse for his irresponsibility than the Duke, though his propensity for banana skins is greater. Yet one expects leaders of governments to reinforce stereotypes and illusions. The Duke could have used his privileged position to arouse consciences and to awaken outrage. However, while there was some truth in his statement about 'absolute poverty' [which he claimed did not exist in Britain because of the welfare state], its overall effect was absolutely appalling, and, in its simplistic view of poverty, it was absolute nonsense.

John Major and the Duke of Edinburgh were symbolic of something which remained a problem and an irritant throughout most of my ministry. Here were people in key positions to influence events, yet who seemed to be so badly advised – if advised at all – that they simply uttered platitudes, and made life more difficult for the people in desperate need.

One of the fashionable phrases at present is 'inclusion'. There is an organisation called 'Inclusive Church' which is concerned about the danger of the Church of England becoming more sectarian and 'excluding' people who do not conform to the current norms. I welcome this stress on inclusion at one level, and much of our work at St Botolph's was influenced by this idea. But I feel that a lot of hard thinking needs to be done in this area, and I was challenged and helped some years ago, after speaking to a conference of clergy in the Diocese of Southwark, by comments from one of them. He wrote:

> If radical Christians are to espouse justice, they cannot espouse liberal notions of inclusion . . . The gospel narratives and the main underlying biblical themes require us to take sides, to march with the oppressed, to work for change in political structures . . . and to revolt against (or subvert) those political structures which use violence, hate and fear to further their purposes.[10]

One of the problems with much 'mainstream' Anglicanism is that it is based on a spurious idea that it stands in the middle, holding a balance between extremes – of which it is wary. But this depends on where we stand in relation to the structures of power, and the middle may only be the middle from a biased perspective, while the extremes may be where we should be. Welcome as it is in the present climate, in which fanaticism and intolerance is increasing all over the place, the language of inclusion does contain some snares and areas of confusion.

Homosexuality

Since the early 1970s the pastoral care of homosexual persons had been a central part of the ministry of St Botolph's. While it has never been a 'gay church', lesbian and gay people have been welcomed, often at periods when this has not been the case in other churches. Blessings of same-sex unions were common at St Botolph's long before they became a matter of controversy in the Anglican Communion as a whole. Malcolm Johnson has been quite open about this, and has said that, during his time as Rector of St Botolph's, he blessed around three hundred same-sex unions, and possibly more. In the interests of honesty and truth, it is important to emphasise that such blessings have been taking place for some time, both here and elsewhere, and we are only now beginning to talk about what it all means – and this is, in fact, the right way round. Practice precedes theory, theology is the second step. As the early South American liberation theologians often said, it 'arises at sundown', that is, it is always a reflection on events, struggles, dilemmas, pastoral practice, without which it cannot exist. So it is often right that we act first and reflect afterwards, trying to make sense of what we are already doing, perhaps revising our positions in the light of experience and criticism. It is those who do the will who will know the doctrine (John 7:17).

We need, too, to consider the implications – theological, spiritual and pastoral – of neglecting this ministry of blessing, implications which were put well some years ago by Jennifer Phillips, former Rector of Trinity Episcopal Church, St Louis:

> A blessing sets something apart as holy and revelatory of God . . . It is not a private matter . . . In a eucharistic community, when many of the lives and relationships of members cannot be celebrated, where

God cannot be publicly thanked for them and asked to assist them, the eucharistic body begins to unravel ... Occasions of celebration become burdened by grief and ultimately members fall away from the table fellowship. Thus the failure to recognise gay and lesbian households as places where God's faithfulness may be known diminishes the whole parish community, homo- and hetero-sexual.[11]

I was honoured to be part of a local church which, for the most part, did not collude with the dominant dishonesty.

However, this truth is denied by ecclesiastical officialdom. Everyone with intelligence and close knowledge of the Church of England knows that blessings of same-sex unions have been happening for many years, and the churches where they are happening are well known, not least to the press. Everyone with close knowledge also knows that the Church of England has been ordaining 'practising' homosexuals for many years, and that such people have often had long and distinguished careers as parish priests, members of the staff of what is now called the Division of Ministry and other parts of the General Synod bureaucracy, bishops' chaplains, and so on. Yet bishops and others speak as if this were not the case. In this climate of dishonesty and denial, it is difficult to have a sensible dialogue. The situation will probably get better, but only because groups and individuals force the issue, often endangering their own future in the Church by doing so. Bishops, unless they are retired, tend to follow later. We should not be surprised at this. People are appointed bishops partly because they are believed – usually rightly – to be 'safe' and to support the current line of duplicity. However, being 'yes men', they will usually change as the climate changes and allows, or even compels, them to do so. This places a heavy responsibility on local groups to keep up the pressure and to speak the truth, in season and out of season.

The decision in November 1992 by the General Synod of the Church of England to allow women to be ordained to the priesthood led the Guardians of the Shrine of Our Lady of Walsingham to issue a statement that women priests would not be allowed to celebrate Mass there. I recalled that one of the arguments used by many opponents of the ordination of women was that it was the first stage of a 'slippery slope' which might end with the ordination of homosexuals. I wrote to the *Church Times*, welcoming the statement from the Guardians, and expressing the hope that they would soon issue a similar statement that 'homosexual priests would not be allowed – or, more accurately, would *no longer* be allowed – to celebrate at their altars'. I was not surprised that my letter did not appear!

HIV and AIDS

The question of homosexuality leads me to that of HIV and AIDS (though it should be remembered that globally many of those with the virus are heterosexual). As a byproduct of work within the gay community, the ministry at St Botolph's involved considerable involvement with people with HIV and AIDS and their families. Although I was not directly involved with this aspect of the ministry, it is important to record it here as it was going on at the same time as my own project. At one point, in the early 1990s, the Rector, Malcolm Johnson, the deacon Pat Wright, and Brother Colin Wilfred SSF were all involved with this area of ministry. For a number of years there was an inter-faith pilgrimage to Lourdes for people with HIV and AIDS, which was led by Malcolm, Rabbi Lionel Blue and Bishop Victor Guazelli, the Roman Catholic Bishop of East London. Pat, a nurse with considerable experience in AIDS units in various London hospitals, was 'seconded' for six years to Swaziland where she trained local nurses and helped to build up the infrastructure of AIDS work there, while Colin Wilfred was employed for several years as an AIDS pastor, based at St Botolph's.

For many people, experience of the HIV and AIDS crisis led to a deepening of faith and discipleship. Ray Gaston, parish priest of All Hallows, Leeds, spoke for many when he wrote:

> my involvement in the AIDS movement in the late 80s really led to my becoming a Christian. I often say, 'People with AIDS converted me to Christ, and none of them were Christians.' The ideologies of the radical left and the social movements that had fed me for many years, after ditching my childhood fascination with faith at 13, were not able to provide me with the spiritual resources and the necessary hope that I sought in the face of the AIDS crisis. The love, compassion and solidarity I saw in those involved and affected by HIV and AIDS was remarkable, and in need of deeper exploration. I came back to church seeking meaning, and slowly the Jesus story helped to

make sense of my experience of AIDS. Sitting in the liturgy, week by week, reading the Gospels, awoke me to the reality of Christ's passion being lived in the AIDS movement – Christ was living with AIDS.

Today, much of this work is under a cloud as the fierce anti-homosexual rhetoric within Anglicanism intensifies to a point close to lunacy. As I write these words, a number of clergy in the Diocese of Chelmsford have announced that they are 'out of communion' with their bishop, John Gladwin, an evangelical with a strong social conscience. Again, the issue is homosexuality. I am horrified, though not surprised in the present unorthodox and deranged climate, that people who think they are evangelical and biblical Christians should wish to be out of communion with their bishop on an issue on which Jesus said nothing whatsoever, while they seem to pay little attention to those issues on which he said a great deal. This is not orthodoxy or biblical Christianity: it is pathological heresy of a kind with which St Paul was only too familiar. The extent of the distortion of what it means to be orthodox was brought home to me on a visit to Los Angeles in 2002 when the local paper reported that a conference of conservative Christians had complained that many churches 'have abandoned scripture by embracing homosexuality, an anything goes theology, and causes such as abortion and *opposition to war with Iraq*' (*Los Angeles Times*, 26th October 2002, my italics). Maybe this comment was more revealing than it intended to be.

Prostitution

Literally outside 'the gate', slightly east of the City boundary, is one of the major centres of juvenile prostitution, in Commercial Street, Old Montague Street and adjoining districts. Work with prostitutes has been a major part of my ministry in the East End, and has given rise to much theological and spiritual reflection. The word 'prostitute' is disliked by many people, who favour the term 'commercial sex worker'. The debate about terminology is not trivial, and it has split the world of the working women themselves. I do not propose to go into that debate here, but it seems important to register its existence. It exposes and opens up an area of contempt towards women, viewed as objects of male desire, as commodities.

Prostitution, like most activities today, is a global reality. It is therefore impossible to isolate Commercial Street from the rest of the world. If we look at the situation of women in Central and South America, we see that prostitution is one aspect of a more dispersed exploitation of women. Melissa Wright's study of the murders of over two hundred women in Ciudad Juarez in Mexico towards the end of the 1990s shows the way in which, in this part of the world, women are seen as flexible and, in the end, disposable labour. Many of the murdered women worked in export-processing maquila factories, of which Mexico has more than 3000. Wright argues that women workers are seen as 'waste in the making'. Often the murdered women are accused of being prostitutes, whether they are or not, since this is a convenient way of saying that they are disposable and that their deaths do not matter. The known fact is that they have to cross stretches of desert to get to main roads and buses. They are, according to Wright, 'the byproduct of a process during which the human beings turn into individual waste'.[12]

Ministry with sex workers raises two issues in social ethics which appear in a wide range of other questions. The first is the issue of how Christians minister with people who are involved in an activity of which they personally disapprove. Prostitution, drug taking, banking, involvement with armaments and the pursuit of war, collusion with capitalist finance – all these raise the same kinds of dilemma, though their similarity is not always recognised. The second issue is whether the Christian task is simply to bear witness to a different lifestyle and a different set of values, or whether we are also to work, with all its mess, ambiguity and imperfection, with trying to make the best of what we have. I suspect that even those who opt for the former find themselves in practice working with the latter. I will try to struggle with these two issues throughout the book, but I should warn my readers that I have not resolved them in my own life, and I wonder if a resolution is possible. So, as the cliché has it, I 'live with the contradictions'!

What is crucially important is that Christians recognise that prostitute women are valuable, important women, made in the image of God. They must not be despised, must not be seen as victims of 'our' compassion, must be treated with respect and seen as equals. When this happens, all kinds of things can change. The ministry of Fr Brian Ralph, based in Bethnal Green, is a dramatic and important example of pastoral care of women in prostitution which is not patronising, and which has certainly helped many women to recognise their own dignity and worth. As a result of her experience of working with Fr Brian and Maze Marigold, Sara Fischer, now a priest in Oregon, founded a group called Rahab's Sisters which works with prostitute women in the Portland area.

In April 2003 a helpful report on prostitution in the East End, authored by Paula Skidmore, was launched, the result of a joint project by Barnardo's, Providence Row Charity and Toynbee Hall, the university settlement in Commercial Street. It was encouraging to see so many people gather at Toynbee Hall for yet another meeting on this subject. It brought back to my mind a similar gathering in the same room to launch Edith Ramsey's report *Vice Increase in Stepney* in 1957. Since then, there have been many such meetings, but most of them have not included a single prostitute. Human beings have been talked about in their absence.

In the East End, prostitution is a well-established historical phenomenon. In the early censuses, from 1851 onwards, many women identified themselves as prostitutes. When I lived in Cable Street at the end of the 1950s, very few of the working women were of local origin. The London Docks attracted young people from all over Britain, and the British Social Biology Council's study in the late 1940s referred to 'the Stepney problem' as a type of prostitution which differed from the London norm. The prostitutes in the Cable Street and Commercial Road districts were much younger, and more likely to be mentally ill, than was the case in London as a whole. By the 1990s, the prostitute district had shifted slightly northward – a process which had begun in the late 1960s with the demolition of the old 'café quarter' in Cable Street – and the women were overwhelmingly from the East London area. The role of drugs had also changed. In the 1950s the women used Drinamyl (dexamphetamine sulphate with amylobarbitone) as a 'wakeamine'. (They were among the first group of users of this drug, manufactured by Smith, Kline & French, although its early use by prostitutes is not well documented.) By the 1990s, the use of crack cocaine and heroin was a key factor, though often it was the 'boyfriend' (pimp) whose drug use provided the economic motive for the work.[13]

Marginality again

Bob Schreiter has reminded theologians that marginality is global, and that 'the experience of a globalised world lies in its peripheries, in the moments of risk and change, in the celebration of survival of yet another day'.[14] In the process of globalising of marginality, the earlier sense of the word as equivalent to 'excluded' or 'overlooked' has been superseded in some quarters by the idea of marginality as a chosen and, in some ways, desirable state of being. Thus Michel de Certeau has written:

> Marginality is today no longer limited to minority groups but is rather massive and pervasive: this cultural activity of the non-producers of culture, an activity that is unsigned, unreadable, and unsymbolised, remains the only one possible for all those who nevertheless buy and pay for the showy products through which a productivist economy articulates itself. Marginality is becoming universal. A marginal group has become the silent majority.[15]

While in this book I shall be writing of marginalisation more in the sense of exclusion, of poverty, and of the experience of being despised and rejected, it is important to recognise this wider perspective.

Exclusion is the result of some agency. It does not simply happen by chance or by accident. Someone, or some cluster of agents, perform the exclusion. Work on health inequality shows that processes of social differentiation actually create social exclusion. So who does the excluding? What forces are at work? It is obvious, for example, that some outer city estates in Britain were designed specifically with exclusion in mind. There is no doubt that the London Docklands Development Corporation quite consciously excluded not only individuals but whole communities, since the entire project of 'regeneration' was based upon the systematic exclusion of those who were in the way of the developers. Again, asylum seekers are excluded by design, but the Social Exclusion Unit was not involved in asylum issues, in spite of the Audit Commission's recommendation that it should be. More generally, as the Latin American Bishops' meeting at Puebla in 1978 stressed, structural poverty is not a chance stage but the product of definite economic, social and political situations and structures.

The language of exclusion often bypasses issues of power, income and wealth, and access to resources, and tends to see inclusion in terms of moral and educational improvement. In this it is similar to the old – and now largely abandoned – approach to race relations in the 1960s, which was dominated by the ideas of host society and assimilation. It blurs social divisions, seeing them as abnormal, and stresses social cohesion. It tends to see exclusion as a property of populations or of places rather than as a dynamic process. If this is so, the answer lies in the labour market or the educational system. In fact, exclusion is a process, not a condition. Linked with this is a concern with control – of 'rough sleepers' (people sleeping in the streets), homeless people, and so on. In much of the rhetoric, exclusion is contrasted, not with inclusion, but with integration, often narrowly conceived as integration into the labour market. This can be seen in current official attitudes to homelessness.

The theologian Jung Young Lee has argued that change and transformation always occur at the margins because that is where creativity flourishes, while the biblical scholar D. C. Duling, in a study of Matthew's gospel, speaks of the marginal character of Jesus' disciples. Others have argued that the experience of marginality is normative for the people of God. Pentecostal youth workers speak of 'border crossings' in their work, while other Christians speak of 'creative boundary living'.[16] Ministry on the margins is rooted in scripture and tradition, in spite of the bias of many churches toward the 'mainstream' of respectability. The Bible makes the experience of marginality normative for the people of God.[17] One of my favourite texts is the statement, in the Book of Jonah, that God 'appointed a worm' (Jonah 3:7). The apostles were seen as 'the rubbish of the world' (1 Cor. 4:13), and Jesus told his followers to invite the poor, crippled, lame and blind to meals (Luke 14:13). The whole theology of incarnation is about self-emptying, about *kenosis*, about God in Christ taking 'the form of a servant'. There is a need for kenotic transformation in all of our lives.

If only the churches had always taken this seriously, history might have been very different. The failure to allow, or enable, marginal voices to be heard has done incalculable damage, not least in the nurturing of imagining alternatives to the way things are. As Walter Brueggemann has written: 'the only ones left who can imagine are the ones at the margin. They are waiting to be heard, but they have a hard time finding a place and a way for their voices.'[18]

In the history of monasticism, marginal movements have inspired the more creative and pioneering developments. Jan Berry, who works in Manchester, has written:

> I am convinced that the way forward for the church is ... to be found ... by looking to the margins – to those small, often

ephemeral but vibrant groups, on the edges of the institutional church; those sitting loose to organised religion, but creating their own theologies, liturgies and sense of community . . . Those at the edges of the church are pushing for an expansion of the boundaries.[19]

In similar vein two writers, influenced by the Anabaptist tradition, have written: 'We believe that in a post-Christendom context, the church will need to learn once again to operate from the margins, so we have chosen to examine marginal expressions of church life as signs of hope.' [20]

The Servant Church

One important issue here is the revived attention to the role of the diaconate, the ministry of a deacon. There has been a remarkable revival of the diaconate in the Roman communion. Of the world's 20,000 Roman Catholic deacons in 2001, more than 13,000 were in the USA. Most members of the Church of England see deacons as trainee priests. Although the Book of Common Prayer instructed preachers at the ordination of deacons to explain 'how necessary that order is in the Church of Christ', it was true for many years that it was 'so necessary that in many dioceses there are no deacons around to speak of between Christmas and Trinity'.[21] In fact the diaconate is both a ministry in its own right and a symbolic pointer to the 'servant ministry' of the whole Church. The word *diakonia* and its associated words occur over a hundred times in the New Testament; *diakonein*, to serve, appears 34 times; *diakonia*, service, 31 times; and *diakonos*, servant, minister or deacon 28 times.

In its origin it is very earthy indeed. *Konia* means dust, *koenein* means to raise dust. *Diakonia* can therefore be seen as a thorough activity of raising dust! It was a great privilege to have worked at St Botolph's with two 'vocational deacons', Pat Wright and James Francis, and, through their ministry, to come to a deeper understanding of the New Testament theme of *diakonia*, often translated as servanthood. The equation of the diaconate exclusively with the 'servant' idea, is, however, incorrect. The major work of John M. Collins showed that in biblical and ancient Christian sources *diakonia* had much wider uses and wider ranges of meanings.[22]

Ideas of 'servant ministry' in recent Church rhetoric have gone way beyond the ordained diaconate. The Church itself, locally and nation-ally, is seen as a 'servant church'. I have no quarrel with this, though it is not adequate as a total view of the Church's ministry. It is worth noting that Jesus told his disciples that they were not to be called servants but friends (John 15:15). The idea of 'the servant church' became popular in the early 1960s, though much thoughtful theological reflection on it has taken place only since the 1990s.[23]

Often this particular idea takes over, and other equally important dimensions of ministry are forgotten. Take, as an example, the parable of the 'Good Samaritan', so often cited as a basis for Christian social action and social care. In 1972, Richard Holloway, holding rather dif-ferent views than he does now, criticised the idea of a 'Samaritan church' as a retreat into good works.[24] (I find myself more in sympathy with the earlier, than with the current, Holloway!) But the use of the parable is highly problematic.

We are, it is said, to follow the example of the 'Good Samaritan'. This leaves out three crucial facts. First, there is no evidence that the Samaritan was 'good', an adjective which is not used in the gospel account. He may have been thoroughly immoral and disreputable. The point was that, when confronted by an urgent crisis, in contrast to the two religious professionals, he did what was needed. Secondly, the parable is Jesus' answer to the question 'Who is *my* neighbour?' The 'I' in the story is not the Samaritan but the man who fell down on the road. It is not primarily about giving, but about *receiving* neighbourly friendship and help from unexpected quarters – in this case from one who was a foreigner and a heretic. And, finally, while it remains an important part of Christian practice, it is only a part; there is much more, and we need, as Ann Morisy suggested years ago, to move 'beyond the Good Samaritan'.[25] It is often more important to build a better and safer road so that thieves do not operate so freely.

An exclusive stress on the diaconal or servant ministry can lead to that type of 'social service religion' of which Evelyn Underhill wrote that it was 'a type of religion which in practice does not wear well'.[26] Yet the diaconate remains a key symbol of an essential part of the Church's ministry. Although in the Eastern Orthodox churches, the role of the deacon has been primarily liturgical, in the churches of the West, the deacon has been seen as playing an important role 'on the margins'. Most vocational deacons exercise a 'servant ministry' in the world, and one of their key liturgical roles is to gather up the prayers of the people at the Sunday Eucharist. The Church of England, as on so many other issues, has been woefully backward in recognising the role of the diaconate, and a recent semi-official handbook on ministry ignores it entirely. By contrast, the number of vocational deacons in the Roman dioceses of the USA grew to 13,764 by 2001. The Second Vatican Council document *Ad Gentes* had referred to the 'sacramental grace of the diaconate', and the late Pope John Paul II had seen the diaconate as a permanent rank within the churches. A document from the Roman Catholic bishops of England and Wales in 1987 stressed the importance of the diaconate as 'a sacred sign of the character of the church as a servant'.[27]

Community-based theology is, partly, about reflection, corporate and personal. But theology has also to be expressed in visible forms of ministry, one of which is what is called the 'vocational diaconate'. In the Church of England – though not in some other parts of the Anglican world – the office of deacon is seen by most people as a stepping stone to priesthood. Most deacons remain so for only a year, and then are ordained priests. When Anglicans speak of the 'transitional diaconate', this is what they mean. What gets lost in this saga is the fact that many Christians feel themselves to be called to the diaconate, not to the priesthood. Two of these, Pat Wright and James Francis, were colleagues at St Botolph's. I think that we were the only Anglican parish in London, possibly in the whole country, to have two vocational deacons on the staff. James has always been heavily involved with issues of homelessness, while Pat has worked in the field of HIV and AIDS.

My sense is that the revival of the diaconate has brought to the surface a number of issues which have, for many years (and, in some cases, centuries), led to confusion within the churches. One of the objections to the revival of diaconal ministry is the argument that there is nothing that deacons can do which lay people cannot do. It is forgotten that this also applies to priesthood and episcopacy. Much work which is associated with priests and bishops is the work of all baptised Christians, and virtually all forms of ministry exercised by priests and bishops can, *in extremis*, be exercised by any Christian. We need to abandon minimalist views of ordained ministry, and see the ordained ministry within the wider context of the ministry of the whole Body of Christ.

What is crucial here is that the deacon – as indeed the priest and the bishop – are symbols of what is the task and ministry of the whole

Church. The whole thing goes wrong when we start to think in functionalist terms of 'who is allowed to do what'.

The Church condescending and indignant

My debt to Stanley Evans, and to his book *The Church in the Back Streets*, is immense. A tiny book, only fifty pages long, and in many ways very out of date, it seems to me to be more relevant now than when he wrote it. I have a tattered copy, much of which now consists of sellotape, and I often go back to it. More than any single work in this area, it shaped my approach to pastoral theology. It is a classic, rooted in his experience in the inner city. He coined the term 'the Church Condescending' as a way of describing how good, dedicated people moved into poor areas to minister *to* (rather than *with*) those whom they saw as belonging to a lower culture.

> Inevitably they saw themselves as missionaries sent to a people of a lower culture, and they can hardly be blamed that they became the executive officers of the Church Condescending. Yet for all that, it is the bitter fruits of the Church Condescending, with all its kindness and desperate desire to do good, that we have inherited … An intelligent man [sic] could have prophesied the reaction of those whose fate it was to be done good to.

'These people' were there to 'be done good to'. (W. H. Auden once caricatured this attitude by saying, 'We are all here on earth to do good to others. What the others are here for, I have no idea.') Evans went on to point out that, at a certain stage, when 'these stupid, ungrateful people don't come', the Church Condescending turns into the Church Indignant.

> The Church Condescending has given birth to the Church Indignant … Does it need to be pointed out that here is nemesis; that at this point a long process has reached its tragic conclusion; that once you reach the stage of despising people, your attitude to them has ceased to be Christian at all, and that you had best haul down your flag and pack your bags, for you have no function left to fulfil.[28]

That syndrome is still alive and well. As I re-read Evans over 40 years on, I wonder how much progress we have made.

A serious response to the 'gated' character of urban society, even including 'gated communities' now, calls for theological activity which takes walls, gates and boundaries seriously. A theology located 'outside the gate' is a vital part of such redemptive work.

Was I any good at it?

I have often found myself wondering whether I was any good at what I was doing, and whether I was 'cut out for it', as the phrase goes. The anthropologist John Jackson, reflecting on his work in Harlem, commented that he 'was terribly shy, and shyness is a self-inflicted death blow to any self-respecting anthropologist'.[29] I know what he means, and I share the shyness, but, for the most part, I found it a pastoral aid rather than a hindrance. There seemed to be something about shyness which could encourage, and help to facilitate, sensitivity, attention and the ability to listen to people who maybe were put off by too direct and too extrovert an approach. Having said that, I am still not sure how good I was at it, but maybe it was a beginning on which others could build, and hopefully improve. All work on margins is full of ambiguity. My friend David Brandon once wrote about his own sense of ambiguity in work with marginalised people: 'My lifelong inheritance is feelings of worthlessness, unrequited love, depression and despair, sometimes struggling with rage, but also ability to touch those socially excluded, similarly devalued and damaged.'[30]

Though our personal histories were different, I feel some considerable closeness to what he wrote. It reflected my experience too.

3

Pointing to Glory: theology, liturgy and the vision of God

Liturgy leads regularly to the edge of chaos, and from this regular flirt with doom comes a theology different from any other.

URBAN T. HOLMES III, cited in Lovanne Kathryn Bachner, *Fire, Story, Water, Feast: an exploration of liturgical theology and the poetics of celebration in the Easter Vigil Liturgy* (PhD dissertation, Emory University 1990, pp. 245–246)

Happy are the people who know the festal shout.

PSALM 89:15

Liturgy as a social act

A major influence on my understanding of the theological centrality, and social significance, of liturgy was the ministry at Holy Trinity, Dalston, a district of Hackney in East London, in the 1950s. Stanley Evans was the parish priest, and the whole life of the parish was focused on the parish Eucharist and the parish meeting, the latter derived from the work of Alan Ecclestone in Sheffield. Celebration and debate, heart and head, were fully engaged in this dynamic Christian community. This was one of the places which helped me to understand the nature of liturgy in shaping the corporate identity of Christian people. In an interview on BBC radio around 1962 (I have the tape but nobody knows exactly when it was recorded), Evans spoke about liturgy and its place in shaping the people of God. Liturgy, he argued, had become separated from the people, become something performed above the people's heads, by clergy or choir. But when people came together as a redeemed community, the whole body could be inspired and inflamed. The crucial part of the interview was his emphasis on the idea of the Christian community as an orchestra.

They are not ever an audience. They are an expressive community, if you like, an orchestra. Now this does not mean . . . that they all play the same instrument or that they all play all the time or at the same time, but they are an orchestra and everybody plays. While the audience response in a theatre is something of great importance, there is still a distinction between the audience and the players. What I am trying to say is that this distinction does not exist in Christian liturgy. We have built up an area in which it does exist and we have destroyed Christian liturgy in doing so.

Shortly afterwards, in 1963, Pope Paul VI's document *Sacrosanctum Concilium* stressed the importance of fully conscious and active participation by the people in the liturgy. A similar point was made later by the Benedictine liturgical scholar Aidan Kavanaugh, who stressed the centrality of liturgy to theology. Liturgy, he argued, constitutes 'primary theology', it is the 'primary theological act'. The origin and heart of theology lie in worship, in the liturgical action.

Kavanaugh also drew attention to the problem of pews, so very modern yet seen by many Christians as 'traditional'. At St Botolph's, not only were we plagued by these wretched structures, but they were the creakiest ones in the world – as any preacher discovered if s/he made a joke or controversial comment, which led to people shuffling their posteriors. The whole church would creak as a corporate entity. But the problem goes way beyond creaking. Kavanaugh wrote:

> Pews, which entered liturgical space only recently, nail the assembly down, proclaiming that the liturgy is not a common action but a preachment perpetrated upon the seated, an ecclesiastical opera done by virtuosi for a paying audience. Pews distance the congregation, disenfranchise the faithful, and rend the assembly.[1]

I believe that we make a disastrous mistake when we ignore the ecology, the environment in which theology occurs. We seem to have taken environmental issues more seriously (albeit only recently) in town planning and in the building of schools and shopping malls than we have in theology or in the life of prayer and discipleship. At St Botolph's, the physical structure of the building, not least the pews, was a major impediment to our spiritual liberation. We were inhibited, confined, repressed by inherited structures. Maybe that was the intention of the architect. On the other hand, we did our best with the structures we had inherited.

Much of my theological work in East London was connected with the idea and the reality of liturgy as a corporate act, as the way in which a community both expresses itself and comes into itself, becomes in germ the reality toward which it strives. I cannot conceive of a Christian theology which is not rooted in this common life of worship and vision. Yet I have been struck, and depressed, by two features of local church life in many places. The first is that theology is seen as something quite separate from worship, a cerebral activity, maybe only necessary for those preparing for ministry, and for those with a particular mental aptitude, 'the clever ones'. The second is a lack of interest in liturgy as that which expresses the community's encounter with God, and therefore as something over which enormous care must be taken. 'Going to church' or 'taking a service' is not the same as the dynamic and profound involvement in the liturgical action. Much conventional Christian worship is anything but profound, and often borders on the sentimental and trivial. My work as a local theologian had to involve serious work and reflection on helping to make the liturgy 'take', empower, inspire, point people to glory. This was really central once the meaning of the liturgy had been understood. In Holmes' words:

> The sacramental life of the church is the heart of the church's performance where the symbols of Christ's passion reach and touch the deep memory of humankind and transform our vision to our roots. We live by the memory of the death and resurrection of Jesus. It is our root metaphor.[2]

Yet so much Christian worship lacks the symbolism, the root metaphors which take us from one place to another. (In Greece, trains, buses and other forms of public transport are called *metaphorai* – they take you from one place to another.) In the liturgy, we are taken forward to share something of the mystery and glory of God. This encounter strikes us as amazing, astonishing, and this sense of astonishment is basic to worship in Jewish and Christian experience.[3]

Two of the features of St Botolph's which attracted me in 1990 were the fact that the church was open more than it was closed, and the fact that the Divine Office was recited, and the Eucharist offered, daily. In the 1970s Malcolm Johnson and David Randall had put a great deal of effort into undermining, and almost destroying, the earlier 'civic Anglican' character of the church, and moving towards a more Catholic, sacramental and liturgical ethos. Even so, there were some members who felt that the liturgy and the work for justice did not connect. One of them, who had come to us from a progressive parish in Toronto, wrote on 27th January 1997:

> our liturgy is done in a vacuum. We talk about justice, we struggle to do justice as a congregation, but what we say in the liturgy has no bearing on what we say, and do otherwise ... We talk about involving ourselves with people, and yet we use a creed that focuses on a cosmic, distant God. We talk about 'standing on the edge', and yet our eucharistic liturgy, week in, week out, reflects nothing but the status quo.

Sadly, that brother left us, disappointed with what he saw as our failure to integrate liturgy and life.

The eucharistic action should be the model for all Christian action, and there has to be the closest connection between what we do in the Eucharist and what we do in the world. For, as the North American bishop Arthur Vogel wrote: 'Through the Eucharist we are extensions of Christ's vulnerability, sustained by the food of his victory: we are not guards placed at the door of his anterooms to protect him from profanation or contact with the world.'[4]

For me, theology makes no sense unless it is rooted in liturgy, in corporate worship and prayer. It is in worship and prayer, most of all and fundamentally, that we are theologians. As the Athanasian Creed puts it, 'The Catholic faith is this: that we *worship* one God in Trinity and Trinity in Unity.' The faith is about worship before it is about doctrine. Liturgy is the primary theological act. It follows that liturgy and worship are key elements of contextual theology.

There is good evidence that what attracted people to the early Christian Church was less their evangelism than the power of their worship and the intensity of their action, particularly their love in action. I have seen this process in today's Church. People are often drawn to a community which takes worship seriously before they understand what is going on, and this is particularly so when the worship is linked with a real sense of community and warmth in welcoming and embracing others.

Awe and wonder

However, this centrality of liturgical prayer has been lost in much theology with its excessive focus on the cerebral. To adapt Marcuse's famous phrase, we have declined into a one-dimensional liturgy. The nurturing and strengthening of the worshipping community, and the recovery of the splendour, awe and wonder of the liturgy is a *sine qua non* of theological existence. The liturgy is an approach to the God who is a consuming fire (Heb. 12:29), and the only possible response is to 'stand in awe' (Rom. 11:20). God is great, mighty and awesome, and 'does great and awesome things' (Deut. 10:17, 21. Cf Ps 89:7; Eccles. 43:29; Mal. 2:5). Much modern liturgy has been too influenced by linear, one-dimensional thinking and, often unconsciously, by a kind of structural functionalism. It has 'no power to make the soul or to break the heart'.[5] Linked with the trend towards subjectivity in the same period, these features have had corrosive and damaging effects on the character of Christian liturgy. The new humanity must sing a new song, says St Augustine, echoing the words of scripture.[6]

I am sure we need to stress the place of awe and wonder in the Church. For places too can be awesome (Gen. 28:17), and we can see heaven opened up anywhere (John 1:51). On the Feast of St Bartholomew (24th August) we often read Genesis 28 with its reference to 'the house of God and ... the gate of heaven' (Gen. 28:17), followed by John 1 – 'you will see heaven opened' (John 1:51). In the account of Jesus' baptism in Matthew 'the heavens were opened to him' (Matt. 3:16). What is central to these references is the idea that any place and any moment can be a place and moment of insight, of revelation, of transfiguration, of the opening of the gates of heaven to us. There is a church in the East End – St Paul's, Bow Common, built in 1961 – which has the words 'This is none other than the house of God and this is the gate of heaven' engraved around the baptistry. What is visible to passers-by on the main Burdett Road is simply 'the gate of heaven', and it is not uncommon for people to get on the 106 or 277 bus at Mile End, and say to the driver, 'Gate of heaven, dear'.

In the midst of an often dreary movement of bureaucratic liturgism, there have been some shining moments – the work of Janet Morley and Jim Cotter, as well as lesser-known figures such as the late William McCrossan ('Liturgical William') in the East End, some of the supplementary material produced by the Church of England and other

Anglican churches, and so on. Yet I still find much of what goes on so restrained, moderate, tame, stiff, lacking in fire, but also lacking in the ability to weep, grieve and mourn. There is a need in our worship, identified by Walter Brueggemann among others, to develop a 'ranged dialectic' of lament and praise, reflecting crucifixion and resurrection.[7]

Weekday worship

The daily worship was at the heart of our life at St Botolph's, though I am not sure that we ever 'got it right'. Perhaps no one ever does. Part of the problem was not of our making. The congregations on weekdays and on Sundays were quite different. Many of the people who came to the daily Mass or joined us for the Divine Office were local workers or students from the nearby university. They were constantly changing. Trying to find times for worship which were convenient to everyone was immensely difficult. There were difficulties too with the varied schedules and commitments of the team itself. Those who worked in the crypt would find it difficult to join us for worship during the day. For a while Pat Wright (one of our two vocational deacons who worked as a night-duty nurse at the nearby Mildmay Mission Hospital) and I used to meet to say Morning Prayer at 7 am. Pat would then go to bed, and I would go about my daily work. Eventually we settled on 9 am as the time which was least inconvenient for most of us to meet for Morning Prayer. We never managed to find a time when we could all guarantee to say Evening Prayer together, which was sad, but, I think, unavoidable unless there was a willingness, and ability, to reorganise our use of time. However, the daily recitation of the Divine Office was so important and, in 'retirement', I miss the discipline and privilege of being able to say the Office regularly with others. I found that the churches of East London, where the daily recitation of the Divine Office was normal, made one think that the whole Church was like that, and it is very sad to realise that, in many places, the idea of this daily rhythm of prayer is unknown to most Christians.

Yet there is something really important here. In the daily reading of the Divine Office, there is a space within which the Word of God may be released. 'The Word of God is not chained' (2 Tim. 2:9), yet, if it is to be released and to be a 'liberating Word', there needs to be a discipline of attention, a persistent brooding on the Word, a genuinely contemplative approach to the Bible. The Word must take root within us. Those who hear the Word and believe have passed from death to life (John 5:25): on the other hand, as Jeremiah said, if the Word is not within us, even the prophets are 'nothing but wind' (Jer. 5:13). For Jeremiah, the words which he absorbed became a fire (5:14).

The fire, however, does need to be kindled and tended, and I think we neglected this. Lindsey Ellin, in her report on her time in the parish in 1992, rightly expressed concern that a church which, in her view, was so radical in many areas of its work, was so conservative and rigid in its worship. I tend to agree with her. I don't think we ever quite got to the point of being able to pray together with that intensity of adoration, anguish, spontaneity and solidarity which comes from closeness in discipleship and sharing of life together. An hour of prayer before the Blessed Sacrament once a week would have really strengthened our sense of solidarity in ministry. Sunday worship too was often lacking in adventure, spontaneity and 'creative chaos'. Members like Ann Hinchliffe and Philip Groom did their best, and achieved considerable results. Yet such a sense of adventure does depend on a real rootedness in a living tradition, and I am not sure that this was present.

Linked with the daily Office and the daily Eucharist, we put a good deal of effort into praying in a disciplined way for the geographical parish, street by street, and for those who lived and worked there, as well as for all the regular members of the congregation. We tried to remember people on their birthdays and on important moments in their lives, and to make sure that our intercessions were thoughtful and intelligent.

For the weekday celebration of Mass, we settled – again after much debate – on the curious time of 1.05 pm. This dated from the days when city offices had clearly defined lunch breaks which began at 1pm, and we allowed five minutes for people to get to the church. By the 1990s this was no longer the case, but it still seemed a time that suited many people. Visitors to London would know that the Mass was offered daily at this time, so we had many people for whom St Botolph's was their 'London church' when they were 'in town'. It seemed important at the weekday Mass to include both relaxed informality and contemplative silence. With an ever-changing congregation, it was impossible to assume that everyone knew the form of the rite, and so flexibility and willingness to adapt was essential. The regular worshippers, for example, were accustomed to give the sacrament to one another, but, if there were a number of newcomers present for whom this practice was unfamiliar, we would change it. We tried to include silence, while being aware that some people had to leave quickly. We tried also to involve the worshippers in the action – reading the scripture lessons, interceding, and so on – with varying degrees of success, in view of the changing nature of the congregation.

We were often joined by people who had no idea of what was going on, and by others who did know, but were drunk or confused or both. I remember one very drunk man who, during the eucharistic prayer, staggered up to the altar and placed a soggy beer-stained five pound note on the corporal. I was at the point of the epiclesis, the invocation of the Holy Spirit, when the priest stretches out her or his hands over the bread and wine, and so it seemed natural to stretch them further towards the man, and so I did an informal laying on of hands within the context of eucharistic consecration. After this, he gracefully retired and went to sleep. After the Mass, a woman, who had never been at the church before, expressed her appreciation for that part of the rite, obviously assuming that it was a normal part of the local liturgical tradition, and happened all the time! (Sometimes it felt as if it did.)

The Sunday Mass

The Sunday congregation had gone through at least four phases in my association with it. In the late 1950s it was mostly local and white, though with some West Indian, African and Indian members who lived in houses close to the church, most of which have now been demolished to make way for offices. By the 1970s, a large part of the congregation was still local residents, but it also included numbers of people, including gay and lesbian Christians, who had fled from less welcoming churches elsewhere in East London. By the 1990s, as a result partly of deaths and partly of 'regeneration', the local residents became a minority in what was increasingly a 'gathered' congregation, still including numbers of gay and lesbian people, but also others who were attracted to St Botolph's for various reasons. Some of these were holding on to the Church but very much on the edge of it, and we seemed to be able to provide a kind of lifeline, and often transitional space, for them. I have many letters, and reminiscences of conversations, confirming this. There were also people who were, or had been, homeless and, as a result of their contact with St Botolph's, had attached themselves to the congregation. Finally, towards the end of the 1990s, there was an influx of professional people with small children who could afford to live in the pockets of residential accommodation around Petticoat Lane.

One of the problems we encountered in trying to minister with a 'gathered', and always changing, congregation was the fact that most of the members only appeared in church on Sundays. This had several consequences. Many had only a vague idea of what went on during the rest of the week, or of what the clergy or project workers did, and often had quite wrong ideas. The fact that, for a long period, 'local' residents – even if the concept of 'local' was extended to the western edge of the City and several miles east into Whitechapel and Stepney – were a small minority meant that there could be little consciousness of, or involvement in, the local ministry of the parish. There was, to my mind, always a certain sense of detachment, of unreality, in the Sunday worship, though what I have described is the norm in many churches in the USA.

I felt throughout my time at St Botolph's that we had far too many preachers. At one point, we had, on the 'team', four priests, two deacons and a lay reader. It was quite possible for a 'regular' attender, who did not come every Sunday, never to hear, or even encounter, one or more of the staff. Consistency of teaching was virtually impossible, and every sermon had to stand on its own. While this was by no means peculiar to St Botolph's, I felt that we failed to engage with the seriousness of the problem in terms of teaching, liturgy and pastoral engagement.

There was too a specifically theological problem. I feel that Christian theologians must play a part in Christian liturgy, and this normally, if not always, includes preaching. It is essential that there is a continuous interplay and dialogue between the theologian as researcher, and the theologian as evangelist, prophet and 'breaker of the word'. While this is not impossible in the kind of liturgical environment which I have described above, it is, in my experience, enormously difficult, not least because part of the theological task is that of ongoing reflection on the pastoral ministry of the community.

This raises the question of the nature of preaching, the role of the sermon, and its relationship to liturgy and theology. Of course, there is a question about whether the 'traditional' sermon is now obsolete, and should be replaced by other methods of catechesis, involving discussion, questioning and so on. Even if – as I would wish – the sermon is retained in a place of importance within Christian worship, it is obvious that it must be supplemented by other approaches and methods. As long ago as 1962, Stanley Evans noted that 'there is no single organisation outside the church, concerned with adult education, which would conceive it right to have two discourses delivered to people every week, where there was neither taking of notes nor asking of questions or discussion, and seriously expect the people to assimilate and digest what was said'.[8] I was very impressed, during regular visits to St Barnabas Church, Glen Ellyn, on the outskirts of Chicago, when Bob MacFarlane was the parish priest, by the fact that, at the daily Mass, the celebrant would say, after the gospel reading, 'Does anyone have anything to say about this?' Sometimes there would be fascinating and profound comments, sometimes silent reflection and prayer. It was such an obvious thing to do, yet it is rare in our churches. As a result the sermon stands in isolation from the rest of the thoughts and struggles of the liturgical assembly.

Eucharist and baptism

When I was a teenager in what were known then as 'the cotton towns' on the edge of Manchester (now called Tameside), the celebration of the Eucharist in most churches suffered from a serious fragmentation and distortion of the tradition. In the Roman communion, and among many Anglican Catholics, the Low Mass on weekdays and early on Sundays was the time when the devout received communion, while the later Sung or High Mass was a service at which the congregation came to 'hear Mass' but only the priest received the sacrament. Among 'low church' and evangelical Anglicans, communion might be quite rare: Morning and Evening Prayer were the major Sunday services. This rarity of eucharistic worship prevailed in most types of Protestantism. Only among the Holiness and Pentecostal churches – the Assemblies of God, the Elim Church, the Church of the Nazarene and others – was 'the breaking of the bread' the central act of Sunday worship, since these churches had gone 'back to the Bible' and took what they found there seriously. The 'Parish Communion' movement, which had spread elsewhere in Britain, was only just beginning to affect Anglican churches in the 1950s in the Manchester area.

Since then, there has been a real revolution in what Wolfhart Pan-nenberg has called 'eucharistic sensibility', and eucharistic liturgy is now valued, and holds central place in many, if not most, churches. However, there has not been a similar revolution in the other great sacrament, baptism. Although the 'private' baptisms on Sunday after-noon, disconnected from the public liturgy and from all church life, are less common (though the 'royal family' is, as on so many other matters, way behind the mood and mind of the Church of which the Queen is meant to be Supreme Governor), the understanding of the centrality of the baptismal liturgy as the great sacrament of initiation into the full membership of the Body is still not understood by many Christians. The understanding of the meaning of baptism is, I believe, utterly central to the future of ministry within and beyond the Christian community.

While many Christians have, since the late nineteenth century, stressed the 'social implications' of eucharistic worship, I am not sure that this has been true of their approach to baptism. The political sig-nificance of baptism has, in recent years, become more urgent with the increases in global and local concerns with water. In both the Eastern Orthodox and Roman rites for the blessing of water, there is a focus on 'new humanity' and 'the renewal of humankind'. But what progress has been made on how this affects the discussion of dams, the diversion of world rivers, the lack of pure water in many countries, or housing damp in East London and elsewhere in Britain? The question of the place of water in social life was a major feature of our work. Like so many other matters, it grew from practical experience in small districts and reflection on them. This is how theology develops.[9]

An issue to which we had given much thought was the reception of Holy Communion by small children. I have felt strongly for many years that to baptise small children, tell them, or their parents and sponsors, that they were now members of the Body of Christ and inheritors of the Kingdom of God, and then to deny them Holy Communion until twelve or more years later, was theologically inde-fensible and pastorally disastrous. If we were not to admit children to communion, it would be better not to baptise them at all. Pastorally and liturgically, it created division at the altar, with first- and second-class Christians, based on age. My colleagues agreed with me, but the issue was largely theoretical, since, most of the time, there were no children. The congregation consisted mostly of single women and men, lesbian and gay couples, and those well past childbearing age. Only when children from other parts of the Anglican Communion – such as the Episcopal Church of the USA where the baptismal theology is better, or children from 'progressive' parishes in Britain – presented themselves, were we faced with the practical question. All this changed a few years ago with the sudden influx into the neighbourhood and congregation of a number of young professionals – the only people who could afford the property locally – with small children. Today there can be between 20 and 30 small children who receive the sacrament at the Sunday Mass.

Some years ago we introduced the Renewal of the Baptismal Covenant in place of the Nicene Creed at all Sundays throughout the Great Fifty Days of the Paschal season. We used the excellent form in the USA Book of Common Prayer. This helped people to see the central importance of baptism in the life of the whole Church. The restoration of the Paschal Vigil, with baptism and renewal of vows at its centre, also made a great difference. I do not believe that we can do Christian theology without taking these liturgical matters seriously.

Hymns

Many Christians take their theology from hymns, so it seemed important to take hymns seriously. The problem here is that many of them are appalling, theologically, politically, linguistically. How can socially responsible Christians sing 'Hide me, O my Saviour, hide, till the storm of life is past', or 'Sweet light, so shine on us , we pray, that earthly joys may fade away'? Can we make sense of the gospels if we sing 'O Sabbath rest by Galilee, O calm of hills above'? Galilee was one of the most violent and troubled places in the ancient world, and Jesus would have been in the synagogue on the Sabbath in any case! One hymn for Ascensiontide includes the lines 'And still the holy church is here, although her Lord has gone'. What kind of theology is this? And then there are the hymns which arise from a particular cultural milieu, and use words which can make no sense to those who now sing them. An example is one of the most popular hymns used by Anglicans in the USA.

> I sing a song of the saints of God, patient and brave and true,
> Who toiled and fought and lived and died

For the Lord they loved and knew . . .
And one was a doctor and one was a queen,
And one was a shepherdess on the green . . .

What idea of sanctity does this communicate to young people in the USA today?

Many of the modern and postmodern hymns are equally bad or even worse: slushy, individualistic, sentimental, lacking in any social or biblical framework. If we are to do good theology in the inner city or anywhere, we have to do something about these dreadful hymns which have possibly done more to undermine Christian action than biblical fundamentalism has done.

Worse still, some of our British hymns are more or less fascist. It is appalling that the words usually sung to Gustav Holst's beautiful tune 'Thaxted' are 'I vow to thee, my country'. It includes the lines: 'The love that asks no question, the love that stands the test'. No orthodox Christian can sing those words without betraying his or her baptismal commitment. Absolute obedience is only to God and God's Kingdom, not to any country. This is particularly disgraceful since it rejects all that the radical Christian community at Thaxted, from the early twentieth century until, at least, the 1970s, stood for. Some years ago the Jubilee Group invited people to write some words that could be sung to this tune by Christians with a clear conscience. The best offering by far was by the Canadian academic William Whitla, 'Let streams of living justice flow down upon the earth'. At my initiative, it was sung at Thaxted, and later at Alan Green's institution at St John's, Bethnal Green, and is now in the hymn book of the Anglican Church of Canada (albeit slightly censored).

These paragraphs have been very negative, and I do not wish to deny that there are many good, wholesome, orthodox, biblically based hymns being written. My point is simply to warn that much damage is still being done by hymns and songs which hinder the work of Christian ministry and Christian social action in the world.

The place of art at St Botolph's

The issues about visual portrayals of Christ, and about the place of art in Christian worship, were raised in the iconoclastic controversy of the eighth century. The key figure in this controversy was St

John of Damascus. Art and music are at the very heart of Christian liturgy. Two features of the art within the church building are worth stressing. The reredos behind the High Altar is a tapestry of the Tree of Life with buildings of the City of London in the background. The artist was asked to portray what she felt was the heart of the ministry of the parish, and the result was a powerful fusion of the Book of Revelation and the structures of today's version of Babylon. At the entrance to the Peace Chapel is a statue of Our Lady, but it is not the familiar statue of Virgin and Child. Instead it shows Our Lady of Sorrows, the mother who looks through the crown of thorns at the pain of the world. Again, so much theology, good and bad, is conveyed through visual art more than through words.

On 19th March 1991 I met Liz Ellis, then the art tutor at St Botolph's Crypt, who was soon to become a close friend and colleague. Liz had been one of the pioneers of art work by homeless people in Britain, and a number of people in 1991 felt that she should travel to the USA to see how artists there were becoming involved with homelessness. With the help of various colleagues, we were able to raise the funds to get her to New York and Chicago. Liz soon became a key figure in my own life and work. Sadly, for reasons which I never fully fathomed, the art work, which to me was so important, seemed to become a low priority at the Crypt. Liz left to do a further degree, and the work was reduced and soon disappeared. In many ways she was the key figure in linking art and imaginative work with the issues around care of homeless people and those with mental health problems.

On 15th September 2001, Liz married Michael Kennedy at the Art Workers' Guild in Queen Square. It was a great honour for me to 'preside' at this event, assisted by Menakshee, the young daughter of Andy Delmege and Bharti Parmar, who came to an agreement with me that if I wasn't doing it properly she would raise her hand! The Art Workers' Guild is an extraordinary place, associated in its origins with John Ruskin and William Morris, but it was the first time that they had ever had a wedding there. Liz, however, was determined that this was the most suitable place for their marriage, and so it was.

On 27th February 1998 we placed the enormous and spiritually amazing painting 'Scene of a Crucifixion with Seven Deadly Sins' behind the High Altar of St Botolph's where it remained throughout Lent. Painted by the Dublin artist Brian Breathnach, it has, to my knowledge, hung in only two places – the James Joyce Centre in

Dublin, and St Botolph's. I had seen it during a visit to the Dublin Theatre Festival some years earlier, and was determined to track down the artist. It seemed to me a remarkable example of 'theology in colour', a piece of theological work presented through a visual portrayal. It shows a naked Jesus hanging on the cross, surrounded by seven naked figures, each one coloured differently. They stand for the seven deadly sins, here portrayed as witnesses of the crucifixion. Jesus is painted in bright yellow, the colour of the sun. Lust is pink, and Anger is red, while Anger's arm is held by the green figure of Envy. Greed, painted blue, is kneeling, pleading for more, while the bloated orange figure represents Gluttony. Pride is coloured purple, and holds his hand above his head – apparently feeling for a halo. (When I led a retreat in an American seminary on the painting, I raised the question of whether the purple figure was looking for a halo, or, maybe, a mitre. The student body collapsed with laughter. Only later did I realise that the Dean had been elected Bishop of New York that morning!) Finally, there is the grey figure of Sloth, with his feet and body turned away, lacking the energy to be there at all, sliding off the picture.

A few days later, on the First Sunday in Lent, Brian preached. He told us of its origin when a spiritual director advised him to examine himself on the seven deadly sins. Being an artist, he decided also to express this in painting.

The church had also been a centre for artists for some time, and exhibitions were common, although some of the key members of the congregation for whom this was a central concern left during the 1990s. But there was no real thinking about how the visual arts related to theology, liturgy, spirituality or our wider Christian mission. Most of the time, the paintings and sculptures which surrounded the worshippers were fairly innocuous and irrelevant to worship. However, occasionally, the art and the worship came into conflict. One such example, in the early 1990s, involved an exhibition on the human body which, not surprisingly, included various naked figures. This offended a very small, but vocal, group within the congregation, some of whom left as a result. I was asked to write a discussion paper on the place of art and on some of the underlying issues. I am not sure that it made much impression, and it did make me think about how we try to relate theology to our worshipping life. I wrote the paper on the Thursday of the third week of Easter when the patristic lesson in the Office of Readings contains these words from Irenaeus:

> If our flesh is not saved, then the Lord has not redeemed us with his blood, the eucharistic chalice does not make us sharers in his blood, and the bread we break does not make us sharers in his body. There can be no blood without veins, flesh, and the rest of the human substance, and this the Word of God actually became . . . How then can it be said that flesh belonging to the Lord's own body, and nourished by his body and blood, is incapable of receiving God's gift of eternal life?[10]

Those words, directed against the early gnostics who saw the flesh as 'intrinsically evil' – to use a term which is all too familiar today – are really important if we are to take art, the use of material things in worship, and the body itself with spiritual and material seriousness.

The commitment to the visual arts at St Botolph's was only a small part of a wider movement within East London as a whole, where, in 1992, it was estimated that around 6,000 artists lived and worked. They included famous figures such as Gilbert and George, Tracy Emin and Sarah Lucas, as well as a wide range of local community artists such as Dan Jones, Liz Ellis and Kinsi Abdulleh. They included also many 'community photographers' – Phil Maxwell, Paul Trevor, David Hoffman and others. I worked closely with many of these local-based artists.

Liturgy and justice

In biblical teaching, worship cannot be separated from the pursuit of justice. Worship without justice is not acceptable to God (Isa. 1:13–17). While a concern with liturgy and justice has increased since, and been nourished and strengthened by, the Second Vatican Council, it antedates that important Council by many years. A key figure in the renewal of liturgy in the Roman communion was the Benedictine Virgil Michel (1890–1938). He founded the journal *Orate Fratres* in 1926, and laid great stress on 'active participation' of the people in the liturgical act. Writing on 'liturgy as the basis of social regeneration' in 1935, Michel said:

> Pius X tells us that the liturgy is the indispensable source of the true Christian spirit. Pius XI says that the true Christian spirit is indispensable for social regeneration. Hence the conclusion: the Liturgy is the indispensable basis of social regeneration.

The social dimensions of the liturgy, stressed for more than a hundred years within Anglican social thought, have become more emphasised in recent thought in various churches. One eminent liturgical scholar wrote in 1982:

> Where else in our society are all of us . . . called to be social critics, called to extricate ourselves from the powers and principalities that claim to rule our daily lives? Where else do economic czars and beggars get the same treatment? Where else are food and drink blessed in a common prayer of thanksgiving . . . so that everybody shares?[11]

When a group of left-wing Anglican priests had met in Bethnal Green, where I was rector, and founded the Jubilee Group at the end of 1974, we invited a fairly unknown graduate student, Rowan Williams, to help compose a manifesto. It began with a quotation from the Russian theologian Nikolay Fyodorov, one of the people who had figured in Rowan's doctoral thesis on modern Russian theology: 'Our social programme is the dogma of the Holy Trinity.' In recent years there has been increasing attention given to the Trinity, not least among feminist theologians. This is not surprising for the Trinity is about relationship, interdependence, co-operation and solidarity. It is about 'the social God'. A few years later I wrote a book with that title.[12] One major consequence of belief in a social God is the realisation that relationship with God must itself be social, not solitary, and so the primary network of such relationship is what we call worship.

The manifesto was a fascinating document, but rather triumphalist, and we rejected it. But it contained some important material which is relevant to the way in which theology and spirituality have their roots in worship:

> We are committed to the struggle for justice, liberty and peace, not because of some secondary interest in social theory, but because of the very foundation of the Catholic Faith . . .

> Because our fathers in the Catholic movement worshipped Christ in the sacrament, they also loved, cared for, and identified with, him in the wretched of the earth . . . What they said in Victorian and Edwardian England, we must proclaim in our situation today. Our commitment to the struggle of the oppressed must be as passionate as theirs, for, while much has changed over the last hundred years,

the poor still starve throughout the Third World and in the streets of our cities.

The heart, the core, the living centre of Christian theology and practice is this sense of rootedness in the being of God. Yet this has to be worked out and engaged with within the contrary structures of our society. So I have found the relationship, which is often also the conflict, between doctrine, liturgy and society, one of my greatest challenges and areas of acute pain and distress in my attempts to be a community-rooted theologian. Yet what else can one be? How can theology be done in isolation, independence, loneliness? St Hilary of Poitiers once said that we cannot preach a loving God if we have to preach a lonely God. Community, solidarity, interdependence: these are central to Christian belief and to the nature of theological work. This is what Vladimir Lossky meant when he said that there is no 'middle way' between the Trinity and hell, for hell is the ultimate loneliness, the terminal point of individualism gone crazy. Or, as William Morris expressed it in the nineteenth century, 'Fellowship is heaven, lack of fellowship is hell.'

4

Wrestling with the Demons: theology and struggle

Theology is a task to be undertaken in solidarity with those who
suffer from the refusal of the powerful to change their policies.

J. ANDREW KIRK in A. E. Harvey (ED.),
Theology in the City (SPCK 1989, p. 20)

Inside my chest
Is a fist, clenching darkness
That has been shaking for a thousand years.

DAVID SHADDOCK, cited in
Denise Levertov, *New and Selected Essays*
(New York, New Directions 1992, p. 15)

. . . the dangers of the storm are real. There is no guarantee at all
of survival or indeed of not being broken.

PETER ROSE, *Reflections on Sailing and Spirituality*
(privately published, 2005)

He [Christ] walks again on the seas of blood,
He comes in the terrible rain.

EDITH SITWELL, 'The Song of Cain'

The necessity of struggle

The practice of theology is not, in conventional western discourse, linked with struggle. In other parts of the world, theology may
be seen as highly toxic, subversive, dangerous, and its pursuit may lead
to death, as it did to Archbishop Romero and to the Jesuits in El Sal-
vador. Their theology was committed, partisan, if you like, biased. In
the West, we have come to prize detachment, 'objectivity', neutrality.
But, as James McClendon pointed out, 'in convictional work, self-

involvement is natural and appropriate, while disengagement requires to be explained'.[1] I have not experienced many examples of such explanation. Most Christians who stand on the edge of major debates, and so support whatever the established order happens to be at the time, do not feel the need to justify or explain their posture. They see it as pursuing a 'middle way', as more 'responsible', more 'balanced' than the 'extremes', or as being 'above the battle', a flawed understanding of transcendence and of spirituality if ever there was one. But most of this is mystification and self-delusion. In fact, they practise a kind of damaged, degraded theology which is disengaged from actual struggles. Genuine orthodox theology must be involved, committed, partisan. A theology which is disconnected from the world is not Christian theology at all.

Indeed, we need to ask: is a detached theology possible? At one level, clearly it is, for there is a lot of it around, and maybe the bulk of what is termed 'theology' suffers from what Oliver O'Donovan has called 'a forced and unnatural detachment'.[2] Yet deeper scrutiny reveals that such 'detachment' is often profoundly *attached* to accepted structures and values. The important question is: can such theology be Christian? Here I feel that the answer must be 'No'. 'One cannot do serious theology . . . in the abstract. Only in the throes of real life situations can fundamental questions of theology, pastoral care and ethics be raised.'[3] So the 'locus', the site on which theology is done, is of critical importance.[4]

Struggle against evil, injustice and oppression is central to our faith and our life, not least because, in Rowan Williams' words, 'hunger and restlessness are part of what [we are] made for'. Many years earlier Karl Barth stressed that grace manifests itself in 'divine impatience, discontent, dissatisfaction'.[5] Political action is inevitable, even if it often takes the forms of apathy, inaction and collusion. These are probably the main forms of political action, though they are rarely recognised as such. When people condemn churches for 'interfering in politics' it is the politics of change that they usually have in mind, not the (far more common and more influential) politics of maintenance and preservation.

It is impossible to escape conflict, but this is not the same as seeking it for its own sake. The East End community activist Maggie Hewitt, reviewing a book by our mutual friend Chris Searle, a teacher and campaigner in the East End for years, claimed that he needed conflict but was unaware of his own position. He was, she argued, 'a kind of Peter Pan figure who doesn't appear to change at all over the years. He is still fighting the system, and he never discusses his relationship to conflict [and] his own propensity to attract controversy.'[6] This comment intrigued me, not only because I knew both the people involved, but also because the same kind of comment has been made about me. It is all too common for an individual to thrive on conflict and controversy in a self-indulgent yet unreflective kind of way, and I have certainly succumbed to this temptation. My friends have sometimes quoted the biblical words, 'From birth you were called a rebel' (Isa. 48:8). As I have grown older, the need for personal honesty, self-scrutiny, understanding of unconscious forces and motives have come to figure more prominently in my life. I have come to be wary of conflictual positions which lack such self-awareness, while recognising, at the same time, that to avoid conflict is harmful to oneself and to 'the cause'. What seems really important here is a kind of courage which is more than simplistic defiance, which recognises the origins of anger and rage, does not value them for their own sake, but is ready to take up adversarial or unpopular positions.

I believe that Christians are, by their baptismal vows, committed to political struggle, to struggle for justice, struggle against evil. Not struggle for its own sake, but because it is only through struggle that we make progress. The pursuit of justice is central to the biblical tradition, where it is rooted in the nature of God. God is a God of justice (Isa. 30:18; Ps. 89:14). Righteousness and justice are the foundations of God's rule (Ps. 89:14). His word about justice is 'a word that shall not return' (Isa. 45:25). The New Jerusalem Bible uses the phrase 'saving justice' (Isa. 51:7–8). Justice, according to the biblical texts, is the only basis for peace: there can be no true peace without justice (Isa. 32:17). We struggle for a community, and a world, where the poor have hope and injustice shuts its mouth (Job 5:16). Worship without justice is not acceptable, neither is peace without justice. Jeremiah condemns those who have 'treated the wounds of my people carelessly and who cry "Peace, peace, when there is no peace"' (Jer. 6:14; 8:11). The prophets condemn conditions where 'the law becomes slack and justice never prevails' (Hab. 1:4). False balances and unjust weights and measures are crucial issues for biblical religion (Prov. 11:1; 20:10). Even fasting is linked with loosing the bonds of oppression, letting the oppressed go free, and sharing bread with the hungry (Isa. 58:6).

Work for justice, in my experience, and in the biblical record, always involves struggle and controversy. This is clear from the case of the prophet Elisha who was critical of conventional certitude, and whose life was rooted in controversy (2 Kings 6:8–23). Controversy is central to biblical religion, and it often involves resistance and what would today be termed negativity, for there is 'a time to break down and a time to build up' (Eccles. 3:3). Christian 'spirituality' involves pressing on and straining forward (Phil. 3:12–13): it is never, in this world, a condition of perpetual calm and peace.

The prophetic task

It follows that churches, locally, nationally and internationally, must always seek to 'maintain justice and do what is right' (Isa. 56:1). They must, with the Psalmist, pray for deliverance to the needy, and for the crushing of the oppressors (Ps. 72:4). But they must also condemn those who 'turn justice to wormwood' and 'trample on the needy and bring to ruin the poor of the land' (Amos 5:7, 11, and 8:4), as well as those who are 'at ease in Zion' (Amos 6:1) and have lost the energy to care. In the context of such apathy, the prophetic role is to remind the Church that the Word of God is living and active (Heb. 4:12–13). There is no escaping this obligation by claiming that only some individuals are called to be prophets. The prophetic task is central to the Church's life, and central to theological work. It is not a vocation: it is a necessary consequence of the baptismal covenant and of Christian discipleship. Christians are called to be 'artisans of a new humanity'.[7]

Christian prophetic witness, in my experience, begins with local struggles and issues. When local Christian communities reflect on the scriptures, and see the contrast between the biblical witness and the current situation, they may be led to 'prophesy against the city'. Here is an example from St Margaret's Church, Scotswood, Newcastle-upon-Tyne, a parish at the heart of a 'regeneration' programme.

> The people of Scotswood had a community in Newcastle, in the city run by the council. And the leader of the council said to the people of Scotswood, 'Give me your homes, so that I can have the land for an urban village, because it is in my city. I will give you better houses for them. Or, if it seems good to you, I will give you a compulsory purchase order to the value of your house.' But the people said to the

leader, 'The Lord forbid that we should give you our community in which our families have lived for generations.' He went back to the council chamber, turned away his face, and would not eat.

His Head of Community and Housing came to him and said, 'Why are you so depressed that you will not eat?' He said to her, 'Because I spoke to the people of Scotswood, and said to them, "Give me your homes for money, or else, if you prefer, I will relocate you into other homes." But they answered, "We will not give you our community"'. His Head of Community and Housing said to him, 'Do you now govern Newcastle? Get up, eat some food, and be cheerful. I will give you the land of the people of Scotswood.'

So she wrote letters in the leader's name, and sealed them with his seal. She sent the letters to the councillors who represented the people of Scotswood. She wrote in the letters, 'Arrange community meetings, and bring the people of Scotswood to them. Seat Going for Growth officers opposite them, and have them bring a charge against them, saying "There is no good home in Scotswood." Then take away their school and break their spirit.' The men and women of this city, the councillors and Going for Growth officers did as she had sent word to them. Just as it was written in the letters that she had sent to them, they arranged the meetings, and seated the people of Scotswood at the table. The Going for Growth officers came in and sat with them, and the Going for Growth officers brought a charge against the community, saying, 'There is no good home in Scotswood.' Then they took away the school and broke their spirit. Then they sent to the Head of Community and Housing, saying, 'The community has been broken, they are leaving.'

As soon as the Head of Community and Housing heard that they were broken and leaving, she said to the council leader, 'Go and take possession of the land in Scotswood, which the people refused to give you for money, for they are no longer there, but are broken.' As soon as the council leader heard that they were broken, he set out to go down to the land in Scotswood to take possession of it.

Then the word of the Lord came to the prophet, saying, 'Go down to meet the Leader of Newcastle City Council. He is now on the land of the people of Scotswood, where he has gone to take possession. You shall say to him, "Thus says the Lord. Have you broken their spirit and also taken possession?" You shall say to him, "Thus says the Lord. In the place where dogs licked up the blood of the people of Scotswood, dogs will also lick up your blood." ' [8]

The story could be repeated, over and over again, about communities all over the country. One of the elements which is central to the story is the indifference of bureaucrats to the views and feelings of ordinary people. Many of us have tended to see indifference as a moral failing which can be dealt with at the level of personal change. There is surely a personal moral dimension, but it is part of a wider pattern of corruption. My view is that it is essential to the workings of the capitalist system, and of the growth of bureaucracy, and that to attack indifference is to attack the system of which it is a vital part. Struggle against 'the social production of indifference' has been an important part of the ministry in the East End.[9]

The struggle against capitalism

Since the 1950s I have been a socialist, and have held the view that capitalism is both a moral evil and an economic and political system which increases deprivation and poverty as it strengthens inequality and privilege. While capitalism has undergone striking shifts in recent years, I see nothing which calls my view fundamentally into question, and much which strengthens it. Of course, there are those who see capitalist globalisation as the 'promise of a unified humanity', yet others, including myself, see rather 'the disturbing view of a fractured world, sharply divided by reconfigured relations of domination'.[10] What has often been ignored is the disastrous effect of capitalism on the human spirit. The vice of avarice, *pleonexia*, the desire to accumulate more and more, has, in classical Christianity – as indeed in Aristotle – been seen as a vice, and in the Catholic tradition it is one of the seven deadly sins. However, in capitalism it becomes a central virtue which is necessary to the effective working of the system. Thus capitalism needs, if it is to function well, to cultivate a type of character which is inclined towards injustice.

If this is true, then capitalism is one of the 'works of the devil' which the Son of God was manifested to destroy (1 John 3:8). I do not believe that this system is reformable – though it can be made more palatable, more humane, within its own limits – or that, as some contemporary 'postmodern' Christians claim, transformation must replace liberation.

Liberation must precede transformation. To call for transformation without liberation is both theologically and politically unsound.

Inner struggle

If I am right that capitalism needs, for its success, persons with an inclination towards injustice, struggle can never be only external. This would be true if capitalism had never existed. We are called to take part in 'the struggle to face both the demons within and the darkness of the historical moment'.[11] I have found that a central element in this interior struggle is related to doubt. Thomas Merton often stressed that doubt was integral to faith, and that faith is not the suppression of doubt. We overcome doubt by going through it.[12] It was Merton's writings which helped me to see that the Christian faith and life was a principle of doubt and struggle before it became a principle of clarity and peace.

The work of ministry and of theology always involves entering into personal struggle, and passing through storms. My friend, and former student, Peter Rose suffered from severe depression, and wrote about what he had learned about coping with this from his long experience as a sailor. In an essay on storms at sea, he wrote that 'the dangers of the storm are real. There is no guarantee at all of survival or indeed of not being broken.' I am sure he is right, and I certainly learned much from Peter — with whom I met regularly during the period of the project — about the need to cope with both storms and fog, both of them experiences of insecurity and loss of orientation. I was greatly helped by the work of the late R. D. Laing who sought to relate experience of psychological distress and the sense of the transcendent, which, as he stressed, 'sometimes' breaks through in psychosis, to the work of 'those experiences of the divine that are the living fount of all religion'.[13] While I strongly reject the view that madness is preferable to sanity, a view which is desperately unkind to people with serious mental health problems, I do believe that 'mental fight' has an important place in spiritual progress. I have learned so much from people who are classified as 'disturbed', perhaps more than I have learned from those who are seen as 'normal'.

There is a 'warfare of the spirit', or 'warfare of the heart' (a phrase which goes back to St Antony of Egypt, the early desert hermit), which is central to theology. God's way is in whirlwind and storm (Nahum

1:3). I remain uneasy with the word 'spirituality' and have opposed the idea of a separate area of existence which goes under that title. Human life is either all spiritual or not spiritual at all. I sometimes regret having contributed to the current cult of spirituality by writing books and articles which get classified under that label, and thus encouraging the idea of spirituality as a special, perhaps religious, mystical, or other compartment of life. Yet the 'life of the spirit', the rooting of our entire life and relationships in God and in the unceasing struggle towards communion with God, is central to my understanding of what it is to be human and Christian. This struggle is one which embraces the whole of life. It is sad that the English word 'spirit' suggests a narrow interpretation, while other European languages use words which are more dynamic and holistic – *geist, esprit, spirito*.

One key biblical text which relates to inner struggle is the Book of Job. Job endured 'months of emptiness and nights of misery' (Job 7:3). He interpreted his suffering theologically. God, he claimed, had crushed him with a tempest and multiplied his wounds (9:17). At the heart of the Job narrative is the theme of trial. The Psalms too speak of being 'distraught' and of anguish of heart (Ps. 55:2–4). Without struggle we are complacent, a condition which is condemned by the prophets (Isa. 32:9–11). Augustine says that Christ is present among those who are 'in severe trial', and goes on to say that 'we progress by means of trial. No one knows himself except through trial.'[14] Neither human life nor the search for God run along smooth and serene paths: they involve tribulation, crisis, conflict and upheaval. We only make progress through conflict. The late Mother Mary Clare SLG once said that she became a contemplative in order to enter more deeply into the heart of the spiritual conflict. I agree entirely with these approaches, and see contemplative prayer as an essential component of the conflict with principalities and powers which is at the heart of the movement of the Kingdom of God.

Struggle and conflict include entering into the mystery of dereliction, doubt, despair and apparent loss of hope which must precede renewal. The season of Lent is rightly seen as a time of struggle, and the collect for Ash Wednesday in the Roman *Liturgia Horarum* brings this out very clearly. Writing these reflections soon after Holy Week, I see more than ever how dangerous and spiritually damaging it is to jump from Hosanna to Alleluia, bypassing the anguish of Gethsemane, the dereliction of Calvary, and the terrible perplexity and amazement of the descent into hell. If we try to bypass the darkness, spirituality becomes a form of *kitsch* – a nice feeling, offering comfort without transformation.

Andrew Shanks has stressed the importance of 'shakenness', while earlier Alan Ecclestone said that the commitment to serious prayer calls for 'a great deal more agony of spirit' than most of us are prepared for.[15] Of course, there is a shakenness which is a sign of instability and spiritual frailty, and we are urged 'not to be quickly shaken in mind or alarmed' (2 Thess. 2:2). There is, however, a profound shakenness which comes from God and which is essential to our progress.

Struggle involves questioning, and a theology which takes this seriously must be a theology of questions, an 'interrogatory theology' as Ched Myers calls it, or even 'a theology of mess' in the words of the East End priest Peter McGeary. The academic theologian Nicholas Lash has stressed that theology is necessarily untidy, and there seems to me to be a parallel here with work in the field of scientific research. The late Sir Peter Medawar pointed out that all advances in scientific understanding begin with a 'speculative adventure, an imaginative preconception of what might be true', with 'the invention of a possible world'. In all scientific work, he argued, there must be a dialogue between two voices, the imaginative and the critical.[16]

The importance of being criticised

A major consequence of this is that theological work must be subjected to regular scrutiny by a group of committed and critical friends. Although I am not always very willing to receive criticism from others, I found it really valuable to surround myself with a network of support and criticism. On 15th February 1992 I received a letter from an old friend in the East End, one of my most valued critics, from whom I know that I will never receive 'smooth things'. It brought home to me the importance of having a community of friends who are also sharp critics and who will submit one's thoughts, ideas and actions to the most rigorous and ruthless scrutiny. Here are some extracts. His letter began:

> Every time I hear from you I tell myself I ought to say things to you that I'm not saying. It's very difficult when you hold a friend in respect yet have critical thoughts about him.

He then went on to identify his concerns.

1. That 'community theology' can hardly be other than a coloniser's notion. However liberated (and liberal, or orthodox, or left-wing) or liberating it thinks itself. I'm afraid I think it will inevitably use people for the sake of the religious institution in the end.

2. That you yourself are in danger of using 'Spitalfields', 'Docklands', 'the homeless', 'the drug scene' and so on to become the approved clerical voice on certain subjects. Of course, you are perfectly entitled and obliged to be as knowledgeable as possible on these heads, but what one sees happening is a kind of focusing on you of everything that is to be expected of the church's Left establishment. It can't be good for you, Ken. You're causing people to expect too much of you, and I'm afraid the time may come – when you've been appointed Master of the Royal Foundation of St Katharine maybe – when you'll be made use of by the set-up.

I feel quite badly about finding fault with you . . . but I have to ask myself, and you: What is the point of another clergyman, however well-intentioned, who doesn't really belong here, although he'd like to think he does, trying to represent whatever local struggles really are going on against Satan and all his works? The situation is too far gone for that to be of any real help. From the point of view of the denizens of the jungle – if they ever hear you – you are just another middle-class pundit putting things into words. The things you say are no more real than the things that Jim Thompson [former Bishop of Stepney], for instance, used to say. It's all epiphenomenal, if you see what I mean.

Of course, if you actually wash someone's feet at the crypt, literally or figuratively even, or let the suffering get to you, and render you speechless, well . . . that's another matter. Maybe you do, Ken, but what that might do to you doesn't come over in the words, if you see what I mean.

For a long time I carried this letter around with me, and read it over and over again. I still find it crucially important, deeply troubling and hurtful, and, at the end of the day, probably right.

One area which has been really valuable, and which I have tried, and am still trying, to take seriously, has been the critical responses to my work over the period. They have fallen into three main categories.

First, there have been hostile attacks or criticisms which, in all honesty, I have to regard as mistaken and based on carelessness or misreading. Typical of this category was a strange article by Caroline (now Baroness) Cox and Rachel Tingle which appeared in a right-wing journal in 1986, and was later developed into a booklet. In the earlier article, these authors wrote about my books: 'In some of these he interprets the main doctrines of the Christian Church in such a way as to abolish all reference to a personal salvation: everything is interpreted in political terms.'[18]

I was appalled when I read this. It did not seem, and still does not seem, that the authors had read my work carefully, if at all, or, if they had, that they had understood it. I have never neglected personal salvation, and many of my writings have been about the person in relationship with God through prayer, contemplation, spiritual discipline and discipleship in the world. At no point have I interpreted Christian theology in exclusively political terms, and have been highly critical of those who do. However, the fact that writers such as these accused me of positions which I had myself often attacked did make me wonder about how they came to these conclusions. Was my writing unclear, even obscure? Were some readers looking for errors and determined to find them, irrespective of what I had in fact written? I am still not sure, but I have reached the conclusion that, apart from trying to write with greater clarity, and responding to misrepresentation or misunderstanding, there is nothing I can do to deal with this kind of response. (I did send one of my critics a copy of my book *True God*, in the hope that it might help her to see what I did believe, but I never received a reply.)

Second, there have been those who have responded, sometimes with distress, to particular comments or interventions which I have made. There have been many of these, most of which antedate my time at St Botolph's. I recall, for example, that many people were outraged when I challenged a programme on Channel Four on 'the anti-racist tendency' in the mid-1980s. I was accused of intolerance and arrogance when I felt I was simply being firm. There were other examples in the 1990s and beyond. My review of the memoirs of the late Bishop David Sheppard provoked much controversy. Although I emphasised the importance of Bishop Sheppard and of his role in alerting the nation to

urban issues, the fact that I was critical of him at all caused much distress. (David Sheppard himself showed no sign of being at all upset.) I
am sure that, on many of these occasions, I may have been mistaken,
but I still worry about the inability of many people, including Christians, to accept, and to respond to, criticism. Maybe I am not very
good at this, but I feel that discussion, criticisms and debate are vital
elements in our life, and within the Christian community, and that we
must learn to deal with them lovingly and honestly. Perhaps I have
been insensitive at times, but I do feel that it is important to speak the
truth in love, and to expect, and welcome, responses which are more
than abuse.

At the same time, it seems important that we learn from experience,
and I do feel that it took me rather a long time to realise that my
polemical style could be very hurtful to individuals. I have tried to
integrate a firmness in criticism with a sensitivity to the feelings of
those whom I criticise. I am still struggling with this, and, to the extent
that I have made any progress, it is largely due to the criticisms and
support of my friends.

Thirdly, there have been those who have pointed to alleged weaknesses, areas of neglect, or serious errors in my theological approach.
Leslie Houlden, whom we commissioned to undertake a critical review
of the work, reported in 1998. The work, he said, was 'amazing in its
many sidedness and its depth', and even claimed that 'nobody springs
to mind who has both his theological fluency and his range of experience, extended over so long a time'. He praised some of the books very
highly, particularly *Drugs and Pastoral* Care (1998), describing it as
'canonical'. However, there were some important criticisms in the
review. Houlden noted that there was a new generation of young clergy
for whom my writing and influence was of no great importance. Their
mentors were elsewhere, and some of them saw me as 'harping on the
past'. He saw me as 'rather an isolated figure' in academic theological
circles, noting that I seemed to be better known in universities and
seminaries in the USA than in Britain. He felt that I had paid little
attention in my work to new thinking about Christology, and that my
documentation of my own work was 'excessive'. Peter Sedgwick, writing around the same time, was concerned that, in much of my writing,
the Church tended to disappear, in spite of the stress on the 'social
dimension' of the faith itself. A more trenchant criticism came from my
old friend Steve Latham, a Baptist minister in Paddington. Looking at

a paper I wrote on theological issues in urban regeneration, Latham protested that there was little theology there, and that Protestant reformed dogmatics had more to offer in terms of the doctrine of regeneration than did Anglo-Catholicism.[19]

Some evangelical friends had been critical of my apparent neglect of the Cross. This was really helpful spiritually, and I realised that, for some time, much of my thought and practice was more 'incarnational' than 'redemptive'. (I should add that not all of these critics were evangelicals. David Nicholls was highly critical of what he once called 'neat incarnationalism' and his thinking led to important changes in my own.) It was partly as a response to this that I wrote *We Preach Christ Crucified* (1994). I have found these criticisms really valuable, though whether I have learned from them is for others to say.

I have been struck, honoured and, at times, slightly puzzled, by the interest taken in my work by Baptist writers – Nigel Wright, Steve Latham, Andy Bruce, Stephen Cave (whose work is still in process), and others. Steve and Andy have been two of my most astute and perceptive critics, and their observations and questions have been really helpful. I still wonder why I seem to receive more useful criticism and correction from Baptists than from Anglicans. I suspect it has something to do with the resurgence of the Anabaptist tradition, a resurgence which figures in the changing Christian presence in the East End.

The struggle against racism

The year 1993 was devastating, not least because of the election of Derek Beackon as councillor for the British National Party (BNP), a fascist party with a long history of support for Nazism and anti-Semitism, in September in Millwall. The response to this event raised the whole issue of the role of the Christian Church in relation to racism, fascism and bigotry. A week before the election, a long letter from me had been published in the local newspaper. It referred to the collapse of political vision, and to the need to transcend local populism. 'Politics in Tower Hamlets now', I wrote, 'is no more than civil war carried on by other means.'[20]

The BNP victory was the first in the country, and caused horror, shame and dismay in the area. Within a few days of the election, a group of us formed a BNP Monitoring Group, co-ordinated by Savi

Hensman, Kaushika Amin and myself. As a result of increased fascist activity, especially in Poplar, Isle of Dogs and Bethnal Green, the group started to meet more frequently, and we continued to meet and share information until the May 1998 local elections. This regular sharing of intelligence and of ongoing scrutiny of local fascist activity, in liaison with other groups, was of real value in the struggle against the fascists.

During the period of intense BNP activity, racial violence increased to an appalling degree. On the night of Tuesday 8th February 1994, Mukhtar Ahmed was beaten up by 25 white youths at the comer of Ramsey Street and Dunbridge Street, Bethnal Green, a few yards from where I lived in the 1970s. On the 11th several hundred of us held a candlelit vigil for him in Altab Ali Park, followed by an inter-faith vigil for all victims of racial violence. The inter-faith situation too was beginning to get difficult, worrying in an area where Jewish, Muslim and Christian people had been getting on well and working together for longer than in most parts of Britain. Yet this can often be deceptive. The history of the East End, as of many areas, is complex: inter-racial harmony in some districts, hostility in others, ambiguity all over the place. Within days of the attack on Mukhtar, a local Liberal Democrat councillor was defending his use of the term 'Paki' in the columns of the local newspaper.

On 14th February 1994 I addressed the Episcopal Urban Caucus Conference in Charlotte, North Carolina. It was a privilege to share the platform with Barbara Harris, the first black female bishop in the Anglican Communion, and with Byron Rushing, a congressman for that part of Boston which includes St Botolph's Street. (Boston means 'Botolph's Town'.) The conference was an important point in the history of the Caucus, and was devoted to the whole issue of anti-racist strategy. The papers were published under the title *To Heal the Sin-sick Soul*. Two years later, on 4th October 1996, I gave the annual Tower Hamlets History Lecture on 'Cable Street in Myth and History', and this was followed, on the 6th, by a rally and march. (A wonderful painting of this, by Dan Jones, was used as the cover of my book *Through Our Long Exile*.) These events, geographically so widely apart, brought home to me something of the importance of seeing how the local and the global connect.

In the light of this history, the recent electoral successes of the BNP in other parts of England has been a cause for great concern, and I felt that there were lessons from the East End which needed recording and which might be helpful to comrades in Burnley, Oldham and the Yorkshire towns. We spent a good deal of time circulating copies of the pamphlet by Sue Mayo and Nic Holtam, *Learning from the Conflict*, on the struggle against the BNP in the East End.[21] It seemed that we had a role in this horrible development of 'gutter fascism', at least in the sense that we had experienced it earlier than most parts of Britain. It seemed that we had a moral obligation to make clear that we were dealing, not with a political tendency with which we differed, but with a demonic reality which was, at its heart, deeply evil. And not only evil, but corrupting, severely damaging many of those who came into contact with it.

The 1993 vote for the BNP was described by the veteran community activist Ted Johns in terms of 'living in the middle of a building site' for ten years, and 'living at the bottom of the well, for a hundred years, with people pissing in it all that time'.[22] By the time I left the East End, in 2004, the BNP had shifted their attention to areas further east in London, such as Barking and Dagenham, to the old mill towns of Lancashire and Yorkshire, and to rural communities far away from the urban cores.

On Saturday 24th April 1999 at 5.57pm a bomb exploded in Brick Lane. It was one of three, planted by the same man, later identified as David Copeland. The others had targeted the African-Caribbean community in Brixton, South London, and the gay community in Soho. Our local bomb was aimed at Salique's Restaurant in Hanbury Street, a meeting place of Bengali leaders and people active in anti-racist work, but not a restaurant well known to tourists or casual visitors. However, a visitor saw the package, thought it was suspicious, and took it to the police office in Brick Lane, a few minutes away. Finding the office closed, he put it in the boot of his car with the intention of taking it to another police station later. The bomb exploded, damaging Café Naz and many surrounding flats and shops. The police cordoned off the area, with the result that people who had been shopping, or had been away from home, were unable to gain access to their homes for a day. I put up an old lady who lived in Brick Lane on my sofa, and provided lavatory access for people who were not allowed to go to the lavatory during the period of the security operation. It was all somewhat bizarre, and I got the impression that the police meant well but had not thought the whole thing through.

The Copeland bombs were part of a longer history of racial violence, about which I have written elsewhere. East London was the pivotal location for racial attacks in the 1990s though the precise locations were shifting. In 1993–94, the period of the BNP campaign, the Newham Monitoring Project dealt with 232 cases of racial harassment, an increase from 198 in 1992–93, while in Tower Hamlets, Anthony Lester QC reported that some Liberal Democrat councillors were 'bringing the party into disrepute' through their racist statements and policies.[23]

September 11th and beyond

More, of course, was to come, internationally in the attack on the 'two towers' on 11th September 2001, and, locally, in the form of the terrorist attacks in July 2005 which occurred after I had left the area. The attacks on September 11th were horrific and indefensible. At the same time, while more than 3000 people died in the USA on that day, according to the Food and Agriculture Organisation, 35,618 children died of starvation throughout the world, a statistic which received no publicity. The struggle for justice needs a cosmic dimension, and we need to move beyond our insularities. I have discussed what is called 'fundamentalism' elsewhere, and further discussion is beyond the scope of this chapter, but most of what I have said above gives an added importance to the need for struggle. It is, in the strictest sense, theological, concerned with the vision of God and of God's justice for the world.[24]

5

Beyond Christendom: theology, spirituality and society

For how could the City of God either take a beginning or be developed or attain its proper destiny if the life of the saints was not a social life?

AUGUSTINE, *City of God* 19:15

We can now understand that the fate of the soul is the fate of the social order, That if the spirit within us withers, so too will all the world we build about us.

THEODORE ROSZAK, *Where the Wasteland Ends*
(Faber 1972, p. xxii)

It is widely accepted that, on the one hand, the 'mainstream' churches are in decline in terms of membership and of spiritual importance, and, on the other, that some kind of spiritual explosion is occurring in our society. Having written about this over thirty years ago, I am under no illusions about its truth, though full of questions about its nature, dimensions and prospects.[1] It is often argued that the churches have been so preoccupied with social and political issues that they have neglected 'the deep things of the spirit', a criticism which, in spite of elements of truth, has always seemed to me to be superficial and rooted in ignorance of theology and spirituality as well as of the churches themselves. It is, of course, true that churches have been intricately involved with social and political issues since the early centuries of the Christian era. There is evidence that, in the earliest Christian period, it was the common life and the mutual love expressed in that life which was a major factor in drawing people to the Church. However, a few centuries later, a mutant of Christianity became the official religion of the Roman Empire. From this point the Church became more political than ever, and this mutant, which became known as 'Constantinian' (after the Emperor Constantine), became the religious expression of the Roman Empire. It expressed, and ritually reinforced, the dominant culture. This role of the Church as ritual reinforcement of the social order has remained, albeit with many erosions of its credibility, to this day. But this is not what bothers the critics. Complaints about the 'politicisation' of the Church are always against the politics of change, never about the far more common politics of maintenance and preservation. Tim Gorringe is right to say that 'protests against the church "interfering" in politics always represent resistance to moral critique and have in principle to be ignored'.[2] I want, in this chapter, to reflect on the 'social tradition' of the Church in relation both to the dominant culture and to other cultures and cultural shifts, particularly in relation to the East End. What do I mean by culture and cultures?

Culture is commonly defined as a configuration of values, symbols, patterns of thought, feeling and discourse.[3] Today a number of words which are related to culture have entered into common use, and some are currently subjected to criticisms of various kinds: words such as cross-cultural, multicultural, counter-cultural, and so on. Many years ago Richard Niebuhr wrote on Christianity and culture, offering a series of possible models for the relationship,[4] and in recent years there has been an upsurge of work in the field of 'inculturation' and cross-cultural issues. The concept of culture itself, while it has been the object of considerable research, is still often used vaguely. Anthropologists have viewed culture as a pattern of meanings and symbols which are transmitted historically. While some writers have tended to see cultures as static and 'pure', this is incorrect. Cultures are always changing, rarely 'pure' and constantly in flux. Like tradition, the only cultures which are free from change and ferment are the extinct ones.

In some quarters, the idea of culture is still seen in an elitist way, as 'high culture', while working-class and poor people are seen as 'uncultured'. Some terms, such as 'youth culture' or 'gay culture', suggest monolithic and unified phenomena, though this clearly is not so. In recent years, much discussion of culture has had an apocalyptic tone. We have heard of the collapse or corruption of culture, the culture of complaint, the culture of narcissism, culture jam, and so on. Many writers refer to a 'new dark age', the collapse of older certainties and of 'traditional values', while thinkers such as Cornel West write of the spread of nihilism, meaninglessness, hopelessness and lack of love.[5]

In these pages I have referred to the changing face of cultures in East London, particularly in relation to the ways in which cultural shifts affect religion and theology. But it is vital, in examining local cultures, that we do not ignore the dominant cultural norms of 'the establishment', and the way in which, for centuries, a form of Christianity has provided ideological underpinning for the *status quo*. This, of course, has had repercussions all over the place, another example of the impact of the international or global on the local. So, while I shall move between the global, international, national and local, I shall be constantly bearing in mind the square mile of the East End in which I worked.

Cultural Christianity

The major problem for churches has not been that of social and political involvement as such, but the fact that some churches have tended to baptise a particular kind of structure and language, that of the *status quo*, and have assumed that it reflects Christian orthodoxy. This was a point raised constantly by the late David Nicholls who was both a valued member of my support group and a major influence on my thought. As an example, Nicholls took the issue of marriage and the family. In his reflections of 1978 on the Lichfield Report, *Marriage and the Church's Task*, he wrote of the danger that churches merely reflected dominant cultural values, interests and assumptions, assuming that they were witnessing to gospel positions, and argued that liberation meant a process of disentanglement in which the captivity of gospel to culture was ended. In his critique of the Lichfield Report, Nicholls drew attention to what the authors called a 'high doctrine of marriage'. But, he suggested 'that this "high" doctrine of marriage is derived not from the New Testament, nor from Christian tradition, but rather reflects contemporary secular rhetoric'. He went on to argue that 'marriage, like the state, is to be seen as a "remedy against sin" as well as an institution which has positive and redemptive aspects ... The commission's understanding of the family derives less from the gospel of Christ than from the gospel of North Oxford and the Dragon School.'

The report had spoken of marriage as 'a foretaste of God's kingdom', yet Nicholls recalled that, according to Jesus, in the Kingdom of God they neither marry nor are given in marriage (Mark 12:25). The report even claimed that in marriage the partners 'give everything and . . . receive everything', a statement which was simply rhetorical nonsense. Nicholls commented:

> It is a monstrous misrepresentation of the commitment in marriage as 'unconditional' or as 'total and unreserved' . . . Such a commitment can be made only to God and to his kingdom. The guest who had 'married a wife and therefore cannot come' did not taste of the heavenly banquet. (Luke 14:20).[6]

There are at least two problems with this 'high' doctrine of marriage and family. The first is that it flies in the face of reality. In one parish in which I worked, there were no people in the congregation who fitted the stereotype of the 'normal' family – a heterosexual couple, married to each other, never married to anyone else, and with two or three children. There were divorced people, one-parent families, lesbian and gay people, single people who had never married, people with a spouse in prison, and so on. But the second problem is theological. Most of the references to family in the gospels are warnings that they are likely to break up as a result of the demands of the gospel. Yet we continually read our cultural assumptions into the gospel.

There are many other examples of what I would call *status quo* theology, and some of this is reflected in East London churches, particularly those of a 'civic' character, and where, for the clergy, ordained ministry is seen as a stepping stone to promotion. But, in my experience, what is equally, if not more, common is the fusing of a modified type of *status quo* theology with social action of a distinctly thoughtful, compassionate, yet reformist kind.

Reformist social theology

Within the general framework of what we might call 'Constantinian theology' there has always been a reformist stream which is prepared to critique particular evils, albeit without attacking 'the system' as such. This kind of social reformism is often referred to as 'liberal'. This is a word of which we should be wary as it is used increasingly as an insult (by its opponents) and vaguely (by its supporters). There is no doubt that the liberal tradition, in theology as in politics, has contributed to human potential and human progress. Its concern with the self and with 'human rights', which it has often defended against the dominant social system, its pragmatic approach to issues, have been of great value. Theological liberalism has helped to keep alive the spirit of critical inquiry, openness to new thinking, resistance to injustice, sensitivity to, and support for, minorities, and so on.

However, the liberal tradition has major weaknesses. It operates within a framework of political (and often theological) optimism, the heir to the eighteenth-century doctrine of progress, and the belief that improvements and reforms can take place without any fundamental threat to, or break with, the existing social structure. But this assumption is not at all evidently the case. If injustices are not accidental but systemic, then to attack one area will be to threaten the whole system, and this will involve conflict. Liberalism cannot cope well with conflict. Saul Alinsky defined a liberal as a person who leaves the room when an argument turns into a fight. The liberal belief in gradual change has no place for a theology of conflict. As Conrad Noel once put it, it believes that the mighty will be put down from their seats so gently that they will not feel the bump when they hit the ground.[7]

Evangelical social witness

I would say that the Anglican social witness, in East London and generally, has tended to lie broadly within this liberal approach. However, there have been some changes. It is important to note the resurgence of an evangelical social conscience over these years. When I arrived in the East End in 1958, I was aware of a shift in some parts of evangelical Anglicanism towards social involvement in specific issues. Christ Church, Spitalfields, under the leadership of Denis Downham, was moving from being a 'gathered' community of Christians who supported 'Reformation principles' to being a local church, seeking to minister to the needs of the community, not least to homeless people, vagrant alcoholics and rough sleepers.[8] Out of this grew the work of Spitalfields Crypt, a centre for people with alcohol problems. Downham's social commitment was continued by his successor Eddy Stride. Other evangelical churches, inside and outside the Church of England, continued to make a clear division between evangelism and social concern, but this was beginning to change, albeit more slowly in some places than others.

The growth of serious evangelical social thought and action has been very marked in East London, among Anglicans, Baptists and some members of Pentecostal churches. The shift in the theological centre of gravity in relation to social thought was very noticeable during the time of the Whitechapel project. Much of this thought and action has moved beyond the reformist and 'rescue' models towards a more radical posture. I would not be surprised if most of the social thought and action within Christian churches in East London in future comes from Christians of an evangelical background.[9]

Spirituality versus social action?

For me, an area which caused great concern, and aroused much interest, particularly during my frequent visits to the USA, was the link between personal spiritual formation, and guidance in this area, and social and political witness. On 14th February 1994 the revised edition of my book *Soul Friend,* originally published in 1977 but arising from work done between 1971 and 1974, appeared. The book was an introduction to the ministry of spiritual direction.[10] The chronological convergence of this with the racist attack on Mukhtar Ahmed really hit me. Indeed these two events raised, in a very practical way, the issue of how 'spirituality' and 'social action' are linked. In the USA, it is common to talk about 'spirituality and social action' as if it were a problem to be solved, and I have found, over the years, that I am welcomed there as someone who has 'held them together' or even 'brought them together'. There is something very troubling and unsatisfactory about this way of speaking and thinking, something which goes to the root of what we think religion is about. I never thought in these terms, and never used that language, until I went to the USA. Prior to this I simply thought of Christian faith and practice as a life which involved prayer, worship and action for justice in the world.

This moment brought back to me an incident which had occurred in Chicago some years earlier. I had spoken at a conference at the South Asian Centre on responses to racial violence. After the conference, a local priest thanked me for my contribution. Just before I left, he said, 'You must often get confused with the other Kenneth Leech who writes books on prayer and spirituality.' I managed to keep a very straight face, and said, 'Yes, I am often confused with him.' I was, at first, amused, but, when I thought about it, became deeply depressed. This good, socially committed priest could not imagine that I might be the same person who wrote on prayer and spirituality. Justice and piety were in different compartments.

The revised edition of *Soul Friend* included, in the new introduction, most of an article which I had written a year earlier, and which had originally been published in *The Tablet* on 22nd May 1993 under the title 'Is spiritual direction losing its bearings?' Reflecting on this article ten years later, Richard Buck said that 'we all sat up with a jolt'. I had, he said, been 'firing [a] bombshell'. Whether people agreed with me or not, he argued, I had put my finger on many crucial points which remained important today, and which 'we ignore at our peril'.[11] I imagine that what he meant, and certainly what worries me, is the danger that 'spirituality' comes to be seen as some kind of compartment of Christian life, something separate from being a Christian, something cut off from the messy world of economics and politics. Much of my work in East London was connected with trying to move beyond the split between spirit and society, piety and politics. This was an issue which John MacMurray raised many years ago. He wrote: 'A spirituality that does not seek to secure its material embodiment is imaginary and unreal. A material life that is not spiritually directed is a meaningless quest for power and more power for its own sake.'[12]

Theology and prophecy

An issue which was raised by Leslie Houlden's critical evaluation of my work was what he described as a tension between theology and prophecy. He illustrated this by contrasting the responses of people who had read my 1998 book *Drugs and Pastoral Care* (who valued its calm 'objectivity') and those (not necessarily the same people) who had, the previous year, read my *The Sky Is Red* (and saw it as sharp, strident and opinionated).[13] I am not sure this is quite how I see it, but certainly there is, in much theological writing, and in the experience of local communities, a perceived tension or even conflict between what are seen as 'pastoral' and 'prophetic' modes of activity. Pastors, it is often claimed, cannot be prophets, and, conversely, prophets make bad pastors. Yet, as Brueggemann has often stressed, to divide things up into prophetic and pastoral is to betray both.

William Stringfellow and East Harlem

This is an issue which arises frequently, and it arose in the difficult relationship of William Stringfellow with the East Harlem Protestant Parish (EHPP) in New York City during the years 1956–64. Stringfellow was an important influence on me, and was involved with the same pastoral, theological and political concerns. A lawyer in East Harlem, his quarrel with the parish led him to leave it after only eighteen months. The EHPP was a flagship for inner-city ministry in the USA, and its work was popularised in Britain by Bruce Kenrick's inspiring book *Come Out the Wilderness* which influenced me and many others to work in the inner city. Kenrick, writing about the work with heroin addicts in East Harlem, stressed that 'the church must suffer and be crucified with those it seeks to serve; and . . . it must keep on being crucified even though the nails bite deep and the hope of resurrection is obscure'.[14]

The EHPP had an important effect in London on ministry where Kenrick himself worked. After the inter-racial conflicts of 1958, Donald Soper, then president of the Methodist Conference, encouraged the formation of a ministry in the Lancaster Road area of Notting Hill based on the ministry in East Harlem. The three ministers who began that ministry – Geoffrey Ainger, David Mason and Norwyn Denny – had all worked in the EHPP with Stringfellow, who had come to East Harlem when he was 28. But he was troubled by its focus on care and neglect of the challenge of the gospel. Kenrick referred to Stringfellow's belief that there was a radical failure to take the Bible and Christ seriously.

Stringfellow described his relationship with the EHPP in his book *My People Is the Enemy* (1964).

> They plunged into all sorts of social work and social action – narcotics, politics, neighbourhood improvement, education, housing, and the rest. They instituted therapy and counselling for addicts, engaged in voter registration, lobbied for new playgrounds, organised PTAs, complained about slum landlords, made themselves a nuisance to those in power around the neighbourhood. It was in many ways an admirable, if idealistic, and in Christian terms naive effort, but they neglected and postponed the proclamation and celebration of the Gospel in East Harlem.[15]

When I first read that, a number of contradictory and confused emotions went through me. One was to say, 'Yes, these are all the things we
have been doing for years and years and years.' The parallels are very
precise. Another part of me said that these are good things and
shouldn't be written off as naive. Nor are they 'just' (just?) social work,
and why should social work be used as a term of abuse anyway? On the
other hand, I recognised that I had been saying this kind of thing to St
Botolph's too, and had felt that nobody took any more notice of me
than the EHPP did of Stringfellow. There is a danger that churches
become nothing more than what Tony Benn once called 'intensive care
wards for capitalism'. They do not challenge the powers, they act as a
casualty station, offer a band-aid ministry, pick up the pieces, comfort
the afflicted without afflicting the comfortable – if they did that, their
government grant would be taken away. Yes, I knew all that, and my
heart went out to Stringfellow. And yet, looking back on it, his
remarks are grossly unfair to those people who are still in East Harlem
today, fifty years after the EHPP was formed.

In one sense this was a classic conflict between prophet and pastor,
or, perhaps, between the prophetic Church and the servant Church.
Stringfellow was playing the role of prophet, the role which Brueggemann once described as a destabilising presence in any community, a
trouble-maker, one who upsets the apple cart. But was it fair? Did he
actually take seriously what the East Harlem workers were trying to
do? One-and-a-half years is not very long to give a parish a chance.
And in fact it is interesting that much of the critique that Stringfellow
made was subsequently incorporated into the parish programme.

What was it about Stringfellow which led him into dispute with this
important experiment in urban ministry? I think there are a number of
things which give us a clue. Stringfellow was a profoundly biblical
person. He was not a fundamentalist, but he was steeped in the scriptures. He wished to develop what Jim Wallis, very much a disciple of
his, later called an 'agenda for biblical people', a kind of biblical consciousness. He felt that there was a neglect of the Bible's challenge to
the contemporary scene, and that the EHPP was deeply conformed to
the world. It is a dilemma that we have all shared, and one with which I
lived at St Botolph's all the time. I suppose one of the differences
between Stringfellow and me is that he found that the conflict was an
impossible one to negotiate and left after a year and a half, and I stayed.

The neglect of the challenge of scripture was fundamental to

Stringfellow's critique. He believed that the parish was playing down, and at times ignoring, the prophetic, confrontational dimension of the Christian message, substituting the servant Church for the prophetic Church. Martin Luther King Jr, in one of his sermons, said that the role of the Church is not to be the servant of the state, still less its master, but always its conscience. It was that which Stringfellow found missing.

The apocalyptic strand in Stringfellow led him into dissent with East Harlem. He felt that they were picking up the pieces, doing good to broken people, but not challenging Babylon. He was essentially a dissenter, often speaking of resistance as the only way to live humanly under a totalitarian regime. He must have been one of the first American writers in the modern period to talk of the need for a confessing Church, a term from the Nazi period. Part of me says that Stringfellow was very impatient and arrogant. There are other dimensions to pastoral ministry than constant polemic and confrontation. There are dimensions of gentleness, care, silence, listening, staying with the suffering. There doesn't seem to be a lot in Stringfellow's writings about that. And it may well be that the EHPP had quite a bit to teach him about those dimensions, and he didn't stay long enough to learn.

I never met Stringfellow, and all I know about him is what I have picked up from the books, the odd tapes, and discussions with people who knew him. But the story is a very familiar one. It is the story of the destabilising presence in a community. It is the story of the clash between the prophetic and the pastoral, the story of what Richard Holloway has called the 'antithetical preacher' who throws kerygmatic parcel bombs through the windows of those who are at ease in Zion. It is an old conflict which is going on still. I am not sure how much of this was to do with incompatible theologies, different views of the relationship of Church and world, different views indeed of what the Church is, or how much of it was to do with personality.

I am always worried about people like Stringfellow, Thomas Merton, Dorothy Day and Conrad Noel, and all those people who were trouble-makers. (I realise that, in worrying about these comrades, I am worrying about myself.) When I look honestly at some of Stringfellow's work, I sense a certain impetuousness, impatience and inability to understand the position of those less charismatic people who simply get on with the boring work and are still in East Harlem now. I see a kind of modern monastic with a strong commitment to poverty; a single-minded chaste vision, and a strong sense of obedience (which, of course, led to disobedience of, and resistance to, the principalities). But what seems to be missing, but which was clearly present in some of the people he fell out with, was the Benedictine tradition of stability: of staying there and not moving, and saying 'God has put me here, and as far as I know hasn't told me to go, so here I stay'. So when I realise that the EHPP is now over fifty years old (it's not called that any more but the storefront churches are still there), that Norman Eddy is still living there, and Bill Webber, who helped set up the ministry, is spending his retirement training black Pentecostal ministers in Sing-Sing prison for the ordained ministry, I look back at Stringfellow's critique and I have to ask: is he really being fair to these people who are still there forty to fifty years on?

The experience of Stringfellow and East Harlem is uncomfortably close to us in all but the geographical sense. The questions I ask about Stringfellow I have to ask about myself. My impression has been that the churches in East London have always had a strong social conscience. However, local crises may put it to the test. There were times when I felt that some Christians were retreating from social involvement into piety and a defensive kind of 'churchiness'. For some Christian groups, there had been no significant tradition of thought or analysis of events and trends in the social, political and economic fields. What was evident, as in East Harlem, was social *action*. Yet action without thought, without theology, can be at best superficial and at worst harmful.

Earlier Anglican social theology

So what does it all mean in terms of a social theology? One of my hopes for the urban theology work in the East End was that it might develop in a similar way, more geared to the present context, to that of St Anne's House in Soho in the 1940s and 1950s. I lived in, and worked from, St Anne's House from 1967 to 1971, and it was there that Centrepoint and the Soho Drugs Group had started. But the building had an earlier and often forgotten history in relation to Christian social thought, closely linked to the work of the Christendom Group. Under the influence of Patrick McLaughlin, Gilbert Shaw and others, it became a vibrant centre for debate about the issues of the day and how they related, or failed to relate, to Christian theology. In a talk on

St Anne's Day, 26th June 1957, the churchwarden, Dorothy L. Sayers, said that 'we are not fully persuaded that the Church as a whole quite realises the situation she is facing today ... It is a new kind of heathendom.' She went on to suggest that 'it is to thinkers and technicians at the top that the Church has to address herself'.

I found this address fascinating, not least because the 'top–down' – even 'trickle down' – approach was so typical of much social thought in this decade and the following ones. If we influence 'the people at the top', eventually it will spread to 'the masses'. (Similar language was used by Dipak Nandy, the first Director of the Runnymede Trust, in 1968.) But, more positively, in a letter to the Church Union on 31st October 1957, Sayers located the work of St Anne's House firmly within the movement of European Catholic social thinking.

> It is well known ... that the work of St Anne's House was inspired by the movement of Catholic revival, known abroad as 'Catholic Action', and that it has been continuously sustained by appeal to and contact with the several agencies of this movement. In consequence, the House has been the centre of communication at once between Christians and non-Christians seeking a faith ... and between Christians of different allegiances ... It is perhaps both a tribute to the House and a comment upon the 'catholicity' even of Catholics in this country, that the reputation of the House should stand so high on the Continent whilst it is so little known or spoken of in England.

This too was fascinating. During the years at St Botolph's, I often got the feeling that what I was trying to do and say was received, and taken seriously, by Anglicans and others in the USA and Canada, more than was the case in the Church of England. This was only an impression, but impressions are important.

There is no doubt that theologians have been concerned with social analysis and social thought for many years, indeed many centuries, but how significant has this been for the 'ordinary Christian', for the person who used to be called 'the man in the street'? Reflecting on his time in Britain, the Argentinian theologian José Miguez-Bonino spoke of his 'impression that the theology developed in and by the academic community was not very significant in the everyday life of the Christian community'.[16] I am sure he was right, and his comment may have been true of much of my own work.

The Anglo-Catholic social tradition

Throughout my time in East London, one of my aims was to articulate a vision of human society arising from and nourished by a Catholic socialist perspective. At the start I was presented with a two-fold problem. First, I was not sure that Anglo-Catholicism as a discrete phenomenon still existed. However, secondly, if it did, I was quite sure that, for the most part, it offered no radical social vision. So I had to speak of resources in need of retrieval rather than of a movement with a clear social vision. It was essential, too, to engage with the movement critically, not to try to restore a world we had lost. The East End situation was certainly hopeful, while that of the Anglo-Catholic 'movement' nationally was rather depressing.

When we speak of the Anglo-Catholic tradition we may mean one of at least three movements. There is, first, the Tractarian movement, which began at Oxford in July 1833. It focused on the spiritual autonomy of the Church and looked back to the early fathers, emphasising catholicity and the revival of the sacramental life. Secondly, there is ritualism which began with the spread of sacramental religion to the new towns and to city slums such as London Docks, Haggerston and other parts of East London. Ritualism became a political issue and priests were imprisoned for ritual and ceremonial offences under the Public Worship Regulation Act of 1874. Or we may think, thirdly, of the Catholic socialist tradition which began with Stewart Headlam and the Guild of St Matthew in the 1870s and continued with Conrad Noel, John Groser, Gresham Kirkby and many others in the twentieth century. Much of this movement too was rooted in the East End.

What became known as Anglo-Catholicism was a fusion of the first and second movements. It was a form of Christianity which emphasised the centrality of the sacraments, especially of eucharistic worship and sacramental confession, and the need for intense personal devotion. Many of the positive aspects of that tradition have now been absorbed into post-Vatican II Roman Catholicism and into many Protestant traditions.

It was in the third phase of the movement, from the late 1870s onwards, that a new theological synthesis was created through a fusion of the theology of F. D. Maurice with the sacramentalism of the Oxford Movement. It was this fusion which created the phenomenon of Anglo-Catholic socialism, most clearly manifested in the establishment of the Guild of St Matthew (GSM) at Bethnal Green in 1877, the first explicitly socialist group in Britain, and which led to the volume *Lux Mundi* and the establishment of the Christian Social Union (CSU) in 1889. From Headlam and the GSM there grew up a rebel tradition associated with such figures as Thomas Hancock (who spoke of 'the banner of Christ in the hands of the socialists' and called the Magnificat 'the hymn of the universal social revolution'), Charles Marson, author of *God's Cooperative Society,* and Conrad Noel, parish priest of Thaxted and one of the founders of the British Socialist Party. From the CSU developed a more genteel and liberal tradition of social critique, pragmatic and reformist in its approach, and very Anglican in its style. Its key figures were B. F. Westcott, Charles Gore and Henry Scott Holland. This tradition of social incarnational sacramental religion dominated mainstream Anglican thought from the 1880s to the death of William Temple in 1944. The publication of *Lux Mundi* in 1889 and of Gore's Bampton Lectures in 1891 were of crucial importance. As Michael Ramsey wrote: 'It was an outcome of the *Lux Mundi* appeal to the Logos doctrine that both democracy and socialism were held to be expressions of the working of the divine spirit.'[17]

The socialism of which these thinkers wrote was of an evolutionary and reformist kind. Westcott defined it as the principle of co-operation as against that of individualism, and said that socialism and individualism corresponded to two conflicting views of humanity. It is true that Westcott gave Christian socialism respectability and legitimacy, and in the process diluted it. That tradition, articulated most memorably in the thought of William Temple, provided the specifically Christian basis for the welfare state – a term first used by Temple.[18] But the Catholic tradition also nourished on its periphery a more revolutionary movement. Conrad Noel ridiculed the CSU as a mere talk shop. 'Here's a pressing social problem: let's read a paper about it.' Noel's Catholic Crusade, formed in 1918 after the Russian Revolution, was committed to involvement in revolutionary struggle. While on many issues it was naïve and uncritical (though no more than many others), it represents the libertarian and prophetic tradition of Anglo-Catholic socialism at its best. Rowan Williams has claimed that of all the early leftist movements it comes closest to liberation theology.[19] The Crusade finally collapsed in the aftermath of the Stalin–Trotsky dispute. When George Orwell wrote that Anglo-Catholicism was the ecclesiastical equivalent of Trotskyism, he was correct in ways that he did not intend, for one of the reasons given by the Communist Party for the expulsion of the early Trotskyists was their association with Noel and the Crusade.[20] There were then two traditions of Anglo-Catholic socialism: a middle-class, reformist, liberal tradition of social reform; and a more grass-roots tradition, rooted in concrete struggles, a tradition of 'socialism from below'.

What kind of social vision emerges from the Anglo-Catholic tradition? First, it is a social vision, a vision of a co-operative society, a community bonded together by a fundamental and unbreakable solidarity, a community of equals. Central to Anglo-Catholic theology is its emphasis on the Church as the body of Christ and as an integral element in the gospel. Michael Ramsey's book *The Gospel and the Catholic Church* (1936) was of fundamental importance in shaping a theological tradition which took seriously both the New Testament and the liturgical renewal and did so in an ecumenical way. It undermined the liberal tradition with its impatience with doctrine and its division between gospel and Church, and prepared the theological ground for what became know as 'Christian sociology'. Ramsey's book included a strong attack on liberal individualism. 'Individualism', he wrote, 'has no place in Christianity, and Christianity, verily, means its extinction.'[21] In fact, individualism has some of its roots in a particular interpretation of Reformation theology, but it is in fundamental conflict with a Catholic vision.

Many years after Ramsey's book, John Robinson was to claim that the doctrine of the body of Christ was 'the specifically Christian clue to the renewal of society', while John Davies saw it as the key doctrine in the Anglo-Catholic resistance to apartheid in South Africa. It is worth remembering that the best-known Anglo-Catholic bishop in the world today is Desmond Tutu. Apartheid involved the belief that Christian love did not have to be expressed in visible material structures. Against this twentieth-century version of the Eutychian heresy, the very traditional Anglo-Catholics of the Reeves-Huddleston generation insisted that Christianity demanded a material and social embodiment. A high doctrine of the Church became a key element in the resistance to 'the novel nonsense of upstart racism'.[22]

It was in its stress on the body, on communion and sharing, and in its rejection of individualism in religion, that the link between Anglo-Catholicism and socialism was forged. 'Those who assist at Holy Communion', insisted Stewart Headlam, 'are bound to be Holy

Communists.'[23] It was not possible to maintain the eucharistic principles of common life and equality without those principles being extended to the social order beyond the sanctuary – unless, of course, one maintained a sacramental dualism which kept sanctuary and street, Church and world, in separate compartments.

Secondly, it is a materialistic vision. It is a vision which is deeply and unashamedly materialistic, which values the creation, which rejoices in the physical, in the flesh, in human sexuality, and which is rooted in the principle that matter is the vehicle of spirit, not its enemy. When Temple said that Christianity was the most materialistic of all religions, he stood within a long tradition of incarnational and sacramental materialism. It not only saw bread and wine as symbols of the transformation of all human resources; it saw the material world as the primal sacrament from which all others derived. Anglo-Catholic theology refuses to tolerate a division between matter and spirit, or any disparaging of matter or the physical. To despise and undervalue the creation is to despise its Creator. Catholic Christianity stands or falls on this sacramental principle: and this must involve a break with those movements of Christian thought which see the spiritual as the antithesis of the material, and concern for social and economic justice as a hindrance to true spirituality. Such dualism is deeply alien to a sacramental materialism. Anglo-Catholic social theology is, I believe, basically at odds with philosophical idealism, and is rooted in a realist and materialist approach to the world.

At the very core of Anglo-Catholic spirituality and of the Anglo-Catholic social tradition is the doctrine of incarnation. But the tradition has not simply emphasised the Word made flesh as the basis of a movement of compassion, care and service: it has emphasised equally the 'taking of manhood into God', the theme of the incarnation as a continuing process of transformation, culminating in the 'deification' of humanity. It therefore offers a type of Christian theology and Christian practice which does not lay so much stress on human fallenness and original sin that it undermines the basis for Christian social action. Rather it lays stress on grace operating in and through the material and historical processes, and on the image of God in all people. It works with a high and hopeful view of human potential, and of the power of grace to transcend the limitations of nature. And this has important political consequences.

Thirdly, it is a vision of transformation, of a transformed society, not simply an improved one. At the heart of Anglo-Catholic spirituality is the eucharistic offering with its twofold emphasis on offering and consecration. Bread and wine, fruits of the earth and work of human hands, products not only of nature but of the industrial process, are, at the eucharistic offertory, brought within the redemptive process. In Smyth's words: 'The bread and wine at the offertory set forth structures in history which have been brought out of the fallen world into the first stage of its redemption.'[24]

In contrast to those who argued that Christian ethics were concerned only with the second stage of wealth, its use, the liturgical offertory sees the movement of creation and of production as equally important. For it is impossible to offer to God the fruits of injustice and oppression, as Irenaeus saw in the second century. Eucharistic worship implies, and indeed depends upon, the process of production as an element in the divine encounter. It involves a rejection of pagan harvest festival religion which, through a theology of vegetable marrows, avoids the hard questions of manufacturing industry and seeks a way to God through matter which bypasses the need for redemption – a point often made by John Robinson.

The eucharist, however, is not only about offering to God the fruits of labour; it is about the transformation, in Thomist language the transubstantiation, of matter to become the material of the resurrection. At the very heart of worship is the reality of change, of the sanctifying power of the Spirit to transform both the material things and the community. A theology which places the transformation of material structures at the heart of its worship is a theology which is open to the need for such transformation in the economic and political life of society.

Fourthly, this tradition is a rebel tradition. The Tractarian movement began as a critique of the Church/Tory alliance and as a protest against state control of the Church. In no other sense can it be said that the Tractarians were social radicals, though the recent work of Simon Skinner has called some aspects of this debate into question. Skinner's thesis is that the early Tractarians already had more of a social theology than is often assumed.[25] Certainly, in their rejection of the politics of the ecclesiastical establishment, they sowed the seeds of a tradition of nonconformity and of dissent in other areas. And this culture of dissent was intensified by the fact that ritualism became a criminal offence in the second phase of the movement. So Anglo-Catholicism and a rebellious spirit became allies. The fact that the rebellion was about the details of church furniture and fashions is not the point: once a movement of nonconformity has been inspired in one area, it can spread to others. It is clear that in a number of slum neighbourhoods – Hoxton and Haggerston, in Portsmouth, in Moss Side and Ardwick, in Sunderland, and elsewhere – Anglo-Catholicism became the religion of the poor and despised, a poor people's Church, a Church of the back streets. Ritualism was, as the churchwardens of St Alban's, Holborn, told the bewildered Archbishop Tait, 'a working men's question'. And this points to a crucial element in Anglo-Catholic history: that the Anglo-Catholic movement in many places broke the identification of the Church of England with the establishment and with bourgeois conformity. Back-street Anglo-Catholicism in some places had a closer affinity with the very poor and dispossessed, with the *lumpen*, than either conventional Anglicanism, the political parties or the trade unions.

But the Catholic socialists of the Noel-Groser-Evans tradition saw pastoral ministry to the poor as only one aspect of the Church's social task: there was the equally important task of nourishing a culture of resistance, a culture which would challenge and confront the false values of mammon. So Father Adderley spoke of the eucharist as 'the weekly meeting of rebels against a mammon-worshipping world order'.[26] At churches like Thaxted in Essex and Burslem in the Potteries, the liturgy was seen as a foretaste of the coming age of justice. These Christian communities recognised that vision and struggle to realise that vision must be nourished at the local concrete level. Without that contextual base among the common people, no social programme could succeed.

One aspect of this rebel tradition has been its ability to establish links of solidarity with marginalised groups without losing its own identity. Examples from the last twenty years or so include the support for Viraj Mendis at the Church of the Ascension in Hulme, Manchester; the solidarity of the church at Goldthorpe with the miners' strike; the identification of St Botolph's itself with the lesbian and gay communities; the close involvement of Anglo-Catholic parishes in Liverpool, Brixton and Bristol in the uprisings of 1981 and their aftermath; and the continuing social commitment of many parishes. This can, of course, be exaggerated. But it is interesting to see the way in which Catholic sacramentalists have been involved at key points in the struggles of oppressed and marginalised groups and communities in our society, especially in the inner urban areas.

Finally, the Anglo-Catholic social vision is one which moves beyond the Christian community and is concerned with the working out of God's purposes in the upheavals and crises of world history. It is Kingdom theology rather than Church theology, a point which I shall develop in Chapter 13. In a sense the relationship of Church and Kingdom and the issues around Kingdom theology — whether the Kingdom of God is this-worldly or other-worldly, social or personal, present or future, and so on — are the key issues in determining whether Christians have any vision for society, and, if they do, how vision and reality connect. Much depends on how we envisage that relationship.

There are close parallels in the debate within Marxism about the relationship of utopian vision and scientific socialism. The dismissal of utopia and its pejorative usage — both by Marx and by his critic Karl Popper — has its parallels in Christian irritation and embarrassment with eschatology. The view that eschatological ideas, millenarianism, adventism, any focusing on the future, is irredeemably escapist, unreal and destructive of political struggle, needs to be questioned. No doubt much visionary thinking is of this kind. But the Anglo-Catholic social tradition, with its deep yearning for the life of the age to come, and its firm conviction that the Kingdom of God is not a purely other-worldly hope, stands as a challenge to contemporary socialism with its conspicuous lack of vision. As Tawney once said of the Fabians, 'They tidy the room, but they open no windows in the soul.'[27]

It is significant, however, that the utopian dimension in socialism is now being reasserted in many quarters, and the need for a recovery of vision and imagination, of dreams and of a politics of hope, is being stressed. One of the insights of the Anglo-Catholic socialist tradition is the recognition that visions and dreams, while they are necessary parts of a politics of struggle, must be constantly tested against experiences of real people and real struggles — against the realities of homelessness, racial oppression, the collapse of communities. Anglo-Catholic social vision has always been worked out in specific neighborhoods, in and through involvement with real struggles. It has begun with the specific and the concrete. And this rootedness in actual struggles is of crucial importance, for, as Gramsci stressed, foresight (or vision) reveals itself not as scientific knowledge but as a practical method of creating a collective will.[28]

The Jubilee Group

I have referred at various points to the work of the Jubilee Group, and it is important to say more here about its role in relation to my theological work and social thought. We had been meeting since 1974, and had become a kind of (international as well as local) support group for one another (which was the original intention) as well as a network of thought. But we were a fairly disorganised, anarchic group of friends, loosely linked by our faith and our commitment to socialist politics. On 6th May 1996 Rick Toews, an anthropologist from British Columbia, arrived to study the Jubilee Group. This was a fascinating experience, and we discovered all kinds of things about ourselves of which we had been unaware. In 2004 the Jubilee Group came to an end, but during my time at St Botolph's it was extremely important as a resource for theological debate.

There were so many gatherings of 'Jubilee people' over these years, and I can refer to only a few of them. One that stands out was on 22nd July 1992, the 50th anniversary of the death of Conrad Noel, founder of the Catholic Crusade. We held the AGM of the Jubilee Group at St Mary's, Somers Town, a church which had been closely linked with the Crusade, and, in 1926, with the General Strike. Archbishop Trevor Huddleston was present, recalling that it was through listening to Basil Jellicoe here as a student that his 'radicalisation' began. John Orens, one of the world experts on 'sacramental socialism', was to give the main address. Knowing that John had as little sense of direction as I do, we chose a church very close to Euston station, and, to make doubly sure, I met him the day before and showed him the exit, and the church. But John did not arrive. After some time of restlessness, Huddleston offered to speak about South Africa until the official speaker arrived. At this point John burst in, having followed my instructions precisely but from the wrong exit of Euston! He proceeded to give a brilliant address. The afternoon session was much enlivened by the presence of Ellis Hillman, a Jewish Marxist councillor who had represented Hackney on the London County Council and the Greater London Council for many years, and who was much inspired by Noel. On 10th April 1996 we held a seminar on John Groser at St George's in the East where he had been parish priest in the 1940s.

What I did during the thirty years of Jubilee's existence, and particularly since the Whitechapel project began in 1990, in trying to keep Jubilee active could be summarised as follows: maintaining a mailing list; producing regular Newsletters and Updates; organising meetings for the East London group and keeping in touch with other groups, in the UK and the USA; printing and/or circulating Discussion Papers – there were over 150 since 1974 – and making sure that these were available; as finance allowed, preparing papers for publication as pamphlets or books, and then trying to make sure that they were sold! (I was not terribly successful, and by 2004 had thousands in my flat); organising the Annual Meeting and Christ the King Lecture in November; responding to inquiries by post, phone, e-mail, etc.; and if there was time, trying to encourage Jubilee people to meet in local or other groups.

Urban theology and theological reflection

During the years in which I worked on this project, a kind of global Anglican urban network had emerged, encouraged and urged on by Andrew Davey at Church House, Westminster, among others. There was a consultation of Anglican contextual theologians at the Episcopal Divinity School in Cambridge, Massachusetts in May 2003. There were important books such as Andrew Davey's *Urban Christianity and Global Order* (SPCK 2001) and Laurie Green's *Urban Ministry and the Kingdom of God* (SPCK 2003). In the USA the work of the Episcopal Urban Caucus had expanded. And, more recently, there was the Commission on Urban Life and Work under the direction of Ann Morisy. Of course, none of this was the direct result of my work, but I think it helped to create a climate in which this kind of theological activity was taken seriously, not least by academic theologians.

My own work involved a good deal of social analysis linked to 'gospel reflection' and to 'discerning the signs of the times'. What does this mean? The term 'theological reflection' has been in use for some decades, but it is not always clear what people mean by it. Recently Elaine Graham and her colleagues have looked at methods of theological reflection, identifying seven possible approaches, each of which played a part in the East End work. One approach, 'theology by heart', is based on interiority, personal life and autobiography, while another involves the use of parables, linking the biblical parables with stories from one's own experience. A third approach is based on the Bible – 'telling God's story', while a fourth, 'writing the Body of Christ', is based around liturgy, community and discipleship. Conversation between cultures, 'speaking of God in public', and 'theology in action', pastoral care and work for justice, are also considered, as is cross-cultural reflection, 'theology in vernacular'.[29]

I found that all these approaches figured in my own work. I certainly found it essential to reflect, in solitude as well as with others, on my own life. Group theological reflection often took the form of sharing stories and linking these with the insights of the gospel. The Bible, used liturgically, read in small groups, and brooded on in silence and solitude, grew more and more important. The worship and pastoral ministry of the local Christian communities was the source and expression of much of the theological work, but increasingly so too was the engagement with other traditions of faith, notably Islam, in cooperative work for justice.

This is theology done by ordinary people within their context, but, if it is to be Christian theology, there has to be an engagement with the Christian tradition as well with the analysis and interrogation of the current world. I have found here that work by scientists has been helpful. Imre Lakatos, in his study of the methodology of scientific research, described a research programme based on a non-negotiable hard core, and an adjustable protective belt. Other scientists, such as the late Sir Peter Medawar, have spoken of the place of vision and imagination in scientific work, while some theologians, such as Nancey Murphy, have seen connections with theological method.[30] I certainly found that we have a great deal to learn from the approach of scientists, many of whom, contrary to the popular stereotypes, are not imprisoned within a framework of 'technical rationality'.

I do not believe that action which is not rooted in, and accompanied by, serious thought and analysis can be satisfactory. Equally, Christian action which is not rooted in, and accompanied by, Christian theology and thought cannot be satisfactory. Every Christian community must be a thinking community, must be, in fact, a theologian.

6

'Doing Theology on Our Knees':
theology and prayer

A theologian is one whose prayer is true.

EVAGRIUS OF PONTUS

True prayer is exposure to the purposes of God. So when we engage in prayer, we find that our instinctive defences against serious thought are melted away. Both the instinct to leave all the problems for others to solve, and the instinct to rush into instant solutions look pretty silly when we pray. We realise that such reactions are essentially frivolous, and do not stand exposure to the reality of God which prayer leads us to experience. It is *not* praying rather than praying that makes people irresponsible.

JOHN DALRYMPLE,
Longest Journey: notes on Christian maturity
(Darton, Longman & Todd 1979, p. 17)

. . . if theology is the untangling of the real grammar of religious practice, the subject is, humanly and specifically, people who pray.

ROWAN WILLIAMS, *On Christian Theology*
(Blackwell 2000, p. 13)

In the 1930s Dietrich Bonhoeffer wrote a letter about prayer to Karl Barth in which he said:

> The kinds of question serious young theologians put to us are: How can I learn to pray? How can I learn to read the Bible? Either we can help them to do this, or we can't help them at all. Nothing of all this can be taken for granted.[1]

When I first read this letter, it brought to my mind a wonderful man in my first parish in East London, who was dyslexic in his own unique way. He often said to me, 'You mustn't take anything for grantage, father.' His words often come into my mind. It cannot be taken for granted today that all who call themselves Christians see prayer as essential, or that this communion through prayer is the source of a new kind of life. Yet this is at the heart of the New Testament and of the Christian tradition. We are called to be transformed, not conformed, in the expectation that we shall see God as he is (Rom. 12:5; 1 John 3:2). St Cyril of Alexandria spoke of the Christian way as 'an entirely new kind of life ... a completely new kind of life', and this life is rooted in, and nourished by, prayer.[2] The roots of this focus on deep inner prayerfulness go way back to ancient Israel. God called the people of Israel to 'wisdom and discernment', called them to be 'a wise and discerning people' (Deut. 4:6). They were told: 'take care and watch yourselves closely' (Deut. 4:9, 15). The adoration of God, and the centrality of the vision of God's glory, was at the heart of Hebrew religion. There was a stress on life for the soul (Prov. 3:22) as well as on knowledge, discretion, insight and integrity (Prov. 8:12; 9:10; 10:9; 20:7). Prayer was central to the ministry of Jesus, as it was in the life of the earliest Christians.

The reason that the title 'theologian' is so restricted in Eastern Orthodoxy – there are only three people who are accorded it – is that theology is identified with a life of outstanding holiness and communion with God. When the Orthodox speak of 'mystical theology', they are not speaking of one type of theology among others, but of the mystical character of all theology.[3] However, in the West, much church life carries on with a minimal emphasis on prayer, while theology is seen as a detached academic discipline, of relevance only to a few, mainly those preparing for ordained ministry. I recall the story of the retiring Archbishop Geoffrey Fisher's complaint to Prime Minister Harold Macmillan in the early 1960s that Michael Ramsey would be a most unsuitable successor to him as Archbishop of Canterbury because he was 'a mystic, a theologian and a man of prayer'! Certainly much written theology has seemed, and still does seem, to be oblivious to prayer or to the relationship with God. Of course, there are many exceptions such as Hans Urs von Balthasar, Rowan Williams, Maggie Ross, Mark McIntosh, and others, but in general, and sadly, I believe that my comment is correct.[4] Yet change has been on the way for some time, and I find myself in the same position as Bonhoeffer expressed in his letter. Most of the Christians, including theological students and pastors, who come to see me want to learn how to pray and how to read the Bible – want, in fact, to be theologians.

The resurgence of interest in 'spirituality' which began in the mid-1960s did bypass the churches for a while. The sociologist Bernice Martin wrote in 1981 – ironically at the very time that many people in the churches were seeking a deeper spiritual life – that 'in the age of the "liberal theologian", the last place anyone will dream of looking for religion is the church'.[5] Her claim is not unusual. Regularly today we hear speakers – many of whom were not alive at the time of which they spoke – dismissing the 1960s as a decade of superficial activism, and seeing the resurgence of 'spirituality' as an occurrence of the 1990s. In fact, during, and since, the 1960s there has been a tremendous growth of concern with the life of prayer, both inside and outside the churches. Yet, in spite of its exaggeration and outdatedness, Martin's claim still needs to be heard. Prayer and *theologia* in its classical sense cannot be taken for granted in much church life.

Of course, the fact that there is a renewed interest in 'spirituality' is no indicator that it is healthy or desirable. More than 25 years ago Jeremy Seabrook claimed that 'a whole generation has been delivered to private enterprise for their most exalted spiritual experiences'.[6] An 'interest' in 'spirituality' may contribute to the life of prayer and union with God precisely nothing. I certainly do not believe that 'strange spirituality is better than no spirituality at all',[7] or that any spirituality is better than none. The New Testament shows no interest in 'spiri-tuality' as such. The word is unknown to earliest Christianity. At the same time, it is clear that 'life in the Spirit' is central to its life and understanding. I think that, in spite of what I have said above, things are changing gradually, and in some places rapidly. Dan Hardy has written that 'the relation between spirituality and theology has become pivotal for religious practice and its intersection with wider concerns'.[8] But this is not only a 'relationship' of an intellectual type. It is a prac-tical, profoundly interior relationship by which all theological work becomes a form of prayer. Maggie Ross has said that, for her, writing is a form of adoration. This resonates with my sense that prayer must become something which impregnates and nourishes the whole of our life.[9] The work of reading and writing must become a kind of prayer, but so must all our activity.

We cannot make sense of prayer without understanding something of the relationship of God to the world, to people and to each of us personally. Prayer is about God, and about relationship, communion, with God. So it is about honesty, integrity and truth. The scriptures teach that God weighs the heart (Prov. 21:2) and that we know God through 'the eyes of the heart' (Eph. 1:18). If this is so, nothing can be hidden from God. We may conceal all kinds of things, parts of ourselves, from other people, including close friends, but we cannot conceal them from God. If this is so, prayer is either the ultimate place of honesty and truth, or it cannot exist at all. It is, as Ann and Barry Ulanov have argued, 'primary speech'.[10] Here, if nowhere else, nothing can be hidden.

So praying is a vital part of being fully human. Alan Ecclestone saw that 'to pray is to make the most of our moments of perception', and stressed the central place in prayer of selfless attention, unwearying patience, passionate commitment, honesty of purpose, and hunger for truth.[11] Ecclestone's recognition of the human character of praying is important. Christian prayer always builds on the human, for we are human before we are Christian.

Many things have helped me in my prayer life, but seven are worth emphasising. First, the recognition that prayer is essentially not our work but God's work in us. One Eastern Orthodox writer went so far as to say that 'prayer is God'.[12] God is the source of our prayer, as Paul suggests in Romans 8. Julian of Norwich believed that God was closer to us than we were to ourselves, for God is the ground in which we stand.[13] Yet this consciousness is not evident in our time: it must be nurtured and nourished, and the provision of space for such nurturing and nourishment is an essential part of the work of local churches.

Secondly, we do not have to be clever, learned or spiritually advanced to pray with depth and passion. Much harm has been done by a 'ladder' approach, which locates contemplative prayer at the top, while most people are confined to the bottom rungs. Both Thomas Merton and Michael Ramsey stressed that contemplative prayer was possible and common among ordinary women, men and children who sought to love God, and was not restricted to the 'advanced' or very holy.

Thirdly, we need, as Dom John Chapman used to say, to 'pray as you can and not as you can't'. God leads us by a variety of paths, and not all forms of prayer are suitable to all people.

Fourthly, it is essential to focus, and this can be done by the use of an icon, a crucifix, a picture, a candle or the tabernacle containing the Blessed Sacrament. We need, as I have suggested elsewhere in this book, to take the ecology of prayer seriously.

Fifthly, we need to get rid of external and internal rubbish and clutter which obstructs and delays the encounter with God. There are helpful words in the Book of Nehemiah, written about the rebuilding of the wall of Jerusalem. 'There is too much rubbish so that we are unable to work on the wall' (Neh. 4:10). A few verses later we read: 'The work is great and widely spread out, and we are separated far from one another' (4:19). These comments are vital for our own lives of prayer: the accumulation of rubbish, and separation from fellow Christians, remain serious obstacles to the work of prayer.

So, sixthly, it is important that we pray with others, pray for others, and support one another.

Seventhly, it should be our aim to 'pray without ceasing', but this does not happen overnight. My experience is that we only come to pray all of the time if we begin by praying some of the time.

When I left London after 46 years, there were only a few things I missed – the underground, libraries, and churches that were open constantly for prayer. While I do not believe that it is only possible to pray in a church, I do believe that one of the main purposes of churches is to be places where prayer can, in Eliot's phrase, be 'valid'. Yet this is becoming increasingly difficult. I have never been willing to work in a church which was not open more than it was closed, and I have never worked in any area which could be considered 'safe'. At Hoxton in the early 1960s, Soho in the late 1960s, and Bethnal Green in the 1970s, we fought to keep the church open, and this battle needs to continue, obstacles and all.

I have also, for many years, been greatly influenced by the spirituality of Charles de Foucauld and the Little Sisters and Brothers of Jesus, with their emphasis on a daily hour of adoration before the Blessed Sacrament, and this is something I have tried to do for some years. I find it extremely important to have this time reserved for silent adoration and nothing else, and there is a great spiritual power in praying in the presence of the reserved Sacrament. In St Mary's Church, Mulberry Street, Manchester, the sacrament is exposed on the altar every day, and there is no time when people are not praying there. In the same city, the Church of the Holy Name in Oxford Road exposes the sacrament for an hour every weekday, concluding with

Benediction. When I worked in East London, I often used to pray in St Mary's Roman Catholic Church in Moorfields where there was also perpetual exposition. I am sure that this focus on the presence of Jesus in the eucharistic elements is of great importance in cultivating and strengthening the life of prayer, and it distresses me that most Anglicans, and indeed most Christians, fail to take this seriously. So churches come to be seen in entirely functionalist terms, as places where certain activities – liturgical, managerial, pastoral, and so on – are performed, but are less and less seen as shrines, prayerful spaces, places in which prayer has been valid. I can see no future for contextual theology in the Catholic tradition which ignores the place of eucharistic adoration. Isaac the Syrian advised people: 'When you fall down before God in prayer, become in your thought like an ant, like the creeping things of the earth, like a leech.'[14] This particular Leech has found prayer extremely difficult, even when he has been powerfully drawn to it, but does try to fall down before God.

In my own life of prayer I have drawn heavily on the contemplative tradition, and have received much support from contemplatives and solitaries. It was wonderful to be visited, in 1993, by Fr William McNamara, a Carmelite who lives in the Colorado desert. He seemed, from his solitude, to understand what was happening in the inner city better than many urban people do. On 6th March 1995 I returned from retreat at Bede House, a centre for Christian spirituality in the Kent countryside, which was set up in 1967 by the Sisters of the Love of God. This community has been one of my main spiritual resources and support networks for over thirty years. I had been associated with Bede House almost from its beginnings, and it had become my favoured place of retreat. It had been of enormous importance to thousands of people since it was opened by Archbishop Michael Ramsey in the late 1960s. (Sadly, like so many creative projects, it has now closed.) I was very conscious, during my time there, of my neglect of silence, solitude, prayer and reflection, and waiting on God. I am so good at telling others how important all this is, but not so good at doing it myself. It is not an uncommon syndrome. I realised too at Bede House how important it is to have had a link with a contemplative community, and that the dialectical relationship between the contemplative and active modes is utterly central to theological work. In September 1995 I made another retreat at Bede House. I was pleased that my times of eucharistic adoration and Bible study had been maintained, but regular intercession had not improved and I had a sense of being overloaded. I had a feeling of being very undisciplined in my prayer life, and this continues.

On 30th June 1999 I went to Bede House for the last time to revise my Rule of Life. This time I felt I needed to take seriously some of the criticisms which one of my closest friends had made of me, as well as areas of weakness and neglect which I have realised myself. It seemed that I needed to do something about regular retreats and quiet days, something which I had felt for decades was so important, and yet had done so little about. I had felt also for some time that my reading was very unbalanced – lots of theology and politics, not much in the way of novels, poetry and so on. I also felt that I needed to practise the discipline of attentive listening to people without interrupting. This reinforced for me the fact that to do theology is bound up with being a particular kind of person, and that the personal qualities and characteristics of the theologian are crucial to the kind of theology which is practised.

I am sure that prayer is vital to the future of pastoral ministry, theology and practical wisdom. If we are bereft of guidance, we perish (Prov. 11:14). As priests, pastors and teachers, we need 'the tongue of a teacher' so that we 'know how to sustain the weary with a word' (Isa. 50:4). None of this can happen without the discipline of prayer. Yet there is abundant evidence that priests and ministers are often neglectful of themselves, not least in the area of ascetical discipline. In his last address to his synod in Milan, St Charles Borromeo advised his clergy: 'Do not neglect the parish of your own soul, do not give yourself so completely that you have nothing left for yourself. You have to be mindful of your people without being forgetful of yourself.'[15]

During these years in Whitechapel, I was often asked to help social and political activists on questions about prayer and reflection. On 30th June 1995 I spent an interesting evening with Stephen Timms's support group in East Ham. Timms is an evangelical Christian who was later to become an important figure in the Blair government. I wondered if he was the only Member of Parliament to have a theological support group. I was asked to speak on the place of prayer in the life of Christians in politics. It was a moving and humbling experience, and I still maintain contact with some of the people who were part of it.

The key issue is prayer. One of the reasons we created the Whitechapel project was our recognition that prayer and contemplation were being neglected in active social and political work. I often find that I am falling into that very trap. My own life of prayer is very weak and fragile, yet the desire for prayer grows more powerful by the day. We need to help and nourish one another in the life of prayer, which is a corporate life, rooted in the work of the Holy Spirit. Of course, prayer, justice and mercy must go hand in hand. St Gregory of Nyssa said that 'when we approach God in prayer, we ask that our debts may be forgiven us. But such words are ineffectual and do not reach the Divine hearing unless our conscience cries in unison with us that it is good to impart mercy.'[16] Yet Walter Wink has warned us that, without the protection of prayer, social activism can become a form of self-justification. Wink argues that prayer is 'the theatre in which the diseased spirituality that we have contracted from the powers can most directly be discerned, diagnosed and treated'.[17]

The New Testament and the early Christians laid great stress on wakefulness and sobriety (1 Thess. 5:6), and prayer calls for alertness and perseverance (Eph. 6:18). It is an expression of life in the Spirit. The term *en spirito*, in the Spirit, is used 164 times in the letters of Paul. Life in the Spirit must be nourished by a discipline of attention. This is why a key element in a prayerful life is listening to, and learning from, God and God's people. I find myself still a beginner at this. Gustavo Gutiérrez said that, when he went to a particular community in Peru, hoping to give, he realised that he was the receiver. The poor people with whom he lived revealed to him the treasures of Christian spirituality which had been hidden from him in the affluent world.[18] On a far less extreme scale, that has been my experience too. But learning the practice of listening, without interrupting, has been one of the greatest struggles of my life. I am a great talker and feel I have lots to say. The discipline of silence and reticence has taken me a long time to learn. In prayer we listen to God, and in conversation we listen to one another, and I see the two as related and inseparable.

I once said, at a meeting of my support group, 'I don't think I have got the balance right between the active side of me and the contemplative.' A woman who had known me for a long time commented, 'By introducing the word balance you have confused the discussion. It is not a question of balance. What you need to learn is how to integrate, to do the things you do in a more contemplative, reflective way. You may end up doing more, not less, but it will be done in a more reflective way.' I am sure she was right. One of the most serious dangers confronting those who minister in the city is that their lives come to be built on frenzy and compulsive busyness. This usually leads to a lack of focus, a tendency to accumulate more and more things, a collapse of reflection, and the cultivation of a personal lifestyle of obligatory tiredness. This then becomes socially infectious so that one may communicate little to others other than one's own exhaustion – not a very kind gift to people who may already have enough problems of their own. The cultivation of a spirit of inner prayerfulness, a climate of the heart in which prayer arises spontaneously, can only be attained by opening the heart to God in times of concentrated prayer. We can only pray all the time if we begin by learning to pray some of the time.

Although the desert was seen historically as the prime site of prayer, St Symeon the New Theologian – the third of the Orthodox 'theologians'! – stressed that the fullness of the vision of God was just as possible 'in the middle of cities' as it was in mountains and cells.[19] The practice of silence and solitude, including the cultivation of inner stillness and inner peace, is a vital component of an urban spirituality. 'God is in heaven and you upon earth, therefore let your words be few' (Eccles. 5:2). We need to learn to be still before God and wait (Ps. 37:7; Zeph. 1:7). Silence and speech complement and nurture one another. Few of us are called to lives of perpetual silence. But all of us are called to the practice of silence as a necessary support for, and strengthening of, our words and actions. The late Audre Lorde argued that, while silence was necessary, we are never whole persons if we stay silent.[20] Silence must nourish speech: speech must grow from silence. Speech which is not so nourished is bound to be superficial, trivial and lacking in attention.

Prayer is central not only to Christian discipleship as a whole, but specifically to the theological task, and this belief has grown stronger during my years in East London. One of the twentieth-century western writers who stressed the integral link between theology and the life of prayer was the late Eric Mascall, who, in one of his books, went so far as to say that 'the really great theologian will also be a saint'.[21] Yet this is what we should expect if the heart of theology is mystical communion with God. The early doctrinal formulations were in fact mystical doctrines formulated dogmatically.[22] The experience of, and adoration of, God came first, and it must come first today. A theology which does not place prayer at its heart is not theology at all. Prayer is vital for the nurturing of that spirit of resistance to oppression and the pursuit of justice. In this sense prayer is a form of protest. Karl Barth used to say that the clasping of the hands in prayer was the beginning of a protest at the disorder of the world. Alan Ecclestone put it so well in 1977:

> The key to such re-shaping of Christian life lies, I believe, as always before, in the way we set about praying. For it is here that the spiritual energy, the sense of direction, the will to adventure, the faith to ensure, the love to embrace, and the hope to continue are all recruited. The very tissues of the Christain body of enterprise in the modern world must lack vitality and fall apart unless we can pray together with a strength greater than that of the disruptive forces which operate in this situation.[23]

7

'The Unsecular City'? Theology, religion and secularisation

> Of all modern delusions, the idea that we live in a secular age is the furthest from reality ... Liberal humanism itself is very obviously a religion – a shoddy replica of Christian faith, markedly more irrational than the original article, and in recent times more harmful.
>
> JOHN GRAY, cited in the *Guardian*, 3rd December 2005

In 1955 I had been a practising Christian for only a short time. One of the most important intellectual influences on me was the philosopher Alasdair MacIntyre, at that time a young lecturer at the University of Manchester. His first book *Marxism: an interpretation*, published in 1953, began in this way.

> The division of human life into the sacred and the secular is one that comes naturally to western thought. It is a division which at one and the same time bears the marks of its Christian origin and witnesses to the death of a properly religious culture. For when the sacred and the secular are divided, then religion becomes one more department of human life, one activity among others. This has in fact happened to bourgeois religion ... Only a religion which is a way of living in every sphere either deserves to or can hope to survive. For the task of religion is to help see the secular as the sacred, the world as under God. When the sacred and the secular are separated, then ritual becomes an end not to the hallowing of the world, but in itself. Likewise if our religion is fundamentally irrelevant to our politics, then we are recognising the political as a realm outside the reign of God. To divide the sacred from the secular is to recognise God's action only within the narrowest limits. A religion which recognises such a division, as does our own, is one on the point of dying.

These words have come to be more important to me as the years go by. I want to emphasise three points that MacIntyre made. First, the division between sacred and secular makes religion simply one department of human life. Second, ritual, one central form of the practice of religion, becomes an end in itself. Third, to divide religion from politics is to regard 'the political' as outside the realm of God. A few years later, MacIntyre gave a talk on the BBC Third Programme entitled 'A society without a metaphysics', which, in some ways, was a microcosm of his subsequent thinking. In this talk he argued that the combination of liberal morality and metaphysical meaninglessness was the characteristic flavour of our time.[1]

However, the unity of sacred and secular raises problems, and one of the tasks of Christians in the coming decades must be to disentangle the truth in MacIntyre's early formulation from distortions of that truth into theocratic states, Christendoms, and refusals to recognise the political autonomy of, and rights within, the 'secular realm'. I have always taken the view that one cannot be a Christian in any coherent sense unless one believes that sacred and secular are one, that religion is concerned with the whole of life, and that there is no part of the world from which God is absent. In this sense, there is no 'secular realm', no zone from which God is or can be excluded. However, like all truths, this can be distorted into fantasy, absurdity and cruelty. Fantasy, in that it can lead to a refusal to face the obvious fact that many millions of people do not believe what I have said, and act as if it were not the case. Absurdity, in that to reject the idea of a secular reality is not the same as pretending that everyone else rejects it. Cruelty, in that, where religious groups are in positions of power, they can confuse belief and practice with the enforcement of both, and the ill treatment or oppression of those who hold a different view.

As usual, the *via media* is a risky and dangerous road. Many years ago, in his book of that title, Eric Mascall pointed out that the *via media*, the middle way, should never be confused with liberalism, comprehensiveness or moderation. Rather it is an attempt to hold together positions which, on the surface, appear incompatible. It is a narrow and precarious road which runs through ambiguities and complexities, and it is easy to fall off it into the comfort of simplification and pseudo-clarity. The *via media* is more closely akin to orthodoxy than to liberalism.[2]

Today it is said that we are in an age which is 'post-Christian', though others would describe it as 'post-secular'. The idea of a 'post-Christian' age, while it is popularly associated with all the other 'posts' which have been identified or proposed in recent years, was in use in the 1930s, though T. S. Eliot, in *The Idea of a Christian Society* in 1939, noted that 'Christian culture' had not been replaced by anything else. In 1977 a General Synod report referred to what it called 'a kind of believing'.[3] Some writers are now inclined to refer to England (more than Britain as a whole) as a 'post-religious society' in spite of much evidence to the contrary.[4] The religious situation in Northern Ireland, Wales and Scotland is more complex. However, the political scientist Anthony King has said that the British are 'now a largely irreligious people'. In one survey cited by King, over one-third of young people were agnostic or atheist – though, quaintly, most of them supported the role of the Queen as 'head' of the Church of England! Belief in God had fallen from 77 per cent of the population to 44 per cent during the period 1968–2004.[5] Studies in other parts of Europe produce similar results. Research in Germany, for example, has suggested that only around 5 per cent of people are active in the churches. These data cannot be ignored, yet alongside them must be placed the extraordinary growth of 'new religious movements', the resurgence of older ones, and the fascination felt by many for 'private' approaches to spirituality. Secularisation and apathy may be the dominant mode, but, at the same time, the religions – or some of them – are increasing.

The concepts of 'secular' and 'secularisation' are also confused and confusing, and, for many years, sociologists have been calling oversimplified interpretations of secularisation into question. Callum Brown's work on what he calls 'the death of Christian Britain' has been somewhat uncritically received, though he makes some important points. However, Brown seems to accept the conventional view that the mid-1960s were of crucial importance in the death he records, claiming that 'quite suddenly in 1963 something very profound ruptured the character of the nation and its people, sending organised Christianity on a downward spiral to the margins of social significance'.[6] 1963 was the year of *Honest to God*, the collapse of the Conservative government as a result of the 'Profumo affair', and other political and cultural events. To isolate that year from its wider historical context is fashionable but misleading. Certainly the overall pattern is one of gradual erosion of the socio-cultural role of the churches in Britain and throughout Western Europe, though not in quite the same form elsewhere.

Yet decline in church attendance, and in basic knowledge about Christianity, cannot be written off as unimportant. Some studies suggest the survival of a residual attachment to Christian faith. A national study in 1973 of 1026 people found that only 12 per cent identified themselves as complete unbelievers, though 64 per cent did not 'practise' any religion. A further study in 1978 reported that 50 per cent of young people claimed to be Christian.[7] A recent survey by *Readers' Digest* reported that 31 per cent thought that Easter was sponsored by Cadburys, while 48 per cent had no idea what it was about. The greatest level of ignorance was among the 16–24 age group.[8]

Data for the Church of England showed that adult membership fell by 19 per cent between 1975 and 1990. By 1991 only 1.1 million were regular Sunday attenders. Other studies suggest a more serious disconnectedness from Christianity. According to a MORI poll for the British Humanist Association in 1996, 43 per cent of those interviewed believed in God, though when MORI did a poll for the Church of England the figure was 88 per cent!

The East End situation

Since I came to the East End almost fifty years ago, I sensed that two features of the relationship between churches and the people were important, and were different from those prevailing in many other parts of Britain. The first was the fact that, with the exception of the Roman Church, most church congregations were small. (The Roman communion was to experience decline later, with the collapse of the 'folk religion' of the Irish working class, first in Britain, and then in Ireland itself.) Whereas, in some other areas, there was a degree of 'cultural churchgoing' – it was 'the done thing' – in the East End this had not been so for many years. As a result, congregations usually consisted of the seriously committed, those who had made a conscious decision and who took their faith seriously, and a declining group of older members for whom the cultural attachment was still present. There were distinct advantages in this situation. You knew where you were. Congregations, small as they often were, meant business. We did not have the problem of the presence of large numbers of members for whom churchgoing was the conventional thing to do, since, in the East End, it wasn't.

Bethnal Green is a classic example. At the *British Weekly* census of

1886, Bethnal Green had the lowest attendance at church of any London parish. The average percentage of the population attending church in London was under 15, but in Bethnal Green it was 12 per cent. (In 1851 it was closer to 7 per cent.) In the late nineteenth century, Charles Booth reported that St Anne's, Hoxton Street – where I once worked – had the smallest congregation in East London. It was around 16, and I recall that, in 1964, it was about the same. 'Secularisation' had hit areas like the East End long before it hit other parts of Britain.

The second feature was that, in terms of social and political commitment, the churches, or many of them, had made an impact on the wider community to a degree much greater than was the norm in many other places. This, for me, called into question any definition of 'secularisation' which restricted itself to church attendance and neglected social impact. Some historians have referred to 'diffused Christianity', and this has certainly been true of the East End since the establishment of new parishes and missions in the nineteenth century.

Today the major growth area for Anglicanism is in Africa. Of the 77 million Anglicans in the world, 2.3 million are in the USA, but 17 million in Nigeria. The Church of England, historically the heart of Anglicanism, is in some respects highly atypical, not least in its relationship with the state, its massive geographical presence, and the fact that the bulk of the membership is lapsed! However, the position is complex. There are problems of decline, obsolescence and stagnation. Some churches and faith communities are in acute decline, while others are increasing. There is decay as well as renewal. The data themselves are varied and at times interpretation is difficult.

The Roman Church

There are major crises throughout the Christian churches, though the forms they take differ. Let us take the case of the Roman Church.[9] The prospects for the Roman Church in the coming years, whether in Europe, North America or the 'third world' are not at all clear. Certainly there has been a growth in membership, as well as a shift in the centre of gravity of the communion towards the southern hemisphere. But perhaps more significant has been the abandonment of the church by large numbers of people, most marked in South America (also one of the areas of growth) as members leave to join Pentecostal churches; in Europe (including Ireland) where the old religious power structures have been eroded, aided by the recent sex scandals among priests (though, more important, by the irresponsible attitude of the hierarchy to them); and, in many places, where the shortage of priests has led to a bizarre situation. In many places now we see a highly sacramental and eucharistic-centred church, where, for much of the time, there are no eucharistic celebrations, and where access to the sacraments is difficult. Can such a situation last much longer? At present Rome seems to be on a suicidal course, but things may change.

In the USA the number of priests has declined by 26 per cent over 25 years, while the Roman Catholic population has increased by 29 per cent to 65 million. Yet at the end of 2005, 3200 parishes were without a regular priest.

The resurgence of religion in East London

The position is complicated by the fact that in many urban areas, religion is not in decline at all. On the contrary there has been a striking increase of religious life, not least among Christian churches. The work done by Greg Smith – from whom I take the title of 'the unsecular city' – over many years in East London has shown that, in Newham, the borough east of the East End, religious practice was actually increasing. In Newham in 1994 there were 198 religious congregations, of which 163 were Christian ones, and 77 religious organisations or centres. About 8 per cent of the population attended religious services, and 10 per cent of the non-Asian population did so (9 per cent and falling was the national average). In addition to the Christian community, Newham contained around 25,000–30,000 Muslims, 20,700 Hindus and over 4000 Sikhs. By 1999 Smith was reporting that there were at least 294 faith-based organisations in Newham, including 181 Christian congregations. The largest number were Pentecostal, and the smallest were Methodist. Smith studied religious groups in Barking Road, the main bus route through Newham, in considerable detail, commenting: 'Today, as I walk the Barking Road, Jesus walks alongside, but in many packages, if not incarnations. It's a bit like the Number 15 bus which travels along the Barking Road. You wait for a Messiah for ages, then three come along at once.'

In Barking Road, which covers around four kilometres, there were at least 44 places of worship. They included the Islamic Centre,

Calvary Charismatic Baptist Church, Mansfield Settlement, Glory Bible Church and Green Pastures Christian Ministry, the Society of St Francis, Memorial Baptist Church, West Ham Central Mission, four new Pentecostal congregations, St Andrew's Church, the Foursquare Gospel Church, the United Reformed Church, another Pentecostal storefront church and a storefront mosque, a Roman Catholic church, St Martin's Anglican church, the Sree Narayan Guru Mission, Emmanuel Enterprises, two mosques, the Church Army Youth Centre (hosting three Pentecostal congregations), Holy Tabernacle Ministries, and the Town Hall (used by the Redeemed Church of Christ Royal Connection Parish). This was simply one, albeit lengthy, road in East London. Secular city?[10]

Much of the religious resurgence generally was among faiths other than Christian, or sectarian mutants from the Christian tradition. For instance, between 1975 and 1990, when membership of the Church of England nationally fell by 19 per cent and of the Roman Catholic Church by 23 per cent, Mormons and Jehovah's Witnesses grew by 50 per cent. Members of Trinitarian churches declined from 8.1 million to 6.8 million, while members of non-Trinitarian churches increased from 330,000 to 460,000. When we look at faiths other than Christian we also have seen significant growths. In the same period Hindus increased by 40 per cent, Muslims doubled and Sikhs trebled.[11] In spite of its surface secularity, London is an immensely diverse religious city, and this pattern is repeated, with changes in detail, in other British cities such as Manchester, Birmingham and Leicester. In the East End, what struck me most was the massive shift in the centre of gravity of the Christian presence toward Pentecostal and post-denominational churches.

The global scene

Increasingly, faiths other than Christian are also numerically strong in North American cities. There are now more Muslims than Anglicans in the USA, Los Angeles has the most complex Buddhist society in the world, and the USA as a whole has been described as 'the most religiously diverse nation on earth'. Yet a study by the City University of New York in 1991 reported that 86.5 per cent of those interviewed saw themselves as Christian – the largest single group (26.2 per cent) being Roman Catholic – while New Age followers were 'statistically insignificant'.[12] When we move outside North America and Europe, the situation is very different. For example, 'faith communities' are responsible for over 50 per cent of all educational and health care work in sub-Saharan Africa.

'Fundamentalisms'

One of the features of the religious resurgence throughout the world, and in East London, has been the growth of 'fundamentalisms'. This too is a difficult concept, and is often used as if it were synonymous with textual literalism. It has, in my view, more to with single-mindedness, with the exclusion of doubt and uncertainty, and with an unintelligent conviction of one's own rightness. The words 'fundamentalist' and 'fundamentalism' (which are unknown in Islam) grew from North American evangelical groups in the period before and after the First World War, and were used with pride by those who coined them. Only later did they become terms of abuse.

The encounter of faiths

Christians are very divided and confused about how they relate to other faiths. My impression from East London was that there was a tremendous amount of co-operation between different 'faith communities', but that, as far as the Christian community was concerned, the theological understanding of what a plurality of faiths means was very weak. This is not a question of which viewpoint one takes on the issue. It is rather about the difficulty in, and maybe the obstacles involved in, coming to a position at all.

My view coincides with that proposed by the controversial Jesuit theologian Roger Haight: that the Spirit of God has been at work in the world from the beginning 'without a causal connection to the historical appearance of Jesus'.[13] This emphatically does not mean that the historical appearance of Jesus is not important, and indeed it is pivotal to Christian faith. It does mean that the work of God is not limited to the incarnation, and that God has been, and continues to be, active in areas of the world and areas of faith and thought in which Jesus is unknown.

I also find myself in agreement with David Tracy that understanding between one faith and another depends on the ability to make an 'analogy' between something in one's own tradition and something in that of 'the other'.[14] If this cannot occur, mutual understanding fails. It follows that rootedness in, and fidelity to, one's own tradition is a necessary prelude to, not *per se* an obstacle to, 'dialogue with the other'. It may well be that the future of Christian – Muslim dialogue lies in the willingness of 'conservative' Christians to engage in it. 'The other' may be a person of different faith, or a person of no faith, a secular person. We need to engage with the *saeculum* but *sub specie aeternitatis*, to engage with this age according to the perspective of the eternal. For Christian theology is not a 'religious dimension' or a 'department' but a way of looking at the world as a whole.

8

'The Time of No Room': theology and homelessness

Give to everyone who begs from you . . .

JESUS, Luke 6:30

Let us then show him mercy in the persons of the poor and those who are lying on the ground.

ST GREGORY NAZIANZEN,
De pauperum amore 38–40, *PG* 35:907–910

The time of the end is the time of no room.

THOMAS MERTON

My involvement with homelessness long antedated the White-chapel project. As a student in the late 1950s and early 1960s, I was involved with several organisations which were working with older homeless men, including methylated-spirit drinkers – the Methodist Church in Cable Street, Spitalfields Crypt, the Brotherhood of Prayer and Action, based at St Botolph's, and, later, the Simon Community (founded in 1963). As a priest in Soho in 1969, I founded Centrepoint, the first all-night shelter for homeless young people, and now one of the biggest organisations in this field in Western Europe. In the 1970s I was involved with the beginnings of the Kipper Project, originally based at St Botolph's. From 2003 to 2004 I chaired UNLEASH (United London Ecumenical Action with the Single Homeless), which had, for over 25 years, sought to be a voice from the churches to politicians and public, as well as an educational resource for Christian and other groups in London. The merger of the Catholic Housing Aid Society and the Churches National Housing Coalition to create a new body called Housing Justice occurred at this time, and we were able to establish the UNLEASH offices with the new body in Marylebone. We employed Alastair Murray and Sophie Kilmister as our first paid workers. This merger of two bodies concerned with housing, and the presence within their premises of UNLEASH, concerned with homelessness, brought out the intimate connection between the two. In 2006 UNLEASH ceased to exist as a separate organisation and was absorbed into Housing Justice.

As my work developed, it became very clear that there was no way of responding to homelessness unless we gave attention to the need for 'social housing'. The Jubilee Group arranged a major lecture in the mid-1990s by Susan J. Smith, Professor of Geography at Edinburgh University, on the future of social housing.[1] Research has shown that we need at least 54,000 new homes each year. In 1994, over 1.7 million houses in Britain were unfit for human habitation, and another 3.8 million were in need of urgent repair. At the beginning of 2005, more than 1 million children lived in poor housing conditions.

Within a few weeks of the beginning of the project in 1991, I and some colleagues met with Michael Fielding, then Methodist Minister in Lambeth, and Doug Shenson, a physician based at Montefiore Medical Centre in the Bronx, New York. Doug had a Rockefeller grant to look at inner-city health care, and was comparing the South Bronx with Tower Hamlets. I introduced him to people and groups here, and hoped that something came of this. These transnational links are important, and Doug was the first of many medical links during this project.

One of the key issues in the beginning of the work was trying to look, theologically and politically, at homelessness. Until recently, the idea that theology and pastoral care were separate areas of activity was dominant in practice, and often in theory, in the western churches. Theology was about doctrine, ideas, formulations, while pastoral care was about compassion, care, doing good. In recent years the pastoral nature of theology itself has been emphasised. Writers such as John Elford have referred to 'the pastoral nature of theology', while Frances Ward has emphasised that Christian discipleship involves 'lifelong learning' in which action and theological reflection are equally necessary.[2]

In 1991 a group of us, all Christians working at St Botolph's, started a theological reflection group. For many years the homelessness work – originally known as 'The Crypt' and later as St Botolph's Project – had adopted a policy that religious belief would not be a factor in employment, though it would have been difficult for those who were fiercely hostile to the Church to work in this setting. However, there was always a hard core of committed Christians working there, and we felt that theological issues were being ignored or glossed over. We did some important work, though at the end of it we felt that we had failed to make any impression on the paid staff of either church or project. About the time that we began our reflection group, Michael Fielding had completed his study of church-based projects working with homeless people in New York City and London. St Botolph's was one of the places he studied, and he concluded that 'religion did not feature' in the work.

So this group of Christians began to meet for theological reflection on issues arising from the work. The core group consisted of Andy Delmege, James Francis, Mark Johnston, Birgit Wagner, Paul Windsor and myself. In November 1993 we produced a paper entitled 'Upstairs, Downstairs: theology at St Botolph's'. The group felt that there was a need for more systematic theological reflection than was possible within the secular ethos of the Crypt. (The title 'St Botolph's Church and Crypt' was in use until the early 1990s, when it was replaced by 'St Botolph's Project', and links with the church were gradually reduced to geographical proximity and the payment of rent.) In our paper we argued that issues about the nature of a 'secular' agency within an ecclesial framework had not been faced; that, as a result, the crypt, was 'physically but not metaphysically related to the church which is "above"', and that there seemed to be a need to find 'a way of glossing over crucial conflicts and differences beneath a kind of liberal (and spiritually neutral) fog'. This never really changed.

When the work began in 1990, homelessness was increasing as well as changing its character. I was appalled at how, even in 1990, prominent figures kept getting it wrong, as on BBC Radio 4's *Any Questions* programme in January when the question of homelessness was raised. I wrote in response:

> I was appalled that four of the more intelligent of our public figures – Fay Weldon, Enoch Powell, Tony Benn and Michael Heseltine – should have been so ill-informed in their answer on *Any Questions* on the subject of homelessness. Most of them focused on the scandalous position of people discharged from psychiatric hospitals on to the streets as if these were the majority of homeless people – although

many people do become mentally ill as a result of homelessness. The two major causes of homelessness were ignored: the shrinking stock of cheap, rented housing, and, in London particularly, the movement of people from Scotland and the North in search of work.

Enoch Powell should know about the former since he helped to draft the infamous 1957 Rent Act, claiming, on 21st November 1956, that 'we are now within sight of, and should in 12 months' time or so be level with, an equation of the overall supply and demand for houses'. Since then cheap rented housing in London has become virtually impossible to find, and poor people are being squeezed out as gentrification spreads. And Tony Benn, who lives very close to North Kensington and Paddington, the heart of the old Rachman empire, has no excuse for not knowing this.[3]

In July 1990 the press reported that the government was to spend £6.9 million on research into homelessness. The news depressed me, and reminded me of the late Saul Alinsky's description of the sociology department of the University of Chicago many years ago. It was, he said, a body which would spend $100,000 to discover the location of all the brothels in the city – information which any taxi driver could have given them for free. In the last 40 years the amount of accumulated data on homelessness has been enormous, most of it collected by voluntary bodies with small budgets. Further research, I felt, would do no more than reinforce the conclusions of earlier studies, and, more important, waste time and money convincing the public that 'something is being done'. It seemed a massively dishonest and irresponsible charade. The real problem was, as always in this as well as in other areas, a lack of political will. It strengthened my desire to set up some independent project where I could be free to act and to agitate.

An issue which grew in media attention and in the concern of local government bodies, both in the USA and in Britain, was that of begging. The *Financial Times* reported on 12th May 1990 that beggars were to be banned from New York underground and main-line stations. The reporter, Martin Dickson, referred to a growing 'Third World air' in parts of the city, and of the 'increasingly sharp polarisation ... into haves and have-nots'. I had known New York City well since 1970 when I spent some time in the parish of St Edward the Martyr in East Harlem, and I went back almost every year since then. (I ended the regular twice-a-year visits to the USA in 2004.) The parallels as well as the contrasts with London are striking. But in 1990 we too were seeing an increase in young beggars and in polarisation. What was, and is, particularly worrying is the polarisation of consciousness, far worse than that which prevailed in the nineteenth century before the publication of *The Bitter Cry of Outcast London*. Then there was perhaps some basis for the claim of ignorance. Today there is rather a deliberate refusal to believe, a conscious averting of the eyes. I felt in 1990 that the erection of a fortress around Downing Street was a kind of sacrament of this new structural blindness. I worry too that Britain continues to 'learn' from the USA in all those areas of social policy where that country has most conspicuously failed, ignoring its successes and the warnings of its most informed commentators. By August 2003 there was discussion in the press about a 'national ban on beggars', arising out of a court case in Manchester. There were differences among homelessness charities about the pros and cons of giving money to beggars. While Crisis took the view that most beggars were homeless and that most of the money given was spent on food, Thames Reach Bondway led a campaign to discourage giving, using posters entitled 'Killing by Kindness'. These raise important spiritual and theological as well as policy issues. I felt that a serious weakness of St Botolph's as a church – St Botolph's Project did a good deal of thinking though in an entirely secular way – was that action, or rather service, tended to replace thought and doctrine.

On 10th April 1991, Yassin Abyan and Mohammed Hersi came to see me to ask for my help with the establishment of a Somali Homeless Project (SHP). Why had they approached me, I asked. 'Because you taught English to our parents' was the reply. My thoughts went back to the late 1950s, when, as a 19-year-old undergraduate, I helped with the evening classes for Somali seamen in the crypt of St Botolph's. Now over forty years later, the children of those students were taking this initiative. Work done in one period often leads to developments many years later. Actually the pioneer of English as a Second Language (now a well-established educational provision) was Edith Ramsey, who started such classes in the East End in 1920 with Somalis especially in mind. The emergence of the SHP coincided with a wider concern among black communities about the increase, and the increased awareness, of homelessness problems among ethnic minorities. During the 1990s and down to 2004, homelessness rose twice as fast among blacks as among the general population. Since the Labour Party came to power in 1997, according to a study by Shelter in 2004, blacks were seven times more likely to be overcrowded. Overall homelesness increased between 1997 and 2004 among blacks by 77 per cent, compared with 34 per cent among the general population.

The 25th anniversary of the founding of Shelter, Britain's national campaign for the homeless, took place towards the end of 1991, and on 4th December I preached at a thanksgiving service at St Martin in the Fields. David Hope, newly installed as Bishop of London, led the service. He and I were students together at St Stephen's House, Oxford, in the early 1960s, so it was good to meet again. Shelter is one of many examples of a national movement which began in a very local way. Its origins lie in the work of the Notting Hill Housing Trust, and in the pioneering work in that district by Bruce Kenrick, whom I have mentioned in Chapter 5. I owe a great debt to Kenrick although we met on only one occasion. His book *Come Out the Wilderness,* an account of the work of the East Harlem Protestant Parish, published in the early 1960s, inspired me, and many others, to commit our lives to inner-city ministry. But it is often forgotten how important Kenrick's work in Notting Hill was in providing the contextual ground out of which Shelter grew. It was a great privilege to preach at this service, and to pay tribute to him. The 4th December is the day on which the Church commemorates St John of Damascus who strongly emphasised the material basis of Christian theology and spirituality. It was so appropriate to thank God for a housing campaign on such a day. 'I do not worship matter', John said in his reponse to the iconoclasts, 'but I do worship the Creator of matter, who, for my sake, became material, who dwelt in matter, and through matter effected my salvation. I will not cease from reverencing matter, for it was through matter that my salvation came to pass.'

On 13th February 2003, the *East London Advertiser* contained three, apparently unrelated, stories. One reported that the battle to save Spitalfields Market, one of our most historic and best-loved sites, had been lost to the property developers. 'The battle is over' was the headline. It ended with a quotation from a representative of the campaigning group SMUT (Spitalfields Market Under Threat), 'We just wanted to show the Corporation of London that it can't trample all over the people of the East End and get away with it.' But that was precisely what it had done. The second described the proposed Minerva Tower, another huge office block which will dominate the landscape around

Aldgate. The third celebrated a police swoop on young prostitutes in the Commercial Street area.

Each of these stories related to districts very close to where I lived, and to each other. They brought home the fact that it is impossible to speak coherently about many issues without a sense of connectedness. We cannot speak of homelessness without speaking of drugs, mental health, health care generally, redundancies, migration patterns, affordable housing, government housing policy, wars internal and external, gentrification, and so on. The onward thrust of the financial district into the East End, the attempt in 'developmentspeak' and in real-estate rhetoric to abolish the East End and replace it by 'City fringe', the encouragement of gentrification and therefore the pushing out of homeless people and prostitutes, as well as poor, working-class people and those in the middle-income groups – all this is part of a connected process. It will be all too familiar to comrades in the USA and elsewhere. Sociologists such as John Eade in London and Chris Mele in New York have been busy examining parallels and contrasts.[4] I feel strongly, after 25 years of regular visits to the USA, that pastoral workers in British and US cities need to maintain and strengthen working links. It is said, in our postmodern jargon, that we cannot see 'the big picture', but only fragments. Nevertheless, while, as I realised 40 years ago, geographical proximity to problems and needs is no guarantee of accuracy of vision, it should be remembered that people who are most involved in local issues may see the 'big picture' more accurately than national figures who may see a broad but illusory one.

Homelessness is increasingly global, affected by changes in the global economy, patterns of migration, and so on. The sociologist Saskia Sassen has written (slightly misleadingly) of a 'sudden growth in homelessness'.[5] UNICEF estimated in 1995 that there were 100 million children living in city streets, of whom half were in Latin America and the Caribbean. Many commentators have warned of the likelihood of millions of displaced persons as a result of the war against Iraq. And who knows where the next victims of the permanent war economy will be found? In the USA, it is estimated that on any night, in the city of Atlanta, there are 11,000 to 16,000 homeless persons. Yet the pattern here is changing. In Philadelphia, in 1960, 75 per cent of homeless people were over 45, and 87 per cent were white. By 1988, 86 per cent were under 45, and 87 per cent were black or from ethnic minorities.

In the USA as a whole it is estimated that there are between 1 and 3 million teenagers living on the streets.

In Britain, and in Inner London specifically, five areas are important: the changing character, and composition, of the population of homeless people; the questions around geography, 'regeneration' and property; the questions about the 'hidden homeless' and 'rough sleepers'; issues about co-option and mergers; and the questions arising from the existence of 'sacred' and 'secular' agencies. Arising out of this, I want to raise the question about whether specifically Christian organisations are still needed.

The changing character of homelessness

First, the changing character of homelessness. I lived close to the point where the fiinancial district ends and an area of acute poverty begins. When I first came to the East End in 1958, the homeless people in this area were almost entirely male, white, often Scottish or Irish, aged over 40, generally with alcohol problems, with a sub-section who lived on bombed sites, derelict buildings and open spaces (of which 'Itchy Park' was a classic example). Since those days, homeless people have included women, younger people, black people, middle-class professional people, and so on. All this is well known. Some of the shifts go back thirty or more years, some of them are more recent. Let me refer to three particular changes.

The racial composition of the homeless population has both shifted and become more visible. White-led projects often claimed that there were no black homeless, when in fact the truth was that black homeless did not come to white-led projects. At the same time, black people were not visible as homeless. This has now changed. The pattern here has been different from that in US cities, partly because of the different relationships between poverty, race and class. In my neighbourhood, for example, where the majority of the population were Bangladeshi, the problem of homelessness was family focused, in contrast to the older white single male pattern.

The appearance of crack cocaine needs more detailed attention than I can give here. Chris Jencks has documented this in great detail in relation to Chicago and other North American cities,[6] while Kevin Flemen of Release in the UK estimated several years ago that 49 per cent of homeless people in London were injecting drugs. (In the general population the figure is 1 per cent.) Certainly, in street work with young sex workers in the East End, the use of crack cocaine has outpaced amphetamines and heroin in recent years.

The numbers of homeless people from middle-class and professional backgrounds increased, the year 1991 being a turning point. In that year there was an increase in repossession of homes because of mortgage arrears. According to government data, homeless families increased by 30 per cent in that year as a result of repossession – in earlier years a very unusual practice. Repossessions grew from about 2000 in 1979 to 23,000 in 1987. In addition, a study in 1996 claimed that 1 in 10 young homeless persons were graduates. Instability and insecurity is now embracing a wide spectrum of groups. The position of homeless families also worsened towards the end of the 1990s, and, according to the Office of the Deputy Prime Minister on 12th December, stood at the record level of 100,000, more than double the total for 1997.

The geography of homelessness

Secondly, the geography of homelessness. In current property-development jargon, the East End of London, as it was once seen as beginning at Aldgate, no longer exists. It is now 'City fringe', one of the many products of the relentless eastward push of the City of London, the financial district within which profits matter more than persons. This itself raises urgent issues. So much work in the field of homelessness is concerned with caring for poor people. Yet we need to remember the words of R. H. Tawney that what thoughtful rich people call the problem of poverty, thoughtful poor people call the problem of riches. On the 'City fringe' we were daily experiencing 'regeneration', sometimes a euphemism for the displacement of the people. We were being told too of the importance of 'affordable housing', but affordable by whom? The 'shrinking stock' of affordable rented housing was noted as long ago as 1962 in the London County Council's Committee of Inquiry into Homelessness, but the position has deteriorated dramatically since those early years. A study in May 2003 by the Joseph Rowntree Foundation confirmed what most people in the field knew – the increasing difficulty of access to affordable housing in Britain. Yet many people still look at homelessness in terms of personal pathology or mental illness, neglecting the crucial issue of access to housing.

Let me give an interesting example of the shifts in geography. From 1990 to 2004, I looked out onto Altab Ali Park a great deal, and, by day and night, I could see exactly who slept there and what went on there. By the late 1990s there were few homeless people sleeping there. However, on the corner of the park, in the rooms below me, were the offices of St Botolph's Project (which went into liquidation in April 2004), and a few seconds across the road were the offices of Centrepoint (which I founded in 1969). A few minutes away was the office of Crisis. About ten minutes' walk to the south were the offices of Thames Reach Bondway, the National Housing Foundation, and Turning Point. Five minutes east were a Salvation Army hostel – almost on the site where the Salvation Army was founded – and the Whitechapel (Methodist) Mission. I estimated that in 2004, even allowing for the collapse of St Botolph's Project, these organisations employed around 600 people. So there were more paid workers in the field of homelessness in this small area than there were homeless people! I draw no particular conclusions from this except the significance of geographical shifts in the access to, and use of, territory.

Rough sleepers and 'hidden homeless'

Thirdly, the issues around rough sleepers and the 'hidden homeless'. It is clear that 'rough sleepers' – people who sleep in the streets – are a tiny percentage of the homeless population, although much attention has been focused on them, and the original government initiative was the Rough Sleepers Unit. Blair, before he was Prime Minister, in January 1997, spoke of the importance of being 'intolerant of homeless people on the streets'. This was the beginning of an attitude which has persisted and become more unpleasant and oppressive. Interestingly, those who objected to it at the time were accused of being alarmist, of having over-reacted, misunderstood, and so on.

Much attention has been on beggars. In Britain, this was a political issue for 'New Labour' before it came to power. 'Clear beggars from streets says Blair' was a headline in *The Times* on 7th January 1997. Six years later, as the courts in Manchester were arguing the case to make begging an imprisonable offence, groups in California were arguing for criminalisation not only of begging but of giving to beggars. Journalists here suggested that the Manchester case could lead to a 'national ban on beggars' (*Independent*, 22nd August 2003). Research on begging is full of uncertainty combined with intense conviction on the part of some of the researchers. A study in 1994 by the London-based project Crisis suggested that 80 per cent of beggars were homeless, and that most of the money was spent on food.

There have been many street counts, although they have not included people in squats or derelict buildings. They have omitted people who were not, literally, asleep. Of course, the numbers have done down. This was, after all, the point of the exercise. But what is the point of the approach? Is it about visibility, or about focusing on such a small group in order to give the impression that 'something is being done'? And does it mean that even this small group of 'rough sleepers' has diminished or that it has simply been pushed on elsewhere, or moved into inaccessible places? To have reduced the numbers of the visible homeless is very convenient to local authorities. According to a report to the Board of St Botolph's Project on 8th July 2002, the London Boroughs of Tower Hamlets and Hackney had no policies on homelessness because their recorded numbers of rough sleepers were less than 10! There are, however, not surprisingly, some oddities here. In the London Borough of Newham in 1999 there were, allegedly, only 11 rough sleepers, yet the Department of the Environment was funding an outreach worker to work with young homeless, expecting him to take on 200 cases per year!

The term 'hidden homeless', highlighted, and possibly coined, by the late Carolyn Ye-Myint in 1992, long before it became part of fashionable jargon, has recently been stressed by writers in New York and elsewhere.[7] Mary Kneafsey, a former worker at St Botolph's Project, suggested to me in 2003 that, with the growth of a new government plan called 'Supporting Persons', the process of getting funding for individuals would get harder. Once benefits could only come via a Post Office account (April 2003), the question of what happened to people with no identification became more acute. No identification, no money, no housing benefit, no accommodation. When we get to asylum seekers and refugees, the situation gets worse. It is a microcosm of 'globalisation', that myth to which governments are so devoted, but whose adverse consequences they do not have to endure.

Recent work has reinforced the seriousness of our present crisis. On Saturday 2nd April 2005, in an independent count in London by the Simon Community, 300 people were found to be sleeping rough in central London; 82 hostels were contacted and 8 bed spaces were available. This was a 33 per cent increase on a survey in the autumn of 2004 which had found 226. However, no bed spaces at all were available for people without income, those out of work and not eligible for housing benefit. Homelessness agencies were becoming increasingly alarmed at the growing proportion of London's street homeless population who were ineligible for benefits. The Simon Community street-work team estimated this to be up to about one-third of those currently sleeping rough. Finding accommodation for these people is now becoming virtually impossible. Increasing numbers of vulnerable people have been forced to sleep rough because they cannot find work and are excluded from claiming benefits. There is an urgent need for temporary emergency accommodation to prevent them from getting used to sleeping rough and permanently joining the community of entrenched street homeless people.

There are a number of different reasons why people are unable to access housing benefits. People in special difficulty include UK citizens who have recently returned from living abroad (and so failing the Habitual Residency Test); European Union citizens who have recently moved to the UK (and so also failing that test); European Union citizens from certain Eastern European recent accession countries; and other people whose immigration status is unclear. As a result of the widespread introduction of charging for services in most central London day centres, those without benefits are now unable to access free food or other services and support which were previously available to them.

'Soup runs' have been criticised for reinforcing street homelessness, a criticism which I have been hearing since the 1960s. It is now being repeated by well-funded homelessness agencies, no doubt to the pleasure of the government and its co-opted spokespersons. To its credit, the Simon Community continues its programme of regular runs providing free food for homeless and destitute people on the streets in central London. That this is still needed is scandalous, but to bring it to an end would be to collude with a systematic programme of denial which would make the word 'scandal' seem mild.

Co-options and mergers

Fourthly, the issues around co-options and mergers. These are two different, but connected, issues here. Alasdair MacIntyre, in *After*

Virtue (MacIntyre, 1981), rewrote Lord Acton's famous dictum. 'All power co-opts', claimed MacIntyre. 'Absolute power co-opts absolutely.' The history of New Labour has been marked, in the area of social policy, by a series of co-options of workers from the voluntary sector or from other non-governmental organisations, some of whom have been given senior and powerful posts within government, while others have been placed in positions of significant influence. As this has occurred, much of their earlier critical thought seems to have dissipated, and they have toed an uncritical and subservient line to New Labour policies and ideology. Fortunately, some have resigned, or been pushed out, and in some cases their critical abilities have returned!

While I am making personal comments (on which I – unlike the British government – would be delighted to be criticised and corrected), let me add that I do find the apparent inability of this government to listen (I emphasise the word 'listen', I am not just saying 'hear') to dissident and alternative voices very disturbing. The problem with New Labour is not so much stupidity, though that is present, as an arrogant authoritarianism, an utter conviction that they are right, and dissenters are just a tiresome nuisance or even (as in the critique of anti-terrorist politics) traitors.

The recent British government White Paper *Winning Back Our Communities* (White Paper 2003) is yet another example of the clumsy authoritarian style of the present government, and of its apparent determination to follow North American policies in all the areas where they have most conspicuously failed. Homeless people are among the most vulnerable members of our society, precisely the people who always suffer greatly at times of economic recession and of overseas war. But military approaches are not peculiar to the approach to Iraq. There has been for some time what the New York sociologist Herbert Gans called a 'war against the poor' and the current proposals seem to be part of this war.

The government could go further along the North American road, and instruct the police to move homeless people from central cities to inhospitable suburbs, a common practice from California to Connecticut. Or they could follow a suggestion from Atlanta and make 'urban camping' illegal – as if being homeless was a holiday. Parts of Britain, such as Manchester, may well follow. The tragedy is that some members of the present government were among the sternest critics of this kind of approach when it came from Conservatives. But turnarounds are hardly new, and will lead to the worsening of situations, something which, at one time, they saw clearly.

The issue of mergers is linked to survival. My former colleague John Downie, in the early months of the twenty-first century, pointed out that agencies of the St Botolph's Project size – 60–80 employees – were finding things difficult financially. Questions such as quality indicators, levels of accountability, the increasing cost of services, and so on, were leading such agencies to look to possible mergers, But whom then do they serve? Projects may merge, get statutory funding, and then become subcontractors for government. Downie commented:

> The choice seems to be one of either becoming a large, not for profit, subcontractor for government, or revitalising our charitable roots with a somewhat reduced service portfolio. The former would allow us to do more overall, and the latter would allow us to meet unmet need, and tackle it in the way we wanted ... It is not just a rational matter: it strikes at our very reason for being.

Within a few years the Project had collapsed.

'Sacred' and 'secular' agencies

Finally, the issues arising from 'sacred' and 'secular' agencies. There is a long history of Christian (and other religious) groups working in this field. Alongside them, and sometimes arising out of them, are groups which are seen as secular. This is well known. Recently, however, there have been a number of developments. There has been an interest in, and promotion of, what the US and British governments now call 'faith communities'. These are probably still mainly Christian, but there are others. The New York Zen Centre, for example, has been active in the field for some time. Common too are church-founded projects which have moved in a secular direction, severing any explicitly Christian links. Sometimes the local church maintains a nominal connection even though most of the workers are not Christians, and there is no interest in Christian theology in the way the project functions. Frank Prochaska's recent study suggests that even explicitly Christian charities function in a secular way, paying little attention to mission or social doctrine.[8] My sense is that there is a good deal of confusion, mystification and ambiguity here, and often a reluctance to confront the issues. There are also examples where churches once provided space and support and then ceased to do so, as in the case of the troubled relationship between St Mary the Virgin in New York City and the Safe Space project, or the work done until 2006 at Salford's Roman Catholic Cathedral.

I feel that the loss of a Christian theological dimension and socio-political critique rooted in theology is a serious matter. Without this, church-based projects can become little more than social-work agencies with a vaguely religious tint, or effectively secular agencies over which churches try (usually unsuccessfully) to exercise some control. Something crucial has been lost.

Take the begging issue, for example. Almsgiving is a spiritual obligation in Judaism, Islam and, arguably, Christianity. If a government makes such an obligation impossible to fulfil, what are the religious communities to do? 'Let us then show him mercy in the persons of the poor and those who are lying on the ground', said St Gregory Nazianzen.[9] If Christians have a duty to share their wealth with the poor, and some of the poor are forbidden by secular law to tell us of their needs, where is the Christian community to go? These isues go right to the heart of the faith. Yet few church-based groups raise issues about this for fear that their funding might be affected. There are biblical insights which must not be neglected. Among the tasks of a shepherd (pastor) are the strengthening of the weak and the work of feeding people in justice (Ezek. 34:15–16), and this must apply to work with homeless people. The instruction not to ill treat or oppress the stranger was repeated at least 36 times in the Mosaic texts. Compassion is not enough. Marianne Sawicki, reflecting on the post-resurrection meals in Luke's gospel, pointed out that, for Luke, the ability to recognise a hungry person is the precondition for recognising the Risen Lord. Knowing how to feed the hungry within a community is crucial to resurrection life.[10]

One area in which a number of us were active during these years was that of developing worship resources for use in relation to housing and homelessness. If Christians cannot pray with intensity and intelligence about burning issues in the world, then we are of all people most miserable and most bereft. In 1992 Christine Allen (now Director of the Catholic Institute for International Relations) and the late Barbara D'Arcy produced a collection of liturgical material called *The Trampled Vineyard* which was immensely valuable.[11]

My question therefore is: are Christian groups still needed in this field of work? If my comments in the preceding paragraph are correct, then the answer is clearly 'Yes'. With a strengthened and courageous Christian prophetic movement, something vital could be regained.

Two important people

Homelessness is not simply an 'issue' or 'problem', but it is about people. I want therefore to end this chapter by remembering two friends who died during the time of my project. Wilf Allen was an important presence around St Botolph's through most of the 1990s until his death in 2002. He worked in the crypt kitchen and was of great support and help to other homeless people. He was an alcoholic who had been helped greatly by Barbara Townley of St Botolph's Project. He had phases of sobriety and rented accommodation, and phases of binge drinking. On one of these binges, he arrived at Mass one Sunday when a Church Army trainee was preaching his first sermon. He was an excellent pastoral worker but his sermon was painful. He was very nervous, read from a text without looking at the congregation, and the delivery was without expression. The congregation lost interest within minutes. After about five minutes, Wilf, very drunk and sitting in the second pew, said, in a voice which could be heard throughout the church, 'What a load of fuckin' crap!' The whole congregation, including the preacher, collapsed in hysterics. The preacher tore up his text and preached a brilliant extempore sermon. He said later that this moment had taught him how to preach. Wilf had no memory of the occasion, but it had a prophetic character.

David Brandon, who died on 26th November 2001, was probably the only British academic to be continuously involved with the study of homelessness for over forty years. It began because he was homeless himself, having run away from a violent father, and slept in doorways near St Botolph's. We met in 1964, by which time he was working with a project for homeless people in central London. David was a deeply spiritual person, with an equally deep distrust of 'spirituality', and he moved from the Society of Friends to Zen Buddhism. As I reflect on our long friendship, four areas seem important: the dignity of all persons, the inevitablity of darkness and depression, the necessity of struggle, and the vision of the future. He combined a fierce confrontational public style with a profound respect and care for individuals, and a deep sense of his own inadequacy. In an unpublished paper he wrote:

My lifelong inheritance is feelings of worthlessness, unrequited love, depression and despair, sometimes struggling with rage, but also ability to touch those socially excluded, similarly devalued and damaged.

In his obituary of David, the psychiatrist Phil Barker brought out the uncomfortable nature of his prophetic style.

David Brandon was the most difficult man I ever met. Our every meeting left me unsettled and ill at ease . . . To the surprise of the pompous, he never forecast his challenges. Sidling up to us, he whipped out his remarkable wit and intelligence, like a Socratic razor, which often cut him as much as any foe. Twenty years ago, at my request, he paralysed a dour Scots audience, unleashing a torrent of abuse upon those who merely spun the fantasy of health care, rather than caring for people. When they tried to defend themselves, he feigned resignation. 'I see. You're the kind of people who would wallpaper the gas chambers.'[12]

David's passionate commitment to truth, and refusal to play political games, was vital to the work against homelessness. I miss him enormously. Like the ancient prophets, he was a destabilising presence in any group, and could divide a room faster than anyone I knew. In a field populated by smooth-talking functionaries, his unreasonableness and uncompromising stance were desperately important. He testified to a homelessness of soul which cannot be met by a fallacious doctrine of 'family' or 'homeland', and which all of us must face if we are to be truly human.

9

'We Preach Christ Crucified':
theology and the Cross

'We proclaim Christ crucified.'

I CORINTHIANS I:23

Some early critics of my work felt that I had neglected the Cross, a criticism which initially shocked me. Over the years, the centrality of the Cross in the life of the Christian, and the need to locate theological work within the context of the dying and rising of Christ, have come to be more and more important in my life and ministry. In part, this has been a kind of theological maturing and deepening. I have never felt that a Christianity without the Cross makes any sense, but my theology has been more incarnationally rooted. I still feel that this is right: the truth that 'the Word was made flesh' is prior to, and necessary for, the significance of the death of Jesus. As Kathryn Tanner has written, we need 'an incarnational model of atonement'.[1] I have come to see, however, that incarnation without redemption is not the gospel. A theology which is rooted in the incarnation alone is inadequate, not least in pastoral ministry. We need, as Sharon Thornton has reminded us, a pastoral theology of the Cross.[2] For me, the deepening sense of the centrality of the Cross was also, and particularly, a product of pastoral care, as well as a needed corrective to some elements in pastoral care itself. But it was in the worshipping community that, for me, the power of the Cross was most evident.

Preaching the Cross and Holy Week

The sharing in the liturgy of Holy Week, in which Christians try to draw closer to Christ crucified and risen, has been more important to me than any intellectual work in bringing these truths home. Some years ago Sheila Cassidy wrote: 'Holding oneself together theologically in Holy Week takes a bit of doing.'[3] This is not surprising, for the liturgy, the texts, the ceremonial and the emotions aroused during their celebration raise all the major issues of life and death, of violence and cruelty, of darkness and desolation, of hope and hopelessness, of dying and, hopefully, rising again. The passion narratives are, in the words of Donald Nicholl, 'extremely primitive, all about money, bread and blood, about hunger and thirst'.[4] They are about events in history. It is dangerous to make the Cross into a symbol or a standard which 'bears no real relation to the historical Cross'.[5] Christian discipleship, theology and pastoral praxis is grounded in the physical crudity of incarnation, crucifixion, resurrection and sacraments.

The proclamation of the Cross is utterly central to Christian faith and life. Luther advised his followers to preach only the wisdom of the Cross. 'Praedica unum: sapientiam crucis.' While this must take place all the time, it is during the great week of the Passion that the preaching of the Cross becomes part of a bigger liturgical action in which we celebrate in action, music and ceremony as well as in word, the dying and rising of Christ. It has been a great privilege to have spent Holy Week and Easter, for most of the last 14 years, in various parishes in the USA. During one of these visits I was asked to lead a course at Colgate Rochester Theological Seminary on the subject of 'Preaching Holy Week'. Although little of this ministry took place in London, it was a really important part of my time as community theologian, and I want to reflect on it within the context of Christology and the following of Christ crucified and risen.

However, while it is the three days leading up to the Paschal Vigil (known as the Triduum) which is associated in the minds of many Christians with the preaching of the Cross, in a way the central act of the Paschal Vigil is the blessing of the font and the baptisms. It is in baptism that we die and rise with Christ, share his death and resurrection, and are joined to the Body of Christ. I believe that we will never see a renewal of Christian theology until we see a renewal of the understanding and celebration of the baptismal liturgy. It is in baptism that we share Christ's dying and rising, are marked with his Cross, are buried with him, and share his resurrection. In baptism we are clothed with Christ (Gal. 3:27). If this is true, as the New Testament teaches, it calls for a real revolution in the way we celebrate, and teach, as well as live, the baptismal reality.

A cruciform church

More than this, Christian life, the life of grace which flows from baptism, is at its heart a sharing in the Cross. The early writer Ignatius of Antioch began one of his letters, 'I greet you in the blood of Christ.' We bear in our bodies the marks of the Lord Jesus (Gal. 6:17), 'carry around the dying of Jesus' so that the life of Jesus may be made visible in us (2 Cor. 4:10). We become like him in his death (Phil. 3:10). It is difficult to stress this too much: Christian life is life in Christ, not simply faith, not even discipleship, though both are essential, but a real solidarity. The theme of participation is central to the Epistle to the Romans. The phrase 'in Christ', *en Christo*, is a key New Testament phrase. There can be no authentic Christian theology apart from this solidarity with Christ crucified.

The Church must be a 'cruciform church', one which follows the way of the Cross.[6] For the Church is Christ's body, shares his wounds, manifests to the world the power of his risen life.

The Cross and the breaking process

The Cross is about being broken. Many years ago I worshipped in a 'storefront church' near London docks, and one of our favourite hymns was 'Jesus, keep me near the Cross'. The chorus is:

In the Cross, in the Cross,
Be my glory ever
Till my raptured soul shall find
Rest beyond the river.

A large West Indian lady, known by all of us as Aunt Matilda, always sang 'ruptured' instead of 'raptured', and her voice was so powerful that all the congregation followed her. Yet in a way she was right. The Cross does involve a rupture, a break, a cleavage. It is a moment of division and disturbance, a point of crisis, a breaking point. The Cross is about trial and conflict. The actual crucifixion of Jesus came as the final event of a life of struggle, temptation and trial, and was the result of an actual trial. Augustine says that Christ is present among those who are 'in severe trial', and goes on to say that 'we progress by means of trial. No one knows himself except through trial.'

We preach Christ crucified

My book We Preach Christ Crucified first appeared in Britain in 1994, and soon after in the USA.[7] Based on Holy Week sermons delivered in several churches in Britain, it was still being reprinted over a decade later. (As I write a Japanese edition has just appeared, while a revised English version has appeared in Britain and the USA.) It differs from my other books in that it is shorter, and in that I retained, as far as possible, the preaching style. While I believe that every sermon is unique, and is preached to, and within the context of, a particular community, my sense is that the fact that this book grew from preaching enabled me to speak through it to many people in a way not unlike that of an actual sermon. My impression is that many readers have used this book as one which they can be read and re-read, an impression reinforced by several reviewers. My impression too is that this book is read by people to whom the others do not appeal.

I spent a long time, in preparation for the sermons and subsequent book, grappling with both the preaching of the Cross and the cruciform character of Christian life. It seemed essential to try to communicate the Christian life as a whole as a putting on of Christ, a sharing in his dying and rising. Like most Christians, I continue to grapple with what this means in our daily lives and in our theological *praxis*.

After its appearance in the USA – where, interestingly, in the first edition, it stayed in print much longer than it did in Britain – I attended Lent groups around that country where congregations were studying it. At All Saints, Pasadena, California, a woman in the congregation, Lee Taylor, wrote an excellent study guide to the book. I was struck by the numbers of people who told me that it had led them to pray, and that they had struggled with, and chewed over, the chapters, often paragraph by paragraph. I was also struck by the fact that, from Stone Mountain, Georgia, through Oklahoma to New York City, it was always the same two of the six chapters which puzzled, confused or troubled people. One was a chapter in which I tried to look at the politics of the Cross, while the other dealt with the darkness which is central to faith. Many Christians found it difficult to look at the Cross politically, partly because we have individualised and 'spiritualised' its meaning, partly because politics has itself fallen into disrepute. For many too the idea that faithful Christians should experience darkness is hard to take: a stress on joy, light and assurance has made such areas as doubt, inner turmoil and the 'dark night of the soul' come to be associated with sin and failure rather than seen as essential elements in the life of faith.

The appearance of this little book seemed important to me for another reason. The tendency for theologians to speak only to one another in a language which at times becomes impenetrable to those outside the academy has always worried me. I hold strongly to the belief that the theologian must preach the gospel in its depth and its simplicity, and that regular contact with 'ordinary people' within the common life of the church is essential. I found the example of the Chicago-based theologian David Tracy helpful here. Although Tracy is often seen – and rightly seen – as a complex theological writer, I was struck by his ability to preach to congregations on the South Side in the most simple language and yet with great profundity. I do not think that there is any future for theology apart from this kind of rootedness among the people.

The way of the Cross

In recent years there has been a remarkable revival in many places, not least in Latin America, of the Stations of the Cross, a way of entering into the Passion journey which involves visual art as well as dramatic action. The Stations are a discipline of following the human, suffering Jesus, a discipline which aids discipleship. In her commentary on her own remarkable Stations, hanging in Christ Church, Eastbourne, the artist Beverley Barr writes:

> Most of the Stations I've seen gloss over Christ's suffering, and show an Arian Jesus swooning elegantly, and, at the deposition, one feels that a good dose of sal volatile will soon bring him round. Mine would not be like that. I felt that we do him little credit if we underplay his sufferings, nor do we do ourselves any favours that way, since how can we recognise that he is with us in our anguish, when we patently feel that he didn't actually suffer for real.[8]

What Beverley sought to communicate through her visual work is exactly what I tried to do in this book: to locate the Cross within the context of the human Jesus and our own humanity. I hope very much that her Stations will be made available to a wider audience, for so much good theology is communicated through art and colour, rather than through the spoken or written word.

This, of course, connects with questions which I tried to grapple with in Chapter 3 in relation to liturgy. Walter Brueggemann has often spoken of the disappearance of lament from much corporate worship. If this happens, a theology of glory replaces a theology of the Cross, and worship becomes deprived of imaginative and creative prayerfulness. The recovery of lament and of the meaning of 'glorying in the Cross' are vital parts of restoring the Cross to the centre of our lives.

The Cross and pastoral care

The second aspect, which I also emphasised in the book, is the centrality of the Cross, not only in preaching and liturgy but in pastoral care. Since then, Sharon Thornton's remarkable book *Broken Yet Beloved: a pastoral theology of the Cross* has appeared. It argues that the Cross is critical to pastoral theology, although she also claims, rightly in my view, that the Cross has been seen in conventional Christian terms as belonging within the sphere of doctrine, not that of 'pastoralia'. Like Thornton, I want to reject this false division. The Cross is indeed central to Christian faith, life, ministry and discipleship.

The crucified Jesus still has a powerful, strange, trans-rational converting power. The lifting up of the Son of Man is the source of salvation, of illumination and of healing power.

Theology and the Cross

The preaching of Christ crucified is at the heart of Christian faith. Yet I was very conscious – and some of my critics were even more conscious – that it seemed that the incarnation played a more central role in my theological work than did the death of Jesus. As I reflected on this, it seemed that this was not only a personal defect in my thought, but it was reflected in much Anglicanism. David Nicholls once termed it 'neat incarnationalism', incarnation without redemption. Putting it more crudely, a newly ordained curate said of his vicar, a well-respected Anglo-Catholic priest, when I asked how he was getting on: 'The trouble is he believes in the incarnation – but I'm not sure he believes in anything else.' He went on to explain that it seemed that an incarnational theology, spirituality and social posture could lead to a pastoral style which 'blessed everything that moved' but never challenged anything. The Orthodox theologian John Behr has written of 'the paschal foundations of Christian theology',[9] and it is certainly true that all Christian theological work is rooted in the mystery of Christ's dying and rising. As the Church itself must be a 'cruciform church' so theology must be cruciform. We must bear the marks of the Lord Jesus, and carry his dying about in our theology.

The purpose of the death of Jesus on the cross, according to the early Christians, was to bring about a new humanity through the breaking down of the wall of division (Eph. 2:14–15). God was in Christ reconciling the world to himself and giving to us the ministry of reconciliation (2 Cor. 5:19). Or as St Cyril of Jerusalem put it, 'On the cross, God stretched out his hands to embrace the ends of the earth.' If the Church is to follow Jesus, it must practise the work of breaking down walls of division, and the work of embracing God's excluded people.

Of all New Testament texts I feel that Philippians 3:10–11 sums up most powerfully the goal of Christian life and of an embodied spiritual theology.

> I want to know Christ and the power of his resurrection, and the sharing of his sufferings by becoming like him in his death, if somehow I may attain the resurrection from the dead.

It is all there: the centrality of Christ, knowledge, power, solidarity in suffering and death, and the hope of resurrection.

10

Koinonia: theology and the common life

Seek the welfare of the city . . . in its welfare you will find your welfare.

JEREMIAH 29:7

Things will not go well in England till all be held common.

JOHN BALL, 1381

Property belongs to the dead world: community is the life of God.

R. M. BENSON, retreat address at Cowley, July 1874

Community, theology and the urban context

A central theme of this book is the connection between theology and the common life of humanity. Joerg Rieger has said that 'the crisis of theology is not primarily an intellectual crisis . . . but the fact that we have separated ourselves from most of humanity'.[1] A central aim of the Whitechapel project was to help develop the life of local communities, or, more usually, to build close links with existing communities and groups. There was nothing unusual or innovative about this in principle, but it does run counter to one stream in the thought and practice of certain churches of various traditions. These churches, whether through theological conviction or through sheer pressure of work, separate themselves from the wider community, concentrating instead on building up the Christian community, and on pastoral and spiritual nourishment within that community. Sometimes this approach is based on a view of 'the world', and, in our context, specifically the urban world, as being a zone of impurity, of danger, of corruption, to which the appropriate Christian response must be that of withdrawal. There is a certain similarity between this approach and the approach of those evangelical radicals such as Ronald Sider who argue for a 'counter-cultural' view of the Church.[2] But their conclusions, interpretations and practice are very different, though often the rhetoric sounds the same. It is worth exploring the crucial differences, many of which are linked to a fundamental conflict about the meaning of the term 'world'.

Let me begin this chapter with a question which crops up constantly in the discussion of the Church and community within the urban context. Is the city a place of corruption, or renewal, or both? Within western societies, there has been a strong anti-urban tradition, even at times an urban demonology in which the city is the scapegoat for all ills. Anti-urbanism goes deep in much of the thinking of the churches. Indeed the biblical tradition itself reflects the ambivalence. The city is soiled, defiled and oppressive (Zeph. 3:1). Cities are often controlled by people who 'make iniquitous decrees' and 'oppressive statutes' (Isa. 10:1), and who leave the hungry unsatisfied (Isa. 32:6). Jeremiah is told 'Do not pray for the welfare of this people' (Jer. 14:11), and the theme of prophecy against the city occurs in both Jeremiah and Ezekiel. Jeremiah's enemies said that he deserved to die 'because he has prophesied against this city' (Jer. 26:11). Yet, we are told, God will change the speech of the peoples to a pure speech (3:9). As co-workers with God, we need to work towards a society in which 'the poor have hope, and injustice shuts its mouth' (Job 5:16). We need to see that our vocation is to be 'the repairer of the breach, the restorer of streets to live in' (Isa. 58:12). There is a central concern among the prophets with a city of righteousness (Isa. 1:26–27).

I have spent much time brooding on the biblical approach to the city, and have concluded that its central teaching is that the city is not beyond redemption, or, to put the point more positively, that the city is potentially, and often actually, a site of holiness and justice. Indeed, the final biblical vision is that of the City of God as a zone of freedom, joy and equality. Only in the city can we attain wholeness of life, equality and the vision of God. Yet, on the way to the fulfilment of this vision, we have to pass through, and confront, the oppressive and corrupting reality of Babylon. We have to move from injustice toward 'community'. But what is 'community'?

We chose the name 'community theologian' before we were clear what we meant by the word 'community'. We were a bit clearer about what we didn't mean! We chose this name, not because we were so pretentious and deluded as to think that I, or any other single person, could represent 'the community', whatever that noble-sounding term might mean, among the many groups, communities, movements, organisations, societies and so on in East London. We chose it out of a conviction that theological work can only authentically be done within a community of commitment and of discourse. A community theologian only makes sense within the framework of the community *as* theologian. That term, 'the community as theologian', was popularised by my good friend Bob Schreiter, and his work has been an important influence on mine. But the identification of a community as theologian is more complex in a secularised culture such as England than it is, for example, in Brazil where a broadly Christian, Catholic or Pentecostal, culture is more pervasive. In the East London context, the community referred to was a small one, a community of voluntary formation. Even so, the hope was that this small community would make links with others in and beyond the immediate area. The root of the word 'community' lies in the idea of 'common'. A community, by definition, holds things in common – perhaps material goods, perhaps a cluster of beliefs and practices, perhaps a particular language, ethnic or religious background, perhaps residential proximity. But without some common bonds, there is no community, simply a collection of individuals.

The community we had in mind was, first, the local Christian community in the Aldgate and Whitechapel districts, but, secondly, those people, mainly, but not exclusively, Christian, who gathered around the Jubilee Group and related 'communities of discourse'. However, the notion of a 'community theologian' or of 'community-based theology' always raised eyebrows and was seen as a novel and innovative one. Those who seek to be theologians usually end up in academic institutions. On the other hand, within the academic centres, there has been a growth in what has become known as 'practical theology', and there is now a sizeable literature on this subject, as well as centres for practical theology at Lancaster University and other places. (Nobody so far has set up a centre for impractical theology, though they certainly exist under other names!)

What we were trying to do was to break with the academic model while maintaining close links with academic institutions. Whether I was, in Laurie Green's words, one of those who was 'fitted to be people's theologians' I do not know. I am not sure that I was really 'fitted', or very good at it, but I hope that my work helped, in a small way, to turn the tide. I was not alone. People like Margaret Kane in the north-east of England preceded me by many years, and Ann Morisy was pioneering community theology in London at the same time as I was. So was Laurie Green himself, as Rector of All Saints, Poplar, for much of my time in the East End.[3]

Early on in the project's life, Nigel Wright, now Principal of Spurgeon's College, the leading Baptist theological centre in London, wrote an article in the *Baptist Times* in which he drew on the work at St Botolph's in order to make some more general observations about the nature of theology. Describing me as 'an Anglo-Catholic of the better type', he commented: 'There can't be many theologians who are directly employed by local churches to ply their trade. For a local church to employ a theologian full time bespeaks an unusual church as well as an unusual theologian.' He went on to suggest that theology must be an activity of the whole church. 'In an ideal world, theology would take place in the midst of ordinary people with their concerns and their wisdom. It would take the form of a constant dialogue of the Christian message with the people, institutions and issues of our time.'[4]

It has been interesting to me that some of the most serious and critical studies of my own thought have come from Baptists, often Spurgeon's College graduates, and that some of the most creative activity on urban ministry in recent years has come from the same tradition. The work of Karen Stallard and Juliet Kilpin in Shadwell and Wapping is one example. Another Baptist, also associated with Spurgeon's College and with the Anabaptist witness, Stuart Murray, has spoken of 'the theologianhood of all believers', and this is certainly a right emphasis.[5]

However, much writing still assumes that all theology takes place in academic institutions. Gareth Jones wrote in 1998 that 'the vast majority of British theologians now work in secular academic institutions'.[6] No doubt this was uttered from an amicable, albeit naïve and limited, perspective, from within the confines of the academy, but I do regard this kind of utterance as amazingly arrogant and ignorant, one which ignores the theology which is going on in communities all over Britain, and as an extreme example of the academic captivity of so much theology. My former colleague Anthony Harvey maybe fell into a similar trap when he described liberation theology as having 'no more than local validity' and was criticised by Ann Morisy for this comment.[7]

It goes without saying that we cannot talk about 'community' without taking the Christian context seriously. The language of 'community' is closely linked with eucharistic language and with descriptions of the Christian body. *Koinonia,* often translated by 'fellowship' but better rendered 'common life', 'community' or even 'solidarity', is a key theme of the second half of the New Testament. It is impossible to discuss community in a Christian context without looking at the expression of what that community is in its liturgy and life.

What is contextual theology?

What is contextual theology? All ideas and practices are contextual in the sense that they arise from reflection on a particular system and culture. Theology is inseparable from, and cannot be done apart from, a community. In Elaine Graham's words, it is 'a performative discipline where knowledge and truth are only realisable in the pursuit of practical strategies and social relations'. Two years later, Mark McIntosh argued that theology needed a 'more embodied and contextual model'.[8]

That all theology has a context is obvious, though often theologians seem unaware of their context, and the word 'context' is itself used without a context.[9] 'Context' is a word similar to, though not identical with 'perspective', defined by Bertrand Russell as 'the view of the world from a given place'.[10] When I use the term 'contextual theology' I refer to theology which is consciously pursued in relation to specific communities or to specific issues in the world; which seeks constantly to understand, and relate to, these communities or issues; and which seeks both to bring to bear the resources of theological tradition upon them, and to learn from them in a way which enriches theology and perhaps calls much of it into question.

Much of the theological reflection with which I was involved went on in small groups which formed around specific issues. One group, which met monthly for several years and became known as 'the death group', arose because several of us at and around St Botolph's were heavily involved with issues of dying and death – through liturgical celebration, nursing, work with people with HIV/AIDS, concerns about the deaths of homeless people in the streets, and bereavement counselling. We covered a wide area in our discussions, and planned to offer some kind of educational resource, initially for the East London churches. Sadly, the group failed for a reason which will no doubt ring bells with others. We relied too much on individual knowledge on the one hand, and on a particular computer programme on the other. The departure of some key individuals left huge gaps in our work, and the problems of recovering material from an outdated programme proved insuperable. As a result, much of our effort came to nothing, though we learned a great deal from our times together. The experience was a warning to us to ensure that all computerised material is preserved in several places, and a reminder that all projects should expect that there will be disasters as well as successes.

'Faith communities'

One major issue that arose in the years at St Botolph's was the relationship of what came to be called 'faith communities' with the ruling political regimes. Later, both George W. Bush and Tony Blair have made much of this relationship, and it has become a major part of their urban strategy. Christians in both countries have responded with mixed reactions. Some have accepted the idea fairly uncritically, while others have insisted that churches cannot ally themselves with governments, or receive money from them, without maintaining the freedom, and the moral obligation, to subject government policies to critique.

During 2001 the issue became central in various Christian papers. On 18th May 2001 *The Church of England Newspaper* published a review of Steve Chalke's book *Faithworks,* accompanied by a photograph of Chalke with Tony Blair. 'Home Secretary vows to work with faith groups' was a headline in the same paper on 22nd June 2001. Chalke played a significant role in trying to mobilise Christians behind Blair and the 'faith communities' project during the build-up to the 2005 General Election.

The terms 'faith groups' and 'faith communities' are somewhat odd, and fairly new, but they generally refer to groups and communities which are part of a religious tradition. This use might suggest that 'faith' is peculiar to religious traditions, and that other people are lacking in faith. Many religious groups have entered into useful partnerships with national and local government programmes, and see themselves as part of the 'social economy'. They seek to create networks of trust and to reduce social exclusion. There is usually a focus on 'social capital' and on the role of religious groups in 'building community'. On the other hand, many government ministers and officials seem to view the role of faith groups in terms of consensus theory, stressing them as agents of, or aids to, 'community cohesion', and ignoring other aspects of their role. The danger of being co-opted and of becoming a stooge of the secular power remains, and has, in my view, grown more serious in recent years.[11]

Regeneration, the City of London and the East End

When people speak of 'community', they often have in mind a geographical area, containing people who are brought together by common bonds of residence, neighbourhood solidarity, shared local problems, opposition to perceived common enemies, and so on. The use of the term 'community' in this geographical sense usually obscures the crucial conflicts of interest among groups. The three major geographical areas with which we were concerned in this project were the financial district of the City of London; the communities around Whitechapel and Spitalfields to the east of the City; and those further east in, and adjacent to, the Docklands developments.

In 1973 Ruth Glass wrote:

> Inner London is not being 'Americanised': it is not on the way to becoming mainly a working class city, a 'polarised' city, or a vast ghetto for a black proletariat. The real risk for inner London is that it might be gentrified with a vengeance, and be almost exclusively reserved for selected higher class strata.[12]

Since then polarisation has become sharper. The architect Richard Rogers, in his Reith Lectures for 1995, claimed that 'cities are increasingly polarising society into segregated communities'.[13]

In 2000 a group of us who were concerned at the eastward push of the property developers started to meet at London Diocesan House. Initially convened by Ann Morisy, at the time advisor for community ministry in the diocese, and then later by Chris Brice, advisor for social justice, the group was first called 'Creep Plus' and later became the 'Faith in the City of London Group'. This was in origin a small gathering to reflect on the outcome of an election in Portsoken Ward in which William Taylor, chaplain of London Metropolitan University, had been elected to the City Corporation. (He was later defeated by the use of the non-residential vote.) The group was in part a support group for William who was seen as a threat by sections of the 'old-boy network', but also as a group which would subject developments in the City to critical scrutiny. Maurice Glassman from the London Metropolitan University and Professor Doreen Massey from the Open University were members, as was my colleague Joe Batty from St Botolph's Project, a City resident. I hope this work continues.

For about fifteen years or so we had regular visits at St Botolph's from urban pastors and students from the Rhineland, always led by my dear friend Klaus Teschner. At some point in the 1980s one of my colleagues, who speaks no German, explained that we had done extensive renovation work on the crypt so that it could be used for work with homeless people. 'We converted the crypt to its new use', he told them. When this was translated into German, the entire group roared with laughter. My colleague was baffled as to what he had said which was so funny. Klaus explained that 'in German, only persons can be converted (*bekehren*); buildings are renewed (*erneuert*) or rebuilt (*umgebaut*)'. Every year, when more pastors would visit us, the joke about the 'converted crypt' would be repeated.

'Only persons can be converted, buildings are renewed.' It is striking that when the language of regeneration is used in English, as in current 'developmentspeak' and other fashionable pseudo-languages, it is used almost exclusively about the environment – buildings, streets and squares – not about people. Of course, people are involved in the process – who else could be? – and, of course, there will be the assertion, at various points in debates and documents, and particularly in the rhetoric of the British government's 'New Deal for Communities', that it is people and communities who matter, but the main focus of the language of regeneration is on the built environment. Indeed, I got the impression in East London that often regeneration meant getting rid of the people! However, there are variations in focus between different parts of government. Thus, while the Home Office tends to see regeneration in terms of law and order and good citizenship, the focus of the Office of the Deputy Prime Minister (an office created under New Labour) is more on the built environment and 'sustainable communities'.

An internet search under 'regeneration' will, however, reveal another aspect of the confusion in language, for, alongside references to urban change, will be found numerous references to regenerative tissue. The terminology used in urban studies is often quite different from that used in medicine, and the same words have different meanings. During the period of the community theology work, the issue of health and 'well-being' was of critical importance. I was privileged to work with the Community Module at the Royal London Hospital Medical College, alongside Geoff Wykurz and Diana Kelly; with Jenny King, a priest-dentist who teaches medical ethics in the college, and with David Widgery, a general practitioner and campaigner who wrote a good deal on the health issues of the East End. David tragically died on 26th October 1992.

A major issue which affected contextual theology in East London was that of water. The River Thames dominates the East End, and questions about water dominated much of the theology I was trying to pursue. Housing damp was a recurring problem, as were water rats around the riverside districts. The whole issue of water is central to health care, as it is to Christian theology with its roots in baptism. More generally, the issue of health inequalities concerned us constantly, and we were made aware on a daily basis of the vast inequalities in health and health care in British society.[14]

The East End and its politics

Today, in most parts of Britain, politics is seen as the work of an abstract and impersonal state, but this was not always so. Before the seventeenth century, politics had a much wider meaning. The East End has a long history of political activity in this wider sense, often involving movements which have had a spin-off effect way beyond the East End itself. The Jewish anarchist movement began here around the journal *Arbeiter Freund*, and the anarchist bookshop still exists, on the site of the original Jack the Ripper murder in Angel Alley, Whitechapel High Street. For many years there was a strong Communist Party in Whitechapel, dominated by Jewish councillors such as Phil Piratin, Solly Kaye, Barney Borman and Max Levitas. Piratin was elected MP for Mile End in 1945 and remained a popular figure for many years. Later, groups such as Socialist Unity, Militant, the Socialist Workers' Party, and, more recently, Socialist Alliance and Respect have had a presence in the area, though opinions differ as to how significant they are.

The Bengali community has a tendency toward socialism, and there have been some attempts to develop a base for debate around the

Bengali approach to socialist politics. I was involved for a while with a group called Samaj Chetona which was trying to create a kind of Bengali equivalent of *New Left Review*, but, as far as I know, it came to nothing. The old Labour Party in Stepney, on the other hand, was dominated by Irish people, and was very right-wing and sometimes racist, though this began to change in the 1980s. The old Liberals were strong in Bethnal Green, and, for a while, in the 1980s, a mutant of the Liberal Democrats was in control of the council in Tower Hamlets. It seemed to me that they represented 'the least progressive, the most prejudiced, and the least visionary stream' within that tradition.[15] I spent much of my time relating to, and working with, political groups, some of which were surprised to find a Christian priest in their midst. These links were really valuable in terms of work over such issues as combating racism, housing and homelessness, and much else.

The Bangladeshi community

The largest minority community in the inner East End is the Bangladeshi community. In parts of Whitechapel they are the majority of the population. By 1991 Bangladeshis were the youngest and fastest-growing ethnic group in the country, with just under half of London's Bangladeshis living in the East End. Much of my work was with Bangladeshi individuals and organisations. I was a patron of St Mary's Centre in Myrdle Street, closely involved with the Kobi Nazrul Centre in Hanbury Street, and a governor of Kobi Nazrul Primary School in Settles Street. I was often invited to speak in Altab Ali Park on the anniversary of the murder of Altab Ali. Earlier I had been involved with the beginnings of the Bangladesh Youth Front and the Bangladesh Youth Movement. I believe that I was the first Christian priest to speak at the East London Mosque, at a conference on drug abuse in the early 1990s.

During the years of the theology project, the Bangladeshi community was changing rapidly. Bangladeshi women were often referred to as 'women in transition', and the radicalisation and politicisation of the community was changing the face both of local politics and of the community itself.[16]

On 12th March 2004 Professor Muhammad Yunus, founder of the Grameen Bank in Bangladesh, arrived in Cavell Street, off Whitechapel Road, as the guest of The East London Citizens' Organisation

(TELCO, on which see below). The word 'grameen' comes from gram, a village. In 1974, when Yunus was Professor of Economics at the University of Chittagong, he lent $27 to 42 people in the nearby village of Jobra. By 2004 the bank had 1178 branches and had given loans to over 2.4 million poor people, mainly rural women, in 41,536 villages in Bangladesh. It was a great joy to meet with him and to discuss microcredit and its wider consequences. As with so many encounters, the meeting with Yunus, and the study of the microcredit practices of the Grameen Bank sparked off all kinds of lines of thought. One of his fundamental principles in establishing the bank was that credit was a human right.[17] Yet access to credit is often determined by social status, by gender, and so on. It suggested links with much of the thinking of groups like the Christian Council for Monetary Justice, which, like many Muslim bodies, is concerned with the injustice of the interest system. Again, there is the whole question of the 'Living Wage', a struggle in which The East London Citizens' Organisation (TELCO), through its energetic worker Catherine Howarth, is heavily involved. And again the issue of water figures prominently, and is a life and death issue in Bangladesh.

So from Jobra to Whitechapel, from microcredit among Bengali women to the critique of the world financial system, from the life of small villages to the Christian and Muslim concern with monetary justice: making such connections, and following the trails which are then opened up, this is a central part of contextual theological method.

The Somalis

Many people associate the East End, in terms of its minority ethnic make-up, exclusively with the Bangladeshi community. But there is also the large Somali community, whose needs are often neglected. This neglect is not peculiar to London, but recurs in Manchester, Liverpool, Tyneside and Cardiff where the Somalis have been present for many years. On 15th and 16th April 1991, Julian Ozanne wrote two perceptive articles in the *Financial Times* drawing attention to the fact that Somalia had 'been deserted to its hapless fate by the outside world'. At this time over half of its population were unemployed and over 40 per cent lived in extreme poverty with a life expectancy of 41–43 years. In 1992, 350,000 died from hunger, illness or war. In Britain, and in London particularly, the Somali community had been augmented by refugees from the troubles. Long established in East London, the Somalis have often been overlooked and ignored by policy makers and others. While larger and more vocal groups have often been successful in drawing attention to problems such as homelessness and racial harassment, and have, rightly, obtained resources for their work, the Somali community has often been forgotten. Two writers in 1992 called them 'the East End's forgotten people'.[18]

By 1992, the Somali Homeless Project (SHP) was functioning, and had an office in the United Reformed Church building in Pott Street, Bethnal Green. Historically, Whitechapel was the heart of the old Somali seafaring community of Britain, and today this long-established community has been supplemented by thousands of refugees – hence the need for the SHP. As late as 1971 there were only ten Somali families in London, as most Somalis were single males, and by 1992 53 per cent of Somalis were single. Between 1983 and 1991 the numbers of Somalis in London grew into thousands. There has been much dispute about the size of the community in East London. While a report to Wapping Neighbourhood in February 1992 produced a figure of 15,000, some feel that the figure is lower. Hostility to, and violence against, Somalis has been considerable, and some have said that they found the East End 'more intolerable than the turmoil they left behind'.[19]

I was involved with Somali issues over the whole period, and four issues are worth mentioning. The first is the use and abuse of the khat plant. Somali men often chew the leaves of the khat plant *(catha edulis)*, which has a long history of use in east and north Africa. It is said that around seven tons arrive at Heathrow airport every week. Its main active constituents, cathinone and cathine, are structurally related to amphetamine, a well-known cerebral stimulant. The notion of psychosis which is now being applied to khat is a slippery one and needs unpacking; and we need to recognise the danger of projecting a simple causal link between any drug and any mental condition. Approaches to it have fallen into two main areas, the biochemical and the sociocultural. The debates have been both about aetiology and about interpretation. The concept of psychosis is not a neutral one. The existence of perceptual change may be seen as a fact; the labelling of such change as psychotic (or mystical or ego-transcending or whatever) is a matter of opinion. The idea of drug-induced psychoses goes back a long way. Amphetamine psychosis was identified by Philip Connell in 1958, LSD psychosis after 1967, and cannabis psychosis increasingly in the 1980s (though in other countries much earlier). Now we have 'khat psychosis'. Up to 1989 there were four cases in the UK, and in 1989 one paper looked at three cases, all in Somali men. A group of us organised a day conference on khat at St Margaret's House, Bethnal Green, on 12th November 1994, which aroused considerable interest.[20]

The second is the issue of female genital mutilation, also known as female circumcision, or, by its supporters, 'purification'. It is claimed that around 100 million women are affected globally. Outside the north-east regions of Africa, many Muslims are not affected by this practice. In the East End, the struggle against this practice was led by Shamis Dirir and the Black Women's Health Action Project.[21]

The third is the issue of the diversity within Islam. It became clear to me, working with Bengali and Somali people of Muslim background, that the approach to Islam varied enormously from one group to another. This seems really important for the future, in which inevitably the complex nature of Islamic societies will be evident.

The fourth is the neglect of the Somali contribution to art and wider cultural issues. It was a great privilege to work with Kinsi Abdulleh, the only Somali female artist in the East End, and my impression is that the role of the visual arts is crucial to further developments in inter-faith work.[22]

Islam in the East End

Most Bangladeshi and Somali people are Muslim, and the Muslim presence in the East End is very large. Inevitably the issues of relations between Muslims, Christians and other religious and non-religious groups figured greatly in our work. This was true in particular of work with young people. In some places Islam seemed able to attract and provide spiritual strength and nourishment for young black men – and I include men of South Asian origin here under the heading 'black' – in a way that most forms of Christianity did not. On the other hand, much attachment to Islam seemed to be 'cultural' and there did seem to be an increase in the number of more or less 'lapsed' Muslims as the hold of culture weakened.

Today there are around 1.6 million Muslims in Britain, and no contextual theology can operate without taking their presence on board, and trying to involve them in the ensuing discussions and debates.

Children and schools

I found myself spending a lot of time with children, not least as a governor of Kobi Nazrul Primary School in Whitechapel, the newest primary school in the East End. For several years I chaired its curriculum and personnel committee. We faced the challenge of a new school where most of the children did not have English as their first language, located in a borough which came bottom in the UK for adult literacy in a recent government report. Our school did very well in this area. Some highlights included the publication of the five-volume *Superphonics* by Ruth Miskin, head of the school for most of my time, on 20th July 2000, and the work of Class 4 (where Sindee Bass was the teacher) on the history of homelessness in the Whitechapel area since the opening of nearby Rowton House (now Tower House) in the nineteenth century. The children had some important discussions, including a session with David Brandon, who was once a resident of Rowton House. They visited a night shelter, wrote poems, had a discussion with Petra Salva of St Botolph's Project and myself, and wrote letters to the Acting Director of Housing for Tower Hamlets on their views about the future of Tower House, which had recently been sold. Later, Class 5 visited St Botolph's as part of their religious study programme.[23]

On 19th June 1993 I spent much of the day being interviewed at length by some eight-year-old children at Hague Primary School in Bethnal Green. They were highly intelligent, and wanted to focus on homelessness, as so many children still do in the area. Many of them were outraged by the persistence of homelessness, an outrage which often dies away as they become conformed to adult life. They wrote an article, not entirely accurate and slightly embarrassing, which rather gave the impression that I was behind everything that went on in this field at St Botolph's. But it was written with care, concern and an astute grasp of many of the realities.

Donald Nicholl once said that theology should always be done in the presence of children. Yet so much of what we call theological debate goes on in compartmentalised groups, often elitist, and most of humankind is left out.

Adult education

Adult education, 'informal education' and community education also figured prominently in our work. Here the history of the East End is enormously important. On 27th February 2003 there was a large gathering in Toynbee Hall, Commercial Street, to commemorate the centenary of the founding there of the Workers' Educational Association (WEA). I was one of the speakers, as the 'local boy', since my flat was almost opposite Toynbee Hall. Indeed, had those attending taken the wrong exit at Aldgate East station, they would have reached either my flat or Whitechapel Library (about which there had been a fascinating programme on Radio 4 a few weeks earlier, stressing its crucial role in informal education, particularly, though not exclusively, among East End Jews). It was at Toynbee Hall that the first Delegate Conference of the WEA took place in December 1903. Gareth Stedman Jones has said that Toynbee Hall has as strong a claim to be seen as one of the antecedents of the Labour Party as Methodism, Taff Vale and William Morris.

Yet it is not just Toynbee Hall but its environs that are important. Within a very short distance of it are sites of key work in adult and community-based education. In fact, all the East End settlements – St Hilda's, Oxford House, St Margaret's House, Eastbourne House, and others – have played major roles in community education, though their relation to socialism is not so clear. The role of radical Jewish groups in education has been documented by Bill Fishman. We might think too of Stewart Headlam, the Bethnal Green curate, who represented that area for years on the London County Council and the London School Board, or of Edith Ramsey, who pioneered courses on 'English as a second language' in the East End in 1920, long before the phrase was known.

The role of 'social Christianity' in its late-nineteenth-century form is clearly evident in the background to these movements. It was a period which converted many 'gentlemen' into social democrats. The term 'socialism' was used vaguely at the time. However, it is clear that books were very important in the growth of socialism in the period 1883–96 The mood was one marked by a liberal and optimistic temper. William Temple, Archbishop of Canterbury 1942–44, was a key figure in WEA, though my impression is that Charles Gore, Bishop of Oxford and founder of the Community of the Resurrection, was more influential in its formation. Albert Mansbridge, founder of the WEA, had met Gore when he was quite young, and his influence was important. The WEA, in some respects, took over the role of the chapels as a base for social education for working-class people.[24]

Today adult education remains a high priority among community projects in the East End, though government and official attitudes are often lacking in imagination and narrow in their understanding of its nature.

From MacMurray to Tony Blair: the rhetoric and politics of community

I have written a good deal on 'community' in earlier studies.[25] While 'communitarianism' is new, it does connect with much earlier activity including laments about the 'collapse of community' (particularly common in the East End and sometimes echoed in the utterances of clergy from the area). Community studies began with Young and Willmott's *Family and Kinship in East London* in the 1950s. In the 1990s we were still being discovered. From the nineteenth century to the present day, the East End has been at the receiving end of constant research, experiments and media coverage. Poverty in the area is regularly being documented. Writing on racial attacks invariably focuses on this area, while it also attracts attention because of health problems. TB notifications are seven times the national average, while problems of access to health care have attracted international attention. Week by week the local papers have headlines such as 'Whitechapel: the shame of London', which reinforce the image of the area as a place of gloom, fear and desolation. Although many local people resent the demonising of the area, the East End remains a place which is written about and its people are 'worked among'.

A philosopher who wrote a good deal about community was John MacMurray, and he has come back to the attention of the media in recent years because of the influence of his writings on Tony Blair. The Australian priest Peter Thomson introduced Blair to MacMurray's thought when they were students at Oxford, and Blair wrote the introduction to a collection of MacMurray's writings. There is no obvious link between MacMurray and East London except that he was a significant influence on many local Christian socialists. It is almost certain that people like John Groser, Stanley Evans and others were influenced by him, although nobody seems to remember any direct influence. When I summarised MacMurray's thought to a colleague in the East End, he commented, 'It sounds like one of John Groser's sermons.' Certainly Alan Ecclestone, who influenced Groser and Evans, said that MacMurray was 'a writer central to my llife and thinking' and that his *The Search for Reality in Religion* was 'the best small book about religion that I know'.[26] He may have affected some East End communists such as Solly Kaye. However, while there is little if any direct link, I believe that the issues with which MacMurray was concerned, are central issues to the life of the East End of London and to the work I tried to do.

Clearly, the issues with which MacMurray was concerned in *Reason and Emotion* (1935) – education, art, sexuality, for example – are concerns which affect us all, but there are issues around each of them in the East End which relate very much to the conflict of values, cultural norms and religious traditions. MacMurray saw the economic base of human community as crucial, but this was because he was a Marxist, and Marxism is distinctly out of fashion today. If he is, as Samuel Brittan claimed, 'Blair's real guru', much of his writing must have been abandoned. He saw that economic systems must support personal life. MacMurray seems not to have envisaged the seriousness and magnitude of the transformations which are occurring today – the globalisation of capital, 'the urbanisation of injustice', the increased patterns of international migration, the growth of multi-racial societies, and the appearance of old and new forms of racism. Although his main works date from the 1930s, indeed from the very years, 1933–36, when Hitler was assuming power and when the East End was plagued by anti-semitism, fascism is dealt with only in the last ten pages of *The Philosophy of Communism*.[27]

For some time Greg Smith and I convened a group which met in Whitechapel, consisting of local community workers, academics from the University of East London (where there was a new department of East London Studies and a new journal *Rising East*, which sadly did not survive in print, though it has now reappeared on the internet), people from the area health authority, and others. We came together around the issues of 'community' and 'communitarianism', aware that the latter was affecting the thinking of Tony Blair and other members of the Labour Party. At the time the group convened, it was Amitai Etzioni whom we had in mind as an influence on Blair's rhetoric on 'community'. (However, it is interesting to note that if you take the socialism out of MacMurray you are left with something not unlike Etzioni!) The group continued to meet for several years to reflect on what the elusive concept of 'community' meant in the East End of today. We tried to ask: What is happening to us? And this presupposed the question: Who are we?

Blair has used the rhetoric of community frequently. Thus on 23rd March 2005 he was cited in *The Times*: 'At the heart of my politics has always been the value of community. From that everything stems: solidarity, social justice, equality, freedom. We are what we are, in part, because of each other.'[28]

However, community is not an unproblematic concept, and many 'communities' are based on the exclusion and rejection of others. One of the most perceptive immediate reflections on the election of Beackon came from the Jewish historian David Cesarani, who claimed that the BNP vote was 'more an assertion of community spirit than a protest against immigration'. For this vote grew out of a community shaped and nurtured, not by classical fascism but by what used to be known as 'Red Poplar', the community of George Lansbury and the rates protesters, a community which was formed by the docks and large factories. In 1993 we saw how, under stress and frustration, this positive and courageous history could be turned against those who did not fit. 'The events in Millwall', commented Ceasrani, 'should compel us to think about what we mean by community.'[29]

Community organising

One valuable recent addition to community activity in the East End has been the appearance of Community Organising. Also known as Broad Based Organising, Community Organising began with the work of Saul Alinsky (1909–72) in the 1940s in Chicago. With the founding of the Industrial Areas Foundation (IAF) in 1940, and the publication of his book *Reveille for Radicals* in 1947, Alinsky's work developed and spread throughout the USA, where it has frequently been revitalised and renewed, not least in Chicago, its place of birth. Since then the tradition has spread to other parts of the world such as India. It did not have a strong presence in Britain until the late 1980s, and the reasons for the delay are worth exploring. They may be connected to the change in the role of the trade unions, to the differing political structures in the two countries, and particularly to the belief, now less widely held, that Alinsky organising was 'peculiarly American'. Indeed some writers claimed that the existence of a labour movement, and strong trade unions, made Alinsky organising unnecessary in the British context.[30] The appearance of The East London Citizens' Organisation (TELCO) has been a welcome addition to the networks of community groups. It has become involved in inter-faith work, in pressure on multinational companies, such as HSBC Bank, for improved conditions for workers, and, through Catherine Howarth's work, in the movement for a living wage.

Christian theology must take place within the turmoil and upheaval of the common life, in the apparent chaos and confusion of the 'breakdown', fragmentation and isolation of communities, in the midst of mess and of rapid change. I do not believe that chaos and community are opposites. Indeed my experience in Whitechapel suggests that often God is in the chaos, and that it is through engaging with chaos that we come to a deeper understanding of the meaning of community.[31]

11

Discerning the Body: theology and the Church

For all who eat and drink without discerning the body eat and drink judgment against themselves.

I CORINTHIANS 14:18

We are returning to the ancient view that the only seed-bed of theological advancement is the experience of the worshipping community.

MARTIN THORNTON, *Essays in Pastoral Reconstruction*
(SPCK 1960, p. 2)

There are very few references in the gospels – three in fact, and all in the gospel of Matthew – to the 'Church' (*ekklesia*). In contrast, there are over a hundred references to the Church, usually described as the Body of Christ, in the rest of the New Testament. The three references in Matthew are concerned with discipline. However, in the Pauline letters, so central to the development of the earliest Christian communities, there is a strong emphasis on 'building up' the body, on peace and mutual upbuilding (Rom. 14:19), and these references seem increasingly to me to be of critical importance for theological work. Theology which does not 'discern the body' (1 Cor. 14:18) is not recognisably Christian. Yet so much of what passes for theology is of this kind – remote, detached, entirely cerebral, individualistic, apparently disconnected from the life of the Christian community.

Today there is much stress in Christian circles, on personal spirituality. Yet there is little, if any, interest in purely personal spirituality in the New Testament letters. As Philip Lee has pointed out, Paul does not show 'the slightest interest in an individual search for God'.[1] Rather the focus is on the building up of the Church, on solidarity in Christ. John

A. T. Robinson described 'the body' as the keystone of Paul's theology.[2]
We are one body in Christ (Rom. 12:5; 1 Cor. 10:17; 12:12). The theme of
building up the body is central to the Pauline letters. The Church itself
is seen as 'God's building' (1 Cor. 3:9). In 1 Corinthians 14, there are five
references to 'building up' (14:4–26). The theme is equally central to
the Letter to the Ephesians where there is emphasis on 'building up the
body of Christ', and on 'the body's growth in building itself up in love'
(Eph. 4:12, 16). It is love which builds up while knowledge simply puffs
up (1 Cor. 8:1). We are called to 'mutual encouragement in the faith'
(Rom. 1:12), to 'mutual upbuilding' (Rom. 14:19) and 'building up the
neighbour' (Rom. 15:2). The Spirit is manifested for 'the common good'
(1 Cor. 12:7). Christians are called to be rooted (*errizomenoi*) and built
up (*enoikodomeumenoi*) in Christ (Col. 2:7). These emphases are central to Christian life. The New Testament knows no 'spirituality' – the
word is unknown, and remained so for many centuries – apart from
the work of the Spirit in building up the common life. If we want to
use the very modern word 'spirituality', we must insist that Christian
spirituality is essentially social, corporate, and rooted in the material
life of the Christian community. There is a solidarity in holiness: if the
first fruits are holy, so is the whole; if the root is holy, so are the bran-
ches (Rom. 11:16). We are not spiritual on our own. We do not function
apart from a wider community, and from learning, and participating
in, its practices.

Paul, in Romans 12, gives a long list of such practices, and I believe
that five of them are particularly important. First, mutual love. We are
to 'love one another with mutual affection' (12:10). Secondly, spiritual
fervour. We are urged to be 'ardent in spirit' (12:11) Thirdly, perseverance in prayer (12:12). Fourthly, hospitality to strangers (12:13). And,
fifthly, transformation not conformity, the theme with which the
chapter began (12:2). Instead of conforming to the standards and practices of the world, Christians are told that should 'not repay evil for evil
... do not be overcome by evil but overcome evil by good' (12:21).
There are many similar passages in the New Testament and throughout
the Christian tradition. Yet much of our practice is in conflict with,
and contradiction of, these calls.

While I have, for many years, believed that Christian theology, as
distinct from the academic study of the history of religious belief and
practice, can only be done authentically within the context of a community, and that Christian theology must be done within the

community of the Church, the Body of Christ, I have come to see equally that to recognise this intellectually is no guarantee that one will practise it. It is so easy to lose patience with the Church, with its slowness, its lethargy, its conservatism, its mediocrity, and to go one's own way, 'without discerning the body'. This can even turn into a kind of contempt for the common life of the body. I found, in East London and elsewhere, that I was falling into this trap over and over again, that my practice contradicted my theory.

One form that this phenomenon can take with priests and pastors is that of throwing themselves into struggles for justice in the world, and, in the process, bypassing the church, local and national, or, often, bypassing the local church, while maintaining links with the national. 'Let's get on with the work, the church can catch up when it is ready' evokes a positive response in many of us. And there is, of course, some truth in this, but it is dangerous in its individualistic focus. The influence on my thinking of such people as Alan Ecclestone and Stanley Evans had led me to see the 'parish', the neighbourhood church-based community, the smallest unit of Christian presence, as playing a crucial role not only in worship, evangelism and fellowship, but also in theological work. However, I found, during my years at St Botolph's, that, while I was becoming heavily involved with a number of East End parishes, and involved, to a lower degree of intensity, with hundreds of parishes and local communities in Britain, Ireland, the USA and Canada, my involvement with the life of St Botolph's itself, and my impact upon its practice, was really quite slight. It is worth examining some of the reasons for this, for, while St Botolph's is not a 'typical' parish, there are perhaps lessons which would be valuable to people elsewhere.

Part of the reason lay in my job description, and part in my own personal failings. When we created the post, we made it clear that I was to work *from* St Botolph's, rather than *in* it. It was to be a base from which to work, a sacramental, prayerful base which would be a source of nourishment and support. I was not to be simply another member of what was, in 1990, a well-staffed team of clergy and laity. I am sure that this was right, and that the freedom to work on the margins and beyond the gates was vital. However, it is vital that individuals in the kind of position that I was in continue to 'discern the body', and I fear I often left it behind. One of the factors in this was the rapidly changing character of both staff and congregation. By the time I left, I had been there longer than anyone on the staff, and longer than the vast majority of the congregation. They had inherited me as 'part of the furniture', and I had become so busy that I had neglected to explain regularly to them what I was up to.

So I felt increasingly, and particularly after the mid-1990s, that the congregational life of the parish and my own work were moving further and further apart. By then the volume of work in the East End and further afield was so great that I did little to maintain and strengthen the links with the parish. It seemed more important to focus on pressing needs in the wider community. While this focus was necessary and right, I realised that I had, in the process, turned my back on the local worshipping community. In retrospect, this was a serious mistake on my part, and it meant that a certain gulf of comprehension was able to develop between us. I feel that I need to warn my younger brothers and sisters not to fall into this trap. The local church, with all its faults, weaknesses, prejudices, and so on, is really important, and we abandon it, or neglect it, at our peril. Authentic theology cannot be done by abandoning the common life of the body.

Alan Ecclestone was, for the late twentieth century in England, a kind of archetypal parish priest. He was the pioneer of the 'parish meeting', a weekly gathering of the congregation and others, at which major theological, political, pastoral and other matters were debated, and which provided an infrastructure of immense power to the activity of the parish community. I tried to encourage this at St Botolph's, but it never worked. The reasons for this are complex, and involved personality clashes, areas of simple incomprehension, real differences about the nature of the church's mission, and many other factors. But two are particularly important. First, the fact that the congregation was increasingly 'gathered' made it difficult to get people to meet except on Sunday after Mass. Only a few stayed, and the time was limited. Secondly, because of this 'gathered' character, there was little involvement, by most of the membership, and often by the clergy, in the life of the neighbourhoods which adjoined the church. As one of the members who lived closest to the church, I found myself in a lonely position, arguing the case for issues, struggles and communities from which most of my colleagues, however sympathetic, were quite remote. I would not say that a parish meeting model can work only in parishes where the bulk of the congregation are local residents, but it certainly makes it easier. We failed in this area. It could perhaps have worked, with more reflection and mutual debate, and it could have helped us in a number of ways. Maybe it still will help after I have gone.

The practical and theological neglect of the church was a major failure, and it was depressing to find that some people had detected it in my work at an earlier stage. One of the most perceptive – and most worrying – criticisms of my theological approach was made by my friend Peter Sedgwick in his contribution to the massive study *The New Theologians*.[3] He said that, in much of my writing, the Church as a material reality seemed to disappear. I was initially both surprised and distressed by this comment, but, on reflection, felt that it was true, and an important weakness which I needed to take seriously. I have always believed that the Body of Christ, the organism which we call the Church, is at the very heart of Christian faith and life. I have seen tragic examples of clergy who have thrown themselves, as individuals, into struggles in the world, leaving their parish congregations to cope by themselves. I was determined that I would not do this, and it was painful to recognise that, in many respects, that is exactly what I had done.

Theologically I have been helped greatly by the work, including the writings, of Elaine Graham, now Professor of Social and Pastoral Theology in the University of Manchester, who has always insisted that 'the praxis of the faithful community constitutes the character and wisdom of theology', while earlier Ian Fraser saw that 'the key to doing theology is the community itself'.[4] On the other hand, there is always a danger that the ecclesial context of theological work can be twisted into an ecclesiastical control of that work. This has been, and remains, a problem in the Roman Communion with its long history of authoritarian control. *The Instruction on The Ecclesial Vocation of the Theologian*, published in June 1990, was in some ways a regressive and distressing document with its emphasis on 'a solid and correct understanding'.[5] Yet the Vatican is by no means unique in the Christian world in its concern to enforce a 'correct line'. We have seen something of this in recent Anglican history.

The Church is central to theological work, and must not be neglected. I do, however, worry about the opposite danger – that of having too 'high' a doctrine of the Church. This may seem strange, coming from one who would be termed 'high church' (though it is not a term I like). There are at least two forms that the tendency I have in mind can take. The first is to substitute the Church for the Kingdom of God, or even to equate the two. The second is to idealise the Church, producing a Church which cannot actually be located anywhere in historical time or geographical space. So while I agree with Stanley Hauerwas that the Church is intended to be 'God's new language', I feel that there is an enormous gulf between the ideal and the reality. We need to deal with the Church as it is, with all its warts, defects and betrayals, while holding fast to the vision of what it can be.[6]

The Church 'as by law established'

Inevitably, the question of the 'establishment' of the Church of England was a problem, and an obstacle, for my work. I have always been opposed to establishment, and have found the alliance between the Church and the monarchy bizarre, obstructive and theologically indefensible. I took the Oath of Allegiance to the Queen – which one has to do in order to minister in the Church of England – with great reluctance, inner turmoil and a sense of sinfulness. I justified it by arguing that it was an oath taken under duress, and that serving God was more important. But it continues to trouble me, and I am relieved that (I hope) I will not have to take it again. It is possible that I am simply neurotic and obsessional, but I think there are important issues at stake here. The Church is not the servant of the state, and the present situation of the Church of England is a scandal and a serious obstacle to the work of the gospel.

So, not surprisingly, the question of, and the movement for, disestablishment of the Church of England figured a good deal in my work over the years in East London. On 7th January 2002 we launched the Jubilee Group's book *Setting the Church of England Free,* a statement of the case for disestablishment. Tony Benn, Simon Barrow, and Tom Hurcombe spoke. We were also joined by Kim Baker, an ordinand from Texas and former lawyer, who was on placement with me for several weeks. I think that the book put the case for disestablishment well, but it was significant that four of the original contributors had died in the period during which the book came to publication – a point not missed by Colin Buchanan in his review of the book. The contributions by Trevor Huddleston, Alan Ecclestone and Valerie Pitt, all of whom had died before the book appeared, were really helpful. Michael Ramsey, former Archbishop of Canterbury, had offered to write the preface, but died before he could do so. The fact that this book took so long, and involved these deaths, is significant. Most people do not see this question as being of major importance. For me, it was, and is, central to the nature of the gospel and the Church. Like my old friend, the late C. B. Moss, I see it as a life-or-death issue for the Church.[7]

From time to time, my attitude to 'establishment' had amusing consequences. On 8th–9th February 1992 I was invited to lead a study day on 'Eucharist and Society' at Sheffield Cathedral. They had also invited me to preach on the Sunday, having forgotten that it was to be a special service for the 40th anniversary of the Queen's Accession! They were embarrassed, I was amused. They explained, in a very Anglican, polite and awkward way, that the Bishop was expecting to preach, and that I could sit in the choir. I explained that I was not a monarchist and would be happier to sit in the Provost's office, which I did.

However, not far away from us, in Limehouse, stands the Royal Foundation of St Katharine. Until the early 1990s the foundation was under the direction of the Community of the Resurrection. Some of the brothers were heavily involved with outreach and with issues in local neighbourhoods, but, over time, the Foundation seemed to become more remote from ordinary people in the East End. As the Community withdrew, I felt these points should be brought to the attention of Queen Elizabeth, the Queen Mother. On 16th July 1991 I wrote the following letter.

Dear Queen Mother,

I understand that you are very much concerned with the future of the Royal Foundation of St Katharine in Stepney. I have known this place very well for about 33 years. I am also very concerned about its future. As you will know, the Community of the Resurrection is leaving soon. I spent a good number of years leading conferences of East End church people there during the 1970s, and I got the strong feeling that it was becoming increasingly very genteel and middle class, and getting very out of touch with the ordinary people of the East End. I believe that it is very important that, whatever happens there in the future, the Foundation should seek to restore the close links with the community in the East End which Fr Groser established in the 1950s and which I remember so well. The recent history of the Foundation has been really rather tragic. I hope that you will do your best to ensure that things improve and that St Katharine's once again becomes an integral part of the life of the area. I will be very happy to be of whatever help I can be in this matter.

To my surprise I received a reply almost by return of post, assuring me that the Queen Mother was very concerned about the matters I had raised. Soon afterwards Malcolm Johnson was appointed Master of the Royal Foundation, to be followed by my old friend Ron Swan. The Foundation was to play an important part in theological developments after my project came to an end.

Theology and local Christian communities

An important aspect of my work from 1991 onwards was theological consultancy to, and support for, groups working on their Christian discipleship, and this was to continue until the end of the project and beyond it. Within a very short time of the beginning of the work, I was asked to act as consultant to a project called Action of the Church Towards a New Social Vision (ACTS). Based in Manchester, ACTS began in 1991 and continued for several years under the auspices of Church Action on Poverty (CAP). It brought together people, mostly linked with local churches, from a number of deprived areas – Ancoats, Hulme and Moss Side in Manchester, Hattersley on the edge of Manchester, Gipton in Leeds, and Meadow Well in the north-east. It was an important piece of local theology, initiated by CAP's conviction that 'those who are excluded in our polarised society should not be excluded from efforts by the churches themselves to refashion Christian social vision'. ACTS was serviced by two excellent workers based in Manchester, Jonathan Dale and Craig Russell.

I spent a large amount of time too working with local parishes and Christian communities in Britain. I found it best to start with Whitechapel and gradually move outwards, without losing the primary geographical focus on the small neighbourhood. As a local-based priest without responsibility to maintain a parish, it was possible to spend time assisting other local-based communities. I spent a good deal of time in the parishes of Christ Church, Spitalfields, St George's in the East, and St Mary's, Cable Street, all of them small but very committed congregations. Towards the end of my time in the East End, I became involved with the 'new breed' of Baptists who had formed 'Urban Expression' in Shadwell, Wapping and Stepney. The Roman Church seemed, throughout my time in the East End, to be in decline institutionally, though there were some remarkable, creative and prophetic members of religious orders – Sister Christine in Poplar, Diarmuid O'Murchu in Spitalfields, the Servite Joe Collela in Stepney, and others – as well as many active lay people.

One moment which sticks vividly in my mind was the inauguration of a new parish, The Divine Compassion, in Newham in East London. Here a number of parishes in Plaistow and Canning Town came together, and the new parish began on 14th June 1996. (I don't think it dawned on some people – including perhaps the local bishop – that the 'divine compassion' was a euphemism for the Sacred Heart of Jesus whose feast day it was.) In fact, the first post-Reformation Franciscan order in the Church of England was the Society of the Divine Compassion, established a few yards from St Philip's Church where the new parish began. It was an honour to be asked to preach at the event. It combined all kinds of elements from different moments of Christian history and geography – Taizé chants, gospel music, African hymns, charismatic choruses, Anglo-Catholic ceremonial splendour. It even provoked an article in the journal *Anabaptism Today* entitled 'Are we all Anabaptists now?' It was a delight to see the evangelical Bishop of Barking, Roger Sainsbury, a former curate of Christ Church, Spitalfields, singing 'Sweet heart of Jesus, fount of love and mercy... And keep us true to Mary and to thee.'

At various points of the work, I realised that there were many groups throughout the country which were doing what I was trying to do. One of them was the Urban Ministry and Theology Project in Newcastle-upon-Tyne. This group works in the East End of Newcastle. Ellen Clark-King has written of this area in her study of the St Anthony's Estate in Newcastle. Built for the early shipyard workers, the area comes high among deprived wards in England and Wales. Aware that she, a middle-class feminist with an academic background, was, for the first time, living on an estate consisting almost entirely of white working-class Geordies, Clark-King undertook a process of serious listening to her neighbours, and particularly to the women, to see what she, feminists and the wider Church could learn from them.

Her conclusions were broadly similar to my own in relation to the East End of London. These churches were not centres of family worship: it was far more common to see grandmothers and grandchildren together than to see mothers and their children, although motherhood and family were central to the women's concerns. The women she interviewed had no problem about addressing God as 'Father', while female imagery and language played no part in their spirituality. The feminist concern with creation and 'bodily focus' played little role, and the natural world impinged 'only peripherally' on spiritual life. God, in their experience, belonged in another realm, though was concerned with this one. 'The God to whom the women pray', she wrote, 'is not in the same room with them or in the same world.' They had a stronger sense of God's transcendence than of immanence. 'The women go to church to be nearer to God, not to be nearer to one another.' She even claimed that they hold 'a dualistic understanding of matter and spirit'. On the other hand, she insisted that feminists and the Church as a whole had a lot to learn from the Newcastle women for whom 'feminism is an alien concept' and God is 'not a God of transformation but of survival'.[8]

In other places, transformation is more central than survival. One of my last engagements, in February 2004, was to speak at the Centre for Radical Christianity at St Mark's, Broomhill, Sheffield, a hopeful example of something which is beginning to happen in a number of places. We need more centres of this kind, which can appeal to those for whom simplistic and conventional forms of Christianity are unattractive and, in the strict sense of the word, incredible, and which can strengthen a genuine critical orthodoxy.

Work with students

Work with students became a major part of the project from a very early stage. The question of how we could be of help to theological and other students had been a difficult one, and during these years a number of us had been looking at possibilities for more useful and creative work of a more collaborative nature. I felt, and still feel, that I was never very good at it. My colleagues, on the whole, did not seem to recognise that there was a problem. It seemed as if having students on placement was just part of the picture, and so, in my view, it went on without serious thought. Students had been coming to St Botolph's for some years, but I felt that there had been no thinking about what it meant. It just happened.

Yet if we were to be of real help to students, it was essential to clear time so that we could attend to them and support them well. This meant that other colleagues had to take over work which did not have to be done by me, and this proved difficult in practice. However, I think we still achieved a lot. Students from all over the world came here. They included students of theology, medicine, youth and community work, social work, social anthropology, urban sociology and geography. There were many students from North American universities. Theological institutions included King's College London, the College of the Resurrection, Mirfield, the North Thames Ministerial Training Course, Westminster College, Oxford (now part of Oxford Brookes University), Cranmer Hall, Durham, and Spurgeon's College. Non-theological ones included Queen Mary Westfield College, the London Hospital Medical College, the University of East London, the London Guildhall University (now renamed the London Metropolitan University) and the Urban Learning Centre. Some of the brightest and most perceptive students came, on an annual basis, from Trinity College, Carmarthen, a college for training teachers. I had students on a three-week placement from Seabury-Western Theological Seminary in Chicago as well as priests working in inner-city areas in the USA. I was privileged too to spend some time with the ordinands from the Stepney Episcopal Area.

I was also involved with supervising, or assisting, student dissertations, ranging from undergraduate essays to PhD theses. Some of these were related to the East End, others to theology or politics. Some examples include: a woman working on a dissertation in the History Department at Queen Mary Westfield on prostitution in East London in the 1950s; a graduate student at the Graduate School of Divinity in Berkeley, California, working on my own thinking; a Baptist minister in East London working on a PhD thesis at King's College, London, on the nature of prophecy in the contemporary Church; a priest in Hackney working on liturgy and community in three adjacent Hackney parishes; an MA student working on the Church in the urban areas since *Faith in the City;* and various students working on applied theology at Westminster College, Oxford, for whom I acted as local area tutor. There were students working on racism and the Church, Church responses to cultural issues in Calcutta and Barking, the history of British Trotskyism, British fascism 1930–50, the black population of Stepney in the 1940s and 50s, spiritual direction (numerous), pastoral work in Soho in the nineteenth and twentieth centuries, and radical Christianity in 1960s Britain.

The time that these commitments took varied. In every case I spent a minimum of one-and-a-half hours with the person, in some cases I spent this time on about four or five occasions. In a few I spent some time each day for several weeks. In the Westminster case I saw the students once a month for two hours. Some of the work with students involved lengthy involvements. One underdeveloped area, because of lack of time and money, was that of help with research and dissertations. I spent a large amount of time meeting with people writing dissertations or doing research in areas with which I was concerned. So, for example, Richard Toews, a doctoral student in social anthropology at Simon Fraser University in Canada, came in May 1996 to study the theology, ideology and social structure of the Jubilee Group. I tried to keep the numbers of students who needed regular and detailed supervision to a minimum, but was involved with many others who needed general guidance and occasional consultations about their work.

The Westminster students were very interesting, though the theology of the academic faculty was much better than their geography. Although I expressed my willingness to tutor students who lived in the East London area, virtually all the ones who came were from South London. Most were ordained in a variety of churches, mainly black-led churches. In order to pursue the Westminster programme the students had to have had a number of years of pastoral experience, and the theological work was rooted in systematic reflection on this experience. I gave up this work after several years, with some sadness, but the fact that there was no geographical, and often no cultural, link with the East End made me feel that it was not workable. As the years moved on, I realised how important it was to think deeply and plan well for how this work with students should be organised. It was very time-consuming, immensely valuable and at times inspiring, and yet so often done in a slipshod and ill-fashioned way. I am still in touch with many of the students, and I hope they benefited from our work and learned from our incompetence.

Work with students was by no means restricted to those studying theology or preparing for ministry. I lived in a ward of Whitechapel where around a quarter of the population were medical, nursing and dental students, based at the London Hospital, while a mile away was Queen Mary Westfield College (QMW), part of the University of London. Even closer to me was the growing London Metropolitan

University, which soon had the highest proportion of Muslim students of any British university. Work with students in these campuses took up a large amount of my time. A Centre for the Study of Migration was established at QMW on 11th November 1995, and I became involved with Dr Anne Kershen in this work. In the same college, I was also involved with the Centre for Bengali Studies, and with the Department of Geography. Often I felt that the geographers understood what I was trying to do better than the theologians. There was also, for a while, a close link with the Community Module of the Medical Science Department, which helped medical students to work in the communities in the East End. Jenny King, a priest-dentist who teaches medical ethics at the London Hospital Medical College, was a member of my support group, and we worked closely together on this and related issues.

An important part of the work with students was their questioning. This was most evident when a student had spent several weeks with us. During September 1992 Lindsey Ellin, a theological student from Cranmer Hall, was on a placement with me, living at the Rectory of Christ Church, Spitalfields. She wrote a most perceptive paper about her time here, which included comments and criticisms (which I don't think were ever taken seriously). She was particularly struck by the fact that, apart from the daily Mass, there were no regular times when the staff met together for corporate prayer, and by the gulf between 'upstairs' (the area of worship) and 'downstairs' (the area of work with homeless people). This was a gulf noted by many students who came.

Questions too were raised in the course of specific gatherings. On 11th March 2003 I spent a stimulating evening with students at the North Thames Ministerial Training Course in the remote suburb of Southgate in North London. The meeting was convened by my former student Ann Coleman. I spoke on the social dimensions of the doctrine of the Trinity. The students were very astute, and two questions gave me much thought. One woman asked me whether I really believed that all human beings were made in the image and likeness of God, and, if so, what was the significance of baptism and of being 'in Christ'. Then a man asked me if, as a result of Trinitarian theology, I felt that Christian social praxis was superior to that of Jews and Muslims. I still don't know how to answer these questions adequately, but I, and all of us, need to struggle with them. I found the work with the North Thames students immensely stimulating.

Equally stimulating were my regular sessions on urban ministry at Spurgeon's (Baptist) College in South London. I was very impressed that, in contrast to most Anglican colleges, there was always a high proportion of working-class and ethnic-minority students. I found these Baptist students very dedicated, but also very open to different ways of understanding theology, mission and pastoral care. While I was visiting Spurgeon's, the Anabaptist renewal was well under way, and we were soon to see some of the results of this in the East End itself.

My doubts and questions about having students at St Botolph's had been well known and documented over the years. They had basically been about whether enough was going on at St Botolph's alone to justify having a theological student on placement. I was really sad to see students sitting about in the church, not quite knowing what they were supposed to do. Several of them said to me that they felt rather abandoned with not much to do, to see, or to respond to. I felt very sorry for them, and felt that we had projected an image of a very active church which they quickly realised was not the case. I therefore did seriously wonder whether we should have students at all if all they were doing was to observe the work of the church. Frankly, not much was going on apart from an hour or so on Sunday, and occasional meetings. Intelligent students realised this very quickly, and some said that they felt they had been 'conned'. As long as we carried on accepting students, we were deceiving them and perpetuating a myth about St Botolph's which had not been true for some years. The myth was probably based on the period from 1974 to 1990 when St Botolph's did play a major role in much pastoral work in East London, but, by 2001, this had not been true for at least ten years. Gradually the numbers of theological students on placement declined, but, sadly, not through a well-thought-out policy, but through lethargy.

I had a range of students on placement with me personally – theological students, overseas clergy, youth and community work, medical, nursing, sociology, and social work students, and others. I also had people doing theological, social, historical, medical and other types of research. All of them took time. I worked with them in a collaborative way, involving local groups and individuals with which I was involved. So, for example, students worked with the Maze Marigold Project, with local parishes, with the London Hospital, with Bengali groups, mental health work, and so on. There was no shortage of work for them to do, or for them to experience. The problem was time. My own workload was heavy, I had no regular assistance, and it was often hard to find time to give adequate supervision. So, for the most part, I said 'No' to requests. Yet other students were stuck in situations where little was going on and where they did not learn much. I am sure Christians in East London and elsewhere need to work hard on this, but it can only be done by a committed group.

One of the most fruitful placements – for me anyway, and I hope for him – was that of William Taylor, who managed to persuade his college, Westcott House, Cambridge, to allow him to have an 'extended placement' covering almost a two-year period, during which he spent a number of days each month in the East End. This took place during 1993 and 1994. William was interested in the impact of economic development on local community initiatives, He worked intensively with the Jungle Project, set up by a group of 8–14-year-olds who lived in the Wilkes Street and Princelet Street area of Spitalfields, and had reclaimed a piece of derelict ground which was named 'The Jungle'. Working with a local youth worker, a storyteller and a sculptor, William developed some significant work with this group of young people. Soon after he was ordained in July 1995 he celebrated his first Mass at Chingford, at which I preached. He later became chaplain of London Metropolitan University at its East London campus, and was, for a time, a City councillor.

A number of theological, medical, social work and other students from the USA spent time with me in the East End over the years, as did various clergy from the USA, some working in similar inner-city parishes, others wishing to learn from a quite different kind of ministry from their own. Four students from Seabury Western Seminary in Evanston spent time with us at the beginning of 1995. One of them, Judith Whelchel, is now a priest in Asheville, North Carolina, where she set up the Church of the Advocate, a 'street church' consisting mostly of homeless people and prostitutes. Jackie Cameron was a medical student, is now a physician and, by the time this book appears, may have been ordained to the priesthood. She came several times, helped with the medical work with homeless people at St Botolph's, worked with a local East End medical practice, and then did an MA in medical ethics at King's College, London. Kim Baker, at the time a seminarian at the Episcopal Seminary of the South West in Austin, Texas, spent three weeks with us, and is now a parish priest in Western New York. Sara Fischer spent a lengthy period working with Fr Brian

Ralph at St Barnabas, Bethnal Green. She became very involved with the Maze Marigold work, and is now a parish priest in Oregon where she has founded Rahab's Sisters, a project working with prostitutes in the Portland area. Gail Keeney Mulligan, a parish priest with a long history of social-action work and ministry with migrant workers, also spent time in Bethnal Green, worked with Maze Marigold, and, after working in the poorest parish in Tulsa, Oklahoma, is now a parish priest in Connecticut. A Google search for her will indicate the extent of her social involvement now. Clare Barry, a deacon from North Carolina, with particular interests in mental health issues, spent time here, based in Wapping. Spurgeon Hays, an Anglican priest who (as his name suggests) was a former Baptist, came in 1998, and was amazed when I took him to the local Baptist church that the pastor was a woman, and a very radical one at that! It was not like the Southern Baptist Church of his upbringing. And there were many more.

It seems to me that there are major areas of potential here for inner-city churches all over Britain if local churches worked closely with other parishes, groups, projects and individuals. Students could gain vastly, for example, from work in a number of the East End parishes and church communities. I helped to lead a conference for new clergy and ministers in East London, led by Liz Varley, then responsible for adult education for the Anglican churches, and Jane Thorington-Hassel of Victoria Park Baptist Church, which was highly successful and opened up to many the enormous range of work going on in the area. It seemed a shame if we did not bring this kind of work to the attention of, and help to make it a resource for, the students who contacted us and who were often not being helped very well at all. Such collaborative work could also have been of benefit to the numbers of parish clergy who were very overworked and, unlike us at St Botolph's, had no ordained or full-time colleagues. Sadly the cluster of issues raised here remains problematic, and I hope some progress will be made in coming years.

The parish

In *The Idea of a Christian Society* (1939), T. S. Eliot argued that the parish was in decay, and linked this with urbanisation. But in the City of London and in the East End, there were other factors at work, related to population movements, the growth of non-Christian faiths, the breakdown of stable residential communities, and so on. The growth of 'ordained local ministry' is meant to be one of the elements in a wider movement of discipleship. Robin Greenwood has written that 'the Local Ministry movement . . . in other parts of the world is referred to as "Total, Common, Mutual or Collaborative Ministry"', though he sadly conceded that 'history may yet label "Local Ministry" as simply the last jar on the shelf in the twentieth-century church's corner shop of remedies for religious *ennui*'.[9] Yet there are vital issues in ministry which arise from within, and is affirmed by, local communities.

In terms of the 'classical parish', St Botolph's was a very odd one. In 2003 a document entitled *Parish Directory* revealed the following data about the composition of the congregation.

Resident in Parish	2
Resident in local area – definite	16
Resident in local area – indefinite	5
Resident outside area	52

In percentage terms this meant that 77.7 per cent of worshippers lived outside the parish and local area, 21.3 per cent could be considered local, with 0.8 per cent possibly local, and 0.35 per cent resident in the parish. It would have been interesting to have had a fuller picture since this list included only 75 persons (one of whom lived in San Francisco!) and it was not clear how it related either to the electoral roll or to the actual membership of the congregation. If more people had been included, I suspect that the numbers of residents in the parish might have increased. Nevertheless it did indicate the largely non-residential character of the worshipping community, a factor which had been increasing since the 1990s.

St Botolph's was very much part of the City of London, and I consistently avoided the meetings of the City Deanery clergy. This was partly because we had already decided that my major work was in the East End. I must confess that it was also due to the fact that I could not bear the stuffiness, the archaic character and the fossilised nature of the City of London. It was clear that those who represented St Botolph's at meetings felt much the same. A report by the St Botolph's representative on the City Deanery Synod to the Annual Parochial Meeting on 26th April 1998 commented drily: 'As usual it has not really debated any issues or made any significant decisions. One meeting every year [out of three] is largely taken up with presenting a prayer book to the Lord Mayor.'

In fact, the world of the City and the world of the East End were millions of miles apart in their perception of the world. One of the papers I found, as I was moving, and throwing away papers, was a report to the City Deanery Synod on the proceedings of the General Synod meeting in February 2004, written by Mrs Sarah Finch, a person entirely unknown to me. I was astonished that Mrs Finch thought that a collect praying that God 'would lead us to seek [Jesus] among the outcasts and to find him in those in need' 'undermined the gospel by encouraging the idea of salvation by good works'. To seek Jesus among the outcasts and those in need is firmly rooted in the gospels and in mainstream orthodox Christian tradition, made very explicit in the early Church fathers such as St John Chrysostom, and expressed frequently in Anglican theology over the last few hundred years, most memorably in Bishop Frank Weston's address to the Anglo-Catholic Congress of 1923 – in words almost identical to those to which Mrs Finch objected. The collect seems to be based on Matthew 25. In no way does it undermine the gospel, indeed it is central to the gospel. I write this sadly, since it is one of the few theological points that I have noticed in all the City Deanery reports that I have read – and it is simply wrong, and, I would say, heretical. I hope in future the Deanery can do a bit better! I wish them well.

Another problem, which did worry me, was the lack of use of me within the parish. During the whole period from 1990 to 2004, I can only recall four occasions when I was asked to do any specifically theological work on behalf of the clergy or congregation. (I omit here sermons and homilies, which are, of course, theological.) One was a comment on the Templeman Report on the future of the church in the City of London. Another was a report, which I wrote in 1996, on the blessing of same-sex unions, an issue with which the parish had been involved then for over twenty years. A third was a comment on a dispute about an art exhibition which raised theological issues about the portrayal of the human body. And a fourth, which arose from members of the congregation, was a presentation about liberation theology and its relevance to the parish. As far as I know, none of these was followed up.

Most of my theological work took place outside the strict framework of the parish. I think the reasons for this were a mixture of my failure to put effort into working within the congregation, tending to leave this to the full-time clergy, and of a certain perplexity among newer members, including clergy, as to what my role was.

Many years ago Alan Ecclestone wrote these words about the Parish Meeting, a weekly gathering of local Christians which was central to the life of the parish in Sheffield where Alan ministered.

> Almost every parish is plagued by unresolved problems or hampered in its work by the necessity felt by some of keeping off certain dangerous questions. This reluctance is not seeking peace in the Christian sense at all. It is merely trying to have peace on the easiest possible terms, and devitalises the church ... The Parish Meeting becomes so much less than it ought to be if it cannot be the place where the personal problems of the church can be faced. Quickness to take offence, over-impulsive retorts, personal dislikes: it is in the wear and tear of such things over the years that the quality of life of church is tested.[10]

I found that the problems which Alan identified were very much present at St Botolph's. The 'unresolved problems', the 'reluctance', the 'quickness to take offence', and the inability or unwillingness to deal with painful issues seemed to be endemic to the parish – as is undoubtedly so in many others. This caused me profound disquiet, at times reaching the point of hopelessness. It was, of course, in part, a disquiet with the structural lethargy of the Church as a whole – hardly a new problem, but it hits you at certain moments with a particular vengeance. One of the results of taking on this work, which involved 'singing for my supper', had been a deepening sense of the need for self-critique and accountability to the wider community. I am sure that the issues of accountability are central to the life of local churches, and they are still not being dealt with. I seemed to have been raising these issues for so many years, but little had developed. I felt that we would make little progress until there was real mutual accountability, including a discipline of scrutiny and real sharing of ministry. I began to feel that I was not going to experience this at St Botolph's, although there were a number of colleagues who were utterly committed to it.

In 1981 Bob Gallagher, a priest in the USA, had written a useful pamphlet on this subject. He wrote of the importance of 'being accountable for our work to some appropriate diocesan authority'. I had never experienced this, or anything remotely resembling this, since I was ordained in 1964, and certainly not at all during my time at St Botolph's. I found this terribly sad, and pastorally appalling, and I am sure that I am not alone. The Diocese of London is perhaps the worst example of lack of accountability and support in the Church of England, though there are far worse examples within global Anglicanism and within the Church as a whole. Dysfunction is the norm in the Church, not an aberration from it.

All the structures of accountability which have been important, and indeed essential, to me have been those which I have created myself. This should not have been the case. Bob Gallagher continued:

> We should be expected to work hard. Brief but frequent reports are needed to encourage reflection as well as accountability. Accountability requires a gentle toughness. We should be expected to work hard at a full parish life of worship, study and action. When we fail, we will need understanding and possibly forgiveness. The time may come when we need to be removed. It is no favour to a priest to let him continue in a situation for which he lacks the vocation or ability. Accountability needs to include both acceptance and confrontation.[11]

If only the churches in England could have taken these words seriously, so much trouble and damage could have been avoided.

I felt that it was important, not least because my work was dependent on what financial support I could raise, that I produced regular and detailed reports of what I had been doing. Leslie Houlden, in his evaluation, felt that 'the amount of self-accounting . . . is surely unique among theologians', and suggested that it might be 'excessive and too time consuming'. It certainly did consume a lot of time, yet I felt it was essential that people knew what I was doing, where my priorities lay, and so on.

What happens in the small and local church is of critical importance for the Church as a whole. The term *ecclesia particularis* was used by the Second Vatican Council to stress the importance of the local small unit of Christian praxis. Yet that unit only functions well if there is mutual solidarity, accountability and some kind of corporate discipline. The question I tried to raise at St Botolph's was: To what extent are we a team with any kind of common purpose? Numerous students on placement had commented that we were not a team at all, just a number of interesting individualists, working in an entirely private way, and, on the whole, getting on OK together. We had noted this, and apparently accepted it. For most of my time at St Botolph's, I felt that we had an inadequate knowledge of what each of us did, thought, believed, felt, of what were the key issues, pressure points, problems and dilemmas. There was a weekly notice board, prominently displayed in the kitchen, but most of the staff never filled it up. As a result, everyone knew what some of us did, week by week, but for the most part, we functioned as isolated individuals, accountable to nobody. At the very least, this was not very helpful for informed intercession.

The question of accountability in the parish hit me with particular pressure because I had become slightly involved with a movement called Gospel Audit, developed by Angela West and Una Kroll, which was concerned to deepen the practice of self-critique and account-ability of individuals to the Body of Christ. So much 'audit' and 'review' in the churches pays little or no attention to the gospel and to the Christian tradition, and is derived from secular management models. Of course, the question of accountability is national as well as local, and affects issues far beyond the Christian community, as Simon Jenkins showed in his critique of contemporary Conservative govern-ment.[12] I am sure that the issues of accountability are central to the life of the Church, and are still not being dealt with. We will make little progress until there is real mutual accountability, including scrutiny and real sharing of ministry. Linked with this was a certain lethargy and resistance to action which seemed to be part of the culture and structure of the parish, and which prevented people from dealing with many issues. It was not uncommon to find a whole history of impor-tant matters which were raised, discussed and then forgotten, until, some time later, they might be raised again. Sometimes action was taken, more often the issue was abandoned, through lack of interest, loss of energy, and no doubt other factors. One of these factors may be a built-in resistance to significant change producing psycho-social mechanisms of cumulative delaying tactics. These are well-known and well-documented mechanisms, albeit not always fully conscious, for ensuring an institution's incapacity to change.[13] The problem through-out this range of connections, it seemed to me, was that there was an unevenness and lack of system about it all. It was haphazard and incoherent. There were many areas which remained mysterious. It was not clear to whom, if to anyone, some of us were accountable, and the degree to which each of us felt accountable to the others was unclear.

Most important, it seemed that St Botolph's was a microcosm of the whole Church, which is why I raise these matters here, for they recur again and again in one parish or community after another.

Work in the USA

During the period of the project, I spent about two months each year in the USA. This relationship with communities in North America had begun in 1978, but during the term of the Whitechapel project, the visits became more important as a way of sharing ideas and developing common links. The connection began on the South Side of Chicago, but quickly expanded to include New York, Washington DC, Atlanta, Idaho, North Carolina, Connecticut, and many other places. It included much work with students training for ministry, and with a wide range of students in many disciplines.

Some years ago, a link was forged between St Botolph's Church and the parish of St James, Capitol Hill, Washington DC. I had known this area for many years, and one year I spoke to the parish about the work in East London. I mentioned that we were located between the financial district and a very poor neighbourhood; that we had been one of the first Anglo-Catholic parishes in England to affiliate corporately to the Movement for the Ordination of Women; and that we had a significant gay and lesbian membership. Fr Richard Downing, the Rector of St James, responded, and said that their parish was also located between the White House and a large ghetto; that they were the first Anglo-Catholic parish in Washington to support the ordination of women; and that they too had a large gay and lesbian membership. The link between the two parishes continues.

On 22nd March 1994 I taught part of a course on racism at the Graduate School of Education at Harvard University. The course was run by my friend Linda Powell, one of the few black professors in that campus at the time, and the students were all training to be teachers, mostly in urban areas. Their responses to my contribution, which formed an integral part of the programme, were fascinating. One raised the question of whether racism can ever be eradicated within a capitalist economic system. Another reacted passionately to my suggestion that, for many involved in racist violence in East London, vandalism had become 'the last available form of social action'. This clearly rang bells with students from Los Angeles and elsewhere. One of the most interesting comments, from a black woman, was that, having read some of my writings prior to the class, she naturally assumed that I was black – and was amazed when I walked into the classroom!

When I laid down the outlines of the course on 'Spirituality and Social Transformation' at Colgate Rochester Divinity School, Rochester, New York for the D Min programme in May 1998, I had a number of aims in mind. I wanted to provide a sound reading programme that reflected as adequately as possible the main traditions within world Christianity which have nurtured the integration of 'spiritual life' and commitment to social change. Of necessity that is a developing project since some areas are still under-documented in terms of published literature. I wished, in my own presentations, to identify some of the main streams. Thus I contrasted the Roman Catholic and Anabaptist traditions, surveyed Anglican social thought as a paradigm, and examined a number of key individuals in Britain and North America. I also wanted, as someone committed to contextual theological work, to draw on my own experience as an Anglican working in London. Most of all, I wanted to give enough time to the students themselves to reflect on the issues of spirituality and social transformation within their own contexts – theological, personal, historical, geographical. It was against this background that I set the two pieces of work, related to a person (perhaps the student her/himself) and a situation. What was I looking for here? Four things: a degree of perception and insight into the person/situation described; theological scrutiny within the specific context described; clarification of the way in which 'spiritual life' was deepened within the social environment and how social commitment was deepened by the spirituality described; and that all the above should be expressed coherently, accurately and as clearly as possible.

There were many other places, incidents and people, and it was really exciting to have been able to develop this two-way link with the USA. I was not the only member of 'the team' to spend time in the USA. Liz Ellis spent several weeks in the parish of the Holy Comforter, Atlanta, where she worked in visual art, photography and sculpture with the congregation, culminating in an exhibition of their art and poetry work in the huge cathedral in Atlanta. Holy Comforter has an important place in my life. Because of the way in which the USA mental health system works, former hospital patients are dispersed into 'the community' and housed in group homes, some of which are wonderful, many of which are little better than glorified 'bed and breakfast' hostels. The neighbourhood around Holy Comforter is dominated by such homes, so most of the congregation, during the time I was there, were ex-psychiatric patients. The parish priest, Mark Baker, himself a carpenter, converted the basement of the church into a workshop, and it was here that Liz worked.

One of the papers which I treasure from my USA visits is a one-page sheet called 'What keeps you coming to Holy Comforter?' It was circulated to the congregation during Mark's time, and it has some remarkable replies, such as the following:

> The Holy Spirit is alive and well here.
> The love here wraps itself around you.
>
> Everyone helps every person, one big family. I feel at home here.
>
> We all grow up here.

One of the most important influences on my understanding of ministry was the time I spent in the Diocese of Northern Michigan. The North American theologian Fredrica Harris Thompsett has said that, in much current thinking about pastoral ministry, the laity has disappeared in what has become a 'clerical reservation'. She too advises that we 'suspend' the use of the term 'lay'.[14]

The last of my regular visits to the USA was in the fall of 2003 as the war against Iraq was building up. As I returned I found Greg Dyke's complaint about the North American media's bias in reporting on the war absolutely right. Dyke accused them of promoting patriotism rather than impartiality. In fact the situation is more complex. There is, for example, the extreme deference to those in power, which was such a contrast to the BBC. Or the tendency to label all criticism or expressions of doubt as 'anti-American'. Or the childish hostility to France, even to the extent of changing the name of 'French fries' to 'freedom fries' and of abandoning other terms (most of which have nothing to do with France). The dominance of the Bush rhetoric was oppressive and omnipresent. British people need to understand that most Americans do not read national newspapers and have only a vague knowledge of who Saddam Hussein is or where Iraq is. I spent much of my time putting people on to Robert Fisk and the British media. I was, however, encouraged at the reawakening of some kind of critical consciousness among a growing minority, often in small towns. Those who love and value the USA must encourage these dissident voices. Here, and elsewhere, the British radio, TV and broadsheets were widely valued. There are few alternative voices.

As I look back over these years in the USA, a number of themes come into my mind. One, sparked off by a comment from Leslie Houlden in his critical review, was the fact that my involvement with academic institutions and seminaries was much greater in the USA than in Britain where I was, in Houlden's words, 'rather an isolated figure' and 'not much associated with academic theological life in this country'. By contrast, I spent much of my time in the USA teaching in universities, seminaries and colleges.

Writing

Writing was central to my work in the East End, but could not have been done, or had any substance, without the work and life which nourished it. *The Eye of the Storm*, which was published in 1992, received the HarperCollins Religious Book Award on 7th December 1993. Its subtitle in Britain was 'spiritual resources for the pursuit of justice', while the USA (original) publisher preferred 'living spiritually in the real world'. (This is in itself worthy of a study!) *Through Our Long Exile: contextual theology and the urban experience* was launched at Eastside Books in Whitechapel Road on 2nd October 2001. Dan Jones, the best-known community artist in the East End, brought the original copy of the pajnting which formed the cover, a magnificent portrayal of the march for the 60th anniversary of the Battle of Cable Street of 1936. *The Sky Is Red: discerning the signs of the times* was published in 1997 and reissued in a revised form in 2003. There were others – *Care and Conflict* (1990), which launched the work, *We Preach Christ Crucified* (1994) and *Drugs and Pastoral Care* (1998). Probably none of them would have been written had it not been for the freedom given to me by the project.

I was also involved in helping some other books to appear. Towards the end of 1995 the symposium *God in the City,* edited by Peter Sedgwick (Mowbray 1995), appeared. This was a collection of work done by the Archbishop's Urban Theology Group, and I gave evidence to it and helped a bit with the final production. Peter Ball's *Journey into Truth: spiritual direction in the Anglican tradition* (Mowbray 1996) was a valuable development from work which I did in the 1970s and built on and extended this, looking in more detail than I did at some key Anglican figures and emphases. Douglas Rhymes' *Time Past to Time Future* (Darton, Longman & Todd 1993) quoted me to an embarrassing degree – which was maybe why *Theology* asked me to review it. His book was sparked off by my *Care and Conflict* (DLT 1990), the book which itself sparked off my work at St Botolph's. Fr Rhymes died on 1st January 1996. Professor Ann Loades edited an anthology called *Spiritual Classics from the Late Twentieth Century* (National Society and Church House Publishing 1995), which included work by six authors, including Cardinal Martini (who was at that time rumoured to be the next Pope) and me!

Should I remain at St Botolph's?

By the year 2000 it had become clear that, for financial reasons, the project was coming to an end. But there were deeper issues about the changing character of the area, of St Botolph's itself, and of the points of focus of my own work. I had been concerned for some years about my relationship with St Botolph's. At times I felt that the original vision of the project seemed to have been lost. There were now few if any people left in the parish who were there when my work began, or who remembered its origins. For most, I was someone whom they had inherited, whose occasional preaching was valued, and whose assistance liturgically was useful, but, with a few notable exceptions, there was little understanding of what I was doing. I had to accept part of the blame for this situation.

I discussed my concerns several times with my Support Group. They felt that I needed to make it very clear to St Botolph's that I was not just an extra liturgical pair of hands, and that the original job description was very clear that I would be based at St Botolph's, and work from it, but would not be involved with the maintenance of the parish and congregation. By the late 1990s this aspect had been largely lost, and I had allowed myself to get caught up in, and limited by, the church machine, whereas a central element in the creation of the post had been to avoid this. It was very important that my contact with the other worshipping communities, Christian and Muslim, in the area was restored and strengthened.

It was inevitable that the relationship with St Botolph's would need to be examined at some stage, and that it might be that a different physical and strategic base would need to be established. It became clear, as we began to consider the future of the work after 2001, with or without my involvement, that the question of whether it should continue to be based at St Botolph's was important. In view of this, we looked carefully at the arguments for and against its continuation.

One aspect of the life of the parish which had worried me, almost from the beginning of my contact with it in the 1950s, was that we never seemed to have made the church seem warm and friendly enough for 'non-churchy' people not to feel awkward and embarrassed when entering it. Of course, this is not peculiar to us or to Anglicanism, and it may be that St Botolph's had done better than most at accepting marginal people as equals. Yet at the moment that should symbolise the equality and solidarity of all people, the moment that we call Holy Communion, it was striking that homeless people, marginal people, people 'outside the gate', were missing. The one exception, significantly, was people who were drunk. Alcohol removes inhibitions, and the congregation had been remarkably kind to people who came to church 'pissed out of their mind'. But it seems at times that, if you are poor and homeless, you maybe have to be drunk to feel welcome in a church – or not to care if you aren't! What is this saying to us? Were not the early disciples on the day of Pentecost mistaken for drunks? Might there not be something important here that we have lost?

Some churches in the USA that I have visited seem to have achieved a sense of solidarity in worship which we have been struggling to achieve. A memorable occasion was a time when I preached at St George's, Patterson, New Jersey when Tracy Lind was the parish priest. There were beds for homeless people in one of the chapels, and a real sense of equality and 'togetherness' at the Mass. People were not divided into 'congregation' and 'clients', as they often are in British and North American churches. I have experienced the same sense of solidarity at the Parish of the Holy Comforter, Atlanta, at the Church of the Advocate in Asheville, North Carolina, and in many other places, including many British churches. But the alienating effect of many Anglican church buildings, particularly those with a 'civic' history, has always troubled me. There is so much work to do here, but if there is no consciousness of the problem, there will not be the work to deal with it.

As we reviewed the work in the mid-1990s the question arose: Should I remain at St Botolph's? There were strong arguments for a continued relationship. While the church was in the City, it was not far from the East End. The staff were still sympathetic to what I was doing, and it was still a place which had credibility and was well known. Moreover, part of St Botolph's *Project* (as opposed to the church) was by then based in Whitechapel, in the same building as me. This was my idea, and I was delighted that, for the first time in many years, the entire building was being used for important work with people. In particular the outreach workers and others were involved locally, and this work had expanded. I had a good working relationship with them. From a personal point of view, the fact that I lived there, and was the only member of staff at St Botolph's who lived very close to the church and whose address and phone number were well known, means that this was an ideal base for pastoral ministry. There was no site which was more significant to Bangladeshi people, and this also seemed to be an argument for maintaining the link with St Botolph's.

There were also arguments against a continued relationship. The church had become very marginal to the East End. Few of the staff or congregation lived in the area, or were involved in East End issues. The Sunday congregation was increasingly eclectic, and probably few of them had any idea about my work and simply saw me as an extra curate. St Botolph's Project had moved further away from the life of the congregation. The close link between the church and the work with homeless people had gone, and there seemed less need, or desire, for someone to contribute theologically to issues of housing and home-lessness at St Botolph's, though I continued to perform this role through UNLEASH and other groups. The original sense of my working within an inter-disciplinary team in church and crypt, how-ever, no longer existed.

More generally, hardly any members of the congregation were involved in any way with my work, though three were heavily involved with the Jubilee Group. St Botolph's already had four ordained people on its staff (two priests, two deacons) as well as me, while most East End parishes were struggling with one priest, or sharing a priest between two parishes. These parishes had far more pastoral work with large residential communities than was the case with the clergy at St Botolph's, and it could be argued that it was very unfair for me to be based in what could be seen as an affluent, privileged and 'cushy' place. From a geographical as well as a theological perspective, I wondered if it might make more sense for me to be based more centrally in Tower

Hamlets where I could be of more use to the parishes and communities in the East End.

My own failures apart, I was aware that the focus of the ministry at St Botolph's had radically shifted in recent years. It now looked west far more than east, as it did before George Appleton became Rector in 1957. Appleton, during his short ministry there, forced the parish to face east, where the ordinary people lived, and to see itself as involved in the needs and life of the East End. That this was, by the mid-1990s, no longer the case was due to a mixture of factors: demographic and cultural changes, changes in personnel, and so on. Most of the houses which were once close to the church on the south side of Aldgate and Whitechapel High Streets had been replaced by city offices. I wrote earlier about our failure to challenge effectively the value system and structures of the City of London. Andrew Henderson, who had written a report on the work at St Botolph's in the late 1990s, referred to its 'prophetic voice' and its 'commitment to social outreach as an expression of the gospel'. He suggested that the parish 'wants to be a bridge between the modern City and the East End'. It was, he claimed, committed to 'the social gospel' and 'has a Catholic tradition'. I am not at all sure that any of this was right by the time he wrote it.[15] In the end, we decided that, in view of the fact that the project was coming to an end, there were more advantages than disadvantages in staying at St Botolph's, but that, for the future, we should be looking for a base further east.

As I look back over these years, there was, in my view, a major theological failure which is by no means peculiar to St Botolph's or to the churches of East London. There was a strong, and right, emphasis on care in almost all the churches with which I worked. I am not sure that there was the same emphasis on commitment. The need for 'Christian proficiency' and for a disciplined, committed 'remnant' was a central theme of Martin Thornton, writing in the 1950s and 1960s.[16] I fear that, in the 1990s, we tended to substitute care for commitment and for building up the Body of Christ.

12

'The Night Sky of the Lord': theology and darkness

Night is coming when no one can work.

JOHN 9:4

In a dark time the eye begins to see.

THEODORE ROETHKE, 'In a Dark Time',
The Collected Poems of Theodore Roethke
(Doubleday/Anchor 1976, p. 117)

And of her darkness I must know and I must know nothing
And in this darkness I must be made and I must be unmade
And of her darkness I must be possessed and dispossessed of
all things.

NICOLA SLEE, 'Litany to a Dark God' in
Praying Like a Woman (SPCK 2004, pp. 140–141)

Darkness and light

There is a dialectic of darkness and light which runs through all living theology. Of course, there are theological systems which seek to exclude, deny or combat the darkness, and which view all forms of darkness as hostile to God. It is here, rather than in biblical literalism, that the real harm of what we call 'fundamentalism' lies. The more I have worked as a priest and pastor, and the more I have tried to make creative and redemptive sense theologically of the pain and anguish which is on all sides of us, as well as within us, the more central has the symbol of darkness become, and I want to try to express this to the extent that I, or anyone, can.

As a young priest in the 1960s, I found that an area for which my 'training' had not prepared me well was that of ascetical theology. We had, of course, had lectures on 'spiritualia', but there had been little attention to the need for a profound exploration of one's own inner depths if one was to be of any real use to people in distress and turbulence. Much of the stress in pastoral theology was on 'doing', on the nuts and bolts of the pastoral task. But, at the heart of the growing drug culture, surrounded by many people who had lost hope, by others who were homeless, suicidal, desperately lost, I realised that the kind of resources which were needed were not so much skills or expertise as inner stability, exposure to brokenness, ability to cope with darkness, and perhaps the dawning awareness that bewilderment was 'another way of knowing', that some truths could only be learned as we become emptied, frightened and confused. In Alan Ecclestone's words, 'there are things that can only be seen in darkened skies, questions only heard in the silence of utter dismay'.[1]

The experience of darkness is particularly acute in people with 'mental health problems' – an experience common to us all, yet experienced most intensely and most painfully by some of us to whom are given such labels as 'psychotic' and 'manic depressive'. The work of theologically rooted priesthood, and of all pastoral care, here as everywhere, is one primarily of presence rather than of skill and function, and at the heart of Christian priesthood is the encounter with darkness, specifically the dying of Christ and his descent into hell, those events which must precede resurrection. We must never seek to evade the darkness with all its confusion and uncertainty.

In pastoral care in dark times and places, silence is critical. If we are to be genuine carers, we need to slow down and absorb situations, to learn how to be passive and receptive. It is true that the Greek word from which 'passion' and 'passionate' derive means 'suffer', but its root is related to passivity. It is the opposite of active. To be active is to do something; to be passive is to do nothing, to receive. I realise that, without a context, these sentences can be dangerously misleading. There are times when drastic action is called for. There are times to speak loudly, times to 'rage against the dying of the light'. I am not recommending silence and passivity as universal postures. I am myself a lifelong activist and much of my energy still goes into campaigns and struggles for justice. All I am trying to do is correct a distorted emphasis in speech and action and to stress that silence and receptiveness are important parts of being human, and of being loving instruments of care. We need to lose our fear of silence, darkness and solitude, and this can only come through patient and disciplined practice.

Of course, I do not wish to convey the impression that everything in pastoral ministry in the inner city is dark and dismal. In any case, not all experience of darkness is negative – there are 'treasures of darkness' (Isa. 45:3)! There were, and are, many shafts of hope, points of ecstasy, rays of light, moments of fun, times of refreshing. Yet now, after almost fifty years of working in inner-city neighbourhoods, I realise how central is the symbol of darkness. This symbol has, however, been associated in conventional religious thinking with 'the inner life' and with 'spirituality', both of which are seen as unconnected with the social, economic and political life of actual communities. I certainly want to contest and reject this view.

The themes of darkness and light occur throughout the biblical texts. Many of the references are to the experience of darkness in the lives of individuals and communities. Thus Abraham experienced 'a deep and terrifying darkness' in the presence of God (Gen. 15:12), while Job experienced darkness at daytime and at noon (Job 5:14; 19:8), but also yearned for it as an escape from the terror of God (23:16–17). Darkness for him raised questions about God's activity, and he cried, 'Can God judge through the deep darkness?' (22:13). The Psalmist wrote of the experience of 'deep darkness' (Ps. 44:19). Jeremiah was brought by God 'into darkness without any light' (Lam. 3:2), an experience marked by the absence of peace and glory, and by the sense that prayer had been shut out (Lam. 3:8, 17, 18). Yet the response to this terrible experience was 'Great is your faithfulness'! (Lam. 3:22–23). The fact that God is surrounded by clouds and thick darkness is, in Psalm 97, linked with righteousness and justice (Ps. 97:2).

Darkness figures throughout the Christian tradition. From Pseudo-Dionysius through *The Cloud of Unknowing* and Dante's 'dark wood' (*silva oscura*) to St John of the Cross and beyond, there is a stress on *apophasis*, that which cannot be said, on 'unknowing', and on the darkness which is at the heart of faith.

'The dark night of the soul'

There is also, of course, 'the dark night of the soul'. The classic statement of the centrality of the dark night within the Western Christian tradition is that of St John of the Cross in the sixteenth century. For John, the dark night was not a state of psychological disturbance such as deep depression, though it could be, and often is, associated with a range of psychological conditions. It is certainly a condition of inner turbulence, upheaval and confusion, characterised by the collapse of familiar ways of praying and feeling, and by the onset of a state of numbness and dereliction. Many recent writers have described the dangers.

> One of the dangers of descending into the Abyss is precisely to be torn apart by the wild chaotic forces that rant and rave there. But if one doesn't take the risk, one risks losing all creative potentialities . . . Only if we confront the chaotic irrational powers at the very depths of our being will we be able to transform them into something meaningful.[2]

Yet, for John, the dark night was an essential part of the life of faith, a sign of progress and of creative, if painful, movement. It was, in fact, a metaphor for Paschal transformation. Pope John Paul II claimed that the dark night represented John's attitude towards all reality, the whole path of faith being seen as a journey through night.[3] As earlier forms of spiritual life died, the person moved into a sphere of freedom as the Holy Spirit increasingly took over her heart and life. John was critical of those who tried to push the person back to the earlier religious disciplines and structures, not realising that they had been transcended and had to be abandoned. His book *The Ascent of Mount Carmel*, of which *The Dark Night of the Soul* is an integral part, is an account of progress, through confusion and upheaval, towards spiritual maturity. The darkness is the light of God experienced from the perspective of human finitude. In the midst of darkness, as Ruysbroeck wrote, one is 'informed and penetrated by a simple light'.[4]

I do not think that responsible Christians can bypass the matters which arise from the dark night. This is a common, if not universal, experience, and any contextual theology must take it into account, socially and personally. It is manifested in such experiences as powerlessness, apparent inability to make progress, and, most intensely, a sense of impasse. In my experience, much pastoral and social ministry includes long periods of uncertainty, perplexity and bewilderment. Many times I have felt an affinity with the prayer of Jehosaphat: 'We do not know what to do but our eyes are on you' (2 Chron. 20:12). (I believe that Dietrich Bonhoeffer said that it was the text on which he preached most frequently in the Nazi period.) More recently, Nicola

Slee has written of 'a sense that darkness, winter, silence and unknowing are necessary counterbalances to the pull of light, summer, speech and knowledge, those activities of the rational conscious mind and of the will'.[5] It was in the midst of the urban uprisings in Liverpool in 1981 that the Passionist priest Austin Smith experienced the features of the dark night, particularly that of impasse, and made a comparison between the Spanish Carmel and the urban ghetto: both gave birth to a new spirit.[6] This has been my experience also. Many times in East London I have found myself reduced to silence, to bafflement, to a state of anguish and inability to respond. This too is a necessary element in lived theology, a theology in which things are not always clear, and the way ahead is often uncertain.

The darkness of God

'When we speak of God', said the late Fr Herbert McCabe, 'we do not know what we are talking about.' In saying this, he was deeply in touch with the Catholic tradition, as represented, among others, by Augustine and Thomas Aquinas, which insisted that God was 'ineffable', and that all talk about God was doomed to falter and be reduced to a state of inadequacy.[7] The darkness of God is central to ancient theology. We are confronted, according to Rowan Williams, with 'a reality drastically and totally beyond the reach of our conceptual apparatus'. Williams went on to say that 'the test of integrity is whether a man or woman has lived in the central darkness of the paschal event'. In a later article, he spoke of the apophatic tradition as 'the acknowledgment of the inadequacy of any form, verbal, visual or gestural, to picture God definitively, to finish the business of religious speech (the acknowledgment that is at work in praise as well) and the expression of this recognition in silence and attention'.[8]

In recent theological writing, the theme of 'the darkness of God' has not been uncommon. Nicholas Lash has said that 'it is the theologian's task to make it difficult to speak of God'. It has, however, been not only common, but central, in Eastern Orthodoxy since the early centuries. As Vladimir Lossky wrote, the 'apophatic' (negative) posture has been 'the fundamental characteristic of the whole theological tradition of the Eastern Church'[9] while the most significant Roman Catholic theologian of the late twentieth century, Hans Urs von Balthasar, wrote that 'because God himself is not an object, God can be experienced by the soul only as dark night'.[10]

What then of the biblical testimony that 'God is light, and in him there is no darkness at all' (1 John 1:5) and that God 'dwells in unapproachable light' (1 Tim. 6:16)? Does not the stress on the divine darkness contradict this important truth? Not at all, it is a consequence of it. Yes, the scriptures insist, God is light. The darkness is not to last for ever. Jesus stressed that 'nothing is covered up that will not be uncovered, and nothing secret that will not become known' (Matt. 10:26). I conclude from this that darkness is a necessary part of our experience of God, that much darkness is temporary, but that there is a more fundamental darkness which is the encounter with God who is eternal light, seen from the perspective of finite humanity. God is revealed in fire and dark cloud: there is no form, only a voice.

Personal darkness

We speak glibly and insensitively about sharing another's darkness. We can never do this fully, for no person can ever know fully what is going on in the deep regions of another's being. Yet there is an affinity and solidarity which develops as a byproduct of a common experience of darkness even though the precise forms may differ. In the very process of entering the darkness of the spirit we come to know and understand better the predicament of those whose darkness is perceived as terrible and as something thrust upon them, something they did not freely choose or desire. Unless this darkness is in some ways shared, no amount of 'training', no acquisition of skills and techniques will help the pastor, priest or carer. All they will do is to provide him or her with more resources with which to do more damage to more people.

The more pastoral contact I had with people in the East End, the more I was struck by what Sharon Thornton has called 'the unexplainable tenacity of the human spirit under extraordinary circumstances'.[11] Margaret Spufford has expressed powerfully what many of us feel about our own lives and those of our friends.

> My circumstances have been in some ways so unpropitious, it seemed at times so improbable that anything worthwhile could be brought of all this pain, that I am not infrequently filled by

amazement and gratitude that anything constructive could emerge from such unpropitious beginnings and roots so damaged.[12]

Yet it is out of darkness and damaged roots that the light and fruitfulness of grace blossoms.

On 13th September 1999 my friend William Young, a most sensitive and imaginative person, organised a gathering at The Marquis of Granby pub near Trafalgar Square to commemorate the birthday and suicide of his friend Sebastian who would have been 21 on that day. The gathering was around the theme of 'Mental Illness and Creativity'. Sebastian was a gifted artist, and his tragic death caused grief to many of us. It was an honour to take part in this, though I had only known Sebastian slightly. The link between mental illness and creativity has been discussed for many years. One of the most moving accounts of a 'journey through madness' is that by Mary Barnes who died in 2001. She believed that however greatly a soul is damaged, there is a part of it which always grows, and which is never beyond the reach of love, and that the darkness and terror of psychosis could be a way towards holiness. Mary was part of the community which grew up around R. D. ('Ronnie') Laing, and which, for a while, was based in East London. Writing in 1965, Laing argued that schizophrenia was incomprehensible. Rather than seek to comprehend, we must recognise distinctiveness, difference, separateness, loneliness, darkness and despair. Two years later he suggested that the person with schizophrenia may have much to teach us about the inner world.[13]

Much of my ministry in East London has been connected, in some way, with issues of mental health, issues which affect us all. For various reasons I have been particularly concerned with manic-depressive illness, and for years have been a member of the Manic Depression Fellowship. Many people have found this group extremely supportive, as others have found similar help through Alcoholics Anonymous. In theory, the local church offers such support, but in practice it is now often other groups which do so, albeit often on church premises. There are theological issues here too, issues about person and community, about wholeness and imperfection, about falling and rising again. It is often on the far margins of the church, or outside of it altogether, that persons in distress find support and solidarity. Theology goes on there too.

There is a particular kind of darkness which comes with the

experience of depression. It is something which I have only experienced slightly, but more deeply through friends. The late Peter Rose, a former student and close friend of mine, suffered from severe depression, yet there were remarkable fruits of his ministry when the depression was most severe. Peter was an experienced sailor, and, in a paper on coping with fog at sea, he wrote: 'Navigating my boat through fog has been a constant metaphor for my journey through faith.'[14]

Corporate or collective darkness

In recent years a number of writers have spoken of a corporate or collective dark night. Several years after Alan Ecclestone published *The Night Sky of the Lord*, John Vincent wrote of 'a time of darkness for the church', while in 1997 Mary Grey, writing of the dark night, saw it as applicable to the Church itself.[15] One North American Anglican priest has written of 'a dark age in parish ministry', while a Roman Catholic priest has referred to a dark night of priesthood.[16] For years people have written of darkness in the political world.[17] It is not too much to say that there is a 'collective dark night of the soul' which, painful as it often is, may well be the prelude to renewed vision.

Darkness and the East End

Throughout the ministry in Whitechapel the experience of darkness was one which I observed and shared. It was evident at an obvious level, historically and politically. The East End was linked historically with images of the dark, from William Booth's 'darkest England' and Jack London's 'people of the abyss' to the present day. Much of the time, communities, interest groups, subcultures, even whole populations, are literally 'in the dark' about what the 'principalities and powers' are up to in their schemes of 'regeneration' and 'renewal'. The experience of being on the receiving end of other people's decisions, linked to the façade of 'consultation', is common, if not universal, in inner cities. It is combined with a sense, historically rooted and verified in experience, that there is 'nothing that we can do', and that those in power – the property developers, central government, transnational companies, or the local state with its 'hangers-on' – will get their way. There is a sense of impasse, of paralysis rather than apathy, the fruit, in many cases, of years of struggle, of banging one's head against a brick wall. Much urban life is shaped, distorted, and at times crushed, by darkness — the darkness of physical and mental illness, isolation, perplexity, exhaustion, insecurity and death. Only a theology which has confronted and not avoided such darkness can be a healing force.

Certainly my years in the East End led me to see the centrality of darkness in ministry. We do not know it all, we are often in the dark, and God is not always clear. We live and walk by faith, not by sight, and often the way ahead is obscure. We live, struggle and work within 'the night sky of the Lord'.

13

'The Regulative Principle': theology and the Kingdom of God

Jesus' proclamation of the Kingdom was unacceptable to most of his listeners, not because they thought it could not happen but because they feared it might, and that it would bring down judgment on them.

JOHN HOWARD YODER, *The Politics of Jesus*
(Eerdmans 1972, pp. 88–89)

For me, and for the networks with which I have been associated over the last fifty years, the primary theological stress has been on the Kingdom of God. I had only been a practising Christian for a short time when, in January 1956, at the age of 16, I read in the *Socialist Christian*, the journal of the Socialist Christian League, an article by Gresham Kirkby entitled 'The earth shall rise on new foundations' (the words come from the Internationale). I had no idea who the author was, but it was the first piece of writing which alerted me to the existence of a revolutionary social and political tradition within Anglo-Catholicism. This article was about the good news of the Kingdom of God as a hope for the transformation of this world, and it argued that, if Christian hope was to respond to the challenge of Marxism, it must include and move beyond, not diminish, the hope that 'the earth shall rise on new foundations'. The article was a turning point in my life as a Christian and a socialist.

Several years later, I met Gresham Kirkby in East London and we became close friends. He was parish priest of St Paul's, Bow Common, from 1951 to 1994, the longest-serving parish priest of any communion in the East End. Gresham Kirkby, to my knowledge, had only ever written one article, and he had been revising it for almost fifty years. The article in the *Socialist Christian*, based on a talk given to the Socialist Christian League in 1955, was the first version. In 1975 he circulated a four-page duplicated sheet to members of the Jubilee Group in which he made some revisions. In June 1977, he read a paper at a conference in Bethnal Green entitled 'The return of the Kingdom of God: the regulative principle of theology'. In 1983, having revised it further, he published an essay in a book which Rowan Williams and I edited, entitled 'Kingdom Come: the Catholic faith and millennial hopes'.[1]

The Kingdom theology of Anglo-Catholic socialism

Kirkby saw the Kingdom of God as 'the regulative principle of theology', a term which he took from Percy Widdrington. In 1922 Widdrington had written:

> The call today is to return to what the New Testament calls 'the Gospel of the Kingdom' – the Kingdom of God, the cardinal doctrine of our preaching, regulative of our theology, and the touchstone by which all the activities of the Church are tested. This will involve a Reformation in comparison with which the Reformation of the Sixteenth Century will seem a small thing ... The Church ... must recognise that it is a means and not an end in itself. Its end is the Kingdom of God. So long as men [sic] serve the Church first and what it should promote second, they are not loyal to the Kingdom of God.[2]

A number of Christians today question whether 'kingdom' is an adequate translation of *basileia* as used by Jesus. Linked with this questioning is the fact that, for many people today, kingdom is associated with conquest, victory and control. Andrew Shanks has suggested simply using the Greek word *basileia,* or translating it as 'jurisdiction', as a way of avoiding misleading modern notions of kings and kingdoms, and in this he is joined by Diarmuid O'Murchu. Beverley Harrison and Peter Selby prefer the word 'commonwealth', and Sharon Welch opts for 'the beloved community'.[3] Whatever phrase we use, I am clear that at the heart of my approach to contextual theology has been the symbol of the Kingdom of God. Following the late Norman Perrin, I say 'symbol' rather than 'concept' because the Kingdom of God in biblical tradition is not a concept which can be analysed and comprehended at the cerebral point, but rather a symbol which swallows us up and within which we live our lives and seek to pursue our vision.[4] I agree that it is 'not possible to define the Kingdom in any extensive way'.[5] The Kingdom of God is, in fact, a way of speaking about God's work of transformation within human time and history, and about our co-operation with that work.

The centrality of the Kingdom of God as the regulative principle of theology was a consistent theme of Anglo-Catholic social thought from the time that Percy Widdrington first used that expression in 1922. In the 1950s Stanley Evans picked up the theme: the real division in the Christian world, he claimed, was about the Kingdom of God. To read Widdrington and Evans today is to see how extraordinarily prophetic and visionary they were. For this is precisely the situation we are in as we confront the new forces and new alignments within the Christian world.

> If we turn to the churches we find a two dimensional split. On the one hand the historic split between east and west has been followed particularly in the west by a denominational fragmentation which is today sustained by references to historical formulae the real meaning of which have been obscured by the passage of centuries. On the other hand, running right across these splits is the other one which, stated simply, divides Christians into those who believe in the coming of some kind of Kingdom of God on earth and those who do not.[6]

The rediscovery of the Kingdom of God

However, Wolfhart Pannenberg in 1977 referred to 'a steady erosion of the notion of the Kingdom of God', while a few years later Charles Kammer claimed that the loss of the centrality of the Kingdom had meant the loss of the social dimension of Christianity. Ten years later Marcus Borg called the Kingdom a 'relatively unused notion within the church'.[7] But they are all mistaken. The rediscovery, among Christians of diverse backgrounds and traditions, of the centrality of the Kingdom of God, not only in the teaching of Jesus but in Christian discipleship, preaching and ministry today has been quite striking, and was well under way at the time Pannenberg was writing. Of course it may still be true that 'everyone forces the Kingdom of God violently into his own theological tradition',[8] but to say that the Kingdom of God is a neglected theme is absurd. As Stanley Grenz has said: 'If we were to point to one topic that above all others has inspired the labours of biblical scholars and theologians in the twentieth century, this topic would no doubt be the Kingdom of God.' The recovery among evangelicals has been particularly significant. George Eldon Ladd was emphasising that the Kingdom was a kingdom within history, whose primary concern was not with the salvation of the individual soul but with the salvation of God's people. There was no purely spiritual salvation. Ladd stressed that the Kingdom would come on earth – renewed, but still this earth.[9]

It is worth identifying some of the key features of this rediscovery, of which the most important is its biblical basis. The Kingdom of God is the heart of the Christian gospel, the central social metaphor of salvation. Its centrality in the teaching of Jesus was unique. There is little doubt about this. John Robinson wrote in 1956: 'The Kingdom of God, rather even than the People of God, is the controlling category for both Old and New Testaments.' He went on to stress that a high doctrine of the ministry must give way to a higher doctrine of the Church, and that higher doctrine of the Church must give way to an even higher doctrine of the Kingdom of God.[10]

That the Kingdom of God is the heart of the Christian gospel and central to the teaching and ministry of Jesus is beyond dispute. Thirty years ago Norman Perrin wrote that 'the whole message of Jesus focuses upon the Kingdom of God', and his view is accepted by virtually all New Testament scholars.[11] The Kingdom is a social metaphor of salvation. Its centrality in the teaching of Jesus, with his particular stress on its nearness, and the call to enter it, was unique, 'completely without parallel in any extant writings'.[12] The term was rare in apocalyptic and Jewish literature, even in the Dead Sea Scrolls, while in Jesus it is central. The terms 'Kingdom of God' or 'Kingdom of Heaven' occur 122 times in the synoptic gospels, of which 90 are from the lips of Jesus himself. In his use of the Kingdom as the central theme of proclamation, Jesus filled it with a new content which was without parallel. He took this 'unusual phrase' and made it his 'central symbol'.[13]

While the actual term 'Kingdom of Heaven' does not occur in the Old Testament writings, and 'Kingdom of God' only a few times, there are 9 references to the Kingdom which is ruled by Yahweh, 41 references in which Yahweh is referred to as King, and many to the commitment of God to the transformation of the world. Certainly the prophets of ancient Israel believed that God's will was to establish dominion from sea to sea (Zech. 9:10). In the gospels, the presence of the Kingdom is shown by the casting out of demons by the Spirit of God (Matt. 12:28). In other parts of the New Testament, it is emphasised that we look for 'a kingdom that cannot be shaken' (Heb. 12:28).

The language of the Kingdom in the teaching of Jesus is in contrast to modern western notions of evolution and gradual penetration. Rather, the parables of the mustard seed and the leaven stress surprise, suddenness. The term 'building the Kingdom of God', while it appears often in Christian writing, has no biblical basis. I criticised this term in 1963. It was used by Pope John Paul II at the end of his visit to Britain in the early 1980s, and appeared in the Roman Catholic Bishops of England and Wales' document *Human Rights in the Catholic Church* in 1998.[14] However, Jesus urges us to 'strive first for the Kingdom of God and his righteousness' (Matt. 6:33). The New Testament does call us to be 'co-workers for the Kingdom of God' (Col. 4:11), and uses the idea of 'building' more in relation to the Church, while the Kingdom is to be recognised, received and proclaimed.

Kingdom and Church

From early times the Kingdom of God was distinguished from the Church. The early Christian text the *Didache*, in its eucharistic prayer, asks that the Church may 'be brought together from the ends of the earth' into the Kingdom.[15] However, in many later writers, the Kingdom is (wrongly) identified with the Church. Augustine is not entirely blameless here, for he said that 'the Church even now is the Kingdom of Christ and the Kingdom of Heaven'. The Anglican theologian R. C. Moberly, writing in 1897, said, of the Church, that 'it does not represent – but it is – the Kingdom of God upon earth'.[16]

Certainly the Church is related to the Kingdom, and many theologians have used the idea of the Church as a 'foretaste', while Karl Rahner stressed the 'provisional character' of the Church, and 'her progressive historical surrender to the coming Kingdom of God toward which she moves like a pilgrim'. Yet the Church is a transitional phenomenon. In the fulfilment of the Kingdom, there will be no temple (Rev. 21:22). What is important is that the Church exists for the Kingdom, always looking beyond itself, something which has been stressed in recent Anglican reports but has not penetrated throughout the local churches.[17]

Kingdom theology and social transformation

The belief that the Kingdom of God does involve the transformation of this world has come to be widely accepted among biblically rooted Christians. Many have misinterpreted 'My Kingdom is not of this world' to mean that it has nothing to do with this world. Gedratis wrote:

> The Kingdom of Christ is indeed not of the world of brokenness, sin and cursing. The Kingdom of Christ is the world of love, peace, blessedness, which is a totally creational possibility, but must be struggled for in the power of his resurrection against the powers of darkness.[18]

An otherworldly or individualistic distortion of the Kingdom undermines the social character of redemption itself. The American evangelical Jim Wallis has argued that where there is no clear proclamation of the Kingdom, the result is large numbers of 'saved' individuals who fit very comfortably into the old order, while, in London, the Baptist minister Steve Latham has described the Kingdom of God as 'the social form which regeneration . . . takes'.[19]

Yet many continue to reject the idea that the Kingdom must involve a new social order. Why is this? The late Ronald Preston often stressed that the Kingdom was not 'a future social order' nor 'the outline of a social order',[20] and he is not alone. Yet the idea of *basileia*, kingdom, does include that of a realm over which God's jurisdiction is absolute. Surely this involves a new social order. Tawney once commented that, although the Kingdom of God was more than a new social order, it could hardly be less. Of course, there is the danger of identifying the Kingdom of God with a particular social order, with capitalism or with a particular form of socialism, but this is different from separating it from the social order altogether.

My view is that the Kingdom must stand in judgement over all social orders, though clearly some are closer to it than others. Brueggemann stresses that the Kingdom is 'a social construction of reality that judges and critiques every other social construction of power and authority', while Hauerwas and Willimon have stressed the conflictual element in Kingdom work. 'In praying "Your Kingdom Come" we are in a power struggle that can become violent because the kingdoms of the world rarely give up power without a fight.'[21]

However, while there is a widespread acceptance of the centrality of the Kingdom, many socially concerned Christians are 'implicationists'. They say that the gospel has 'social implications'.[22] I find 'implication-ism' confusing theologically and unhelpful politically. It suggests that the gospel is about one thing but has implications for something else: for example, that the gospel is really about individual salvation but has social implications. The implications seem to be secondary, derivative and, through a common logical jump, optional. I want to urge that the Kingdom of God is central, not peripheral, to the gospel, and that Kingdom and gospel are, at heart, about social reality and social rela-tionships. We need to see ourselves as part of the process of recognition of, and co-operation with, this new social reality. In short, the gospel is not concerned with implications but with redemption.

14

'Keep on Walking': the future of contextual theology

Those who do not change their minds in the course of a decade have probably stopped thinking altogether.

SIR MICHAEL HOWARD, *The Causes of War*
(Temple Smith 1983, p. 6)

The world is turning upside down. And those who are losing altitude in the transaction are not well pleased. But as those who have been held down for so long are allowed to rise, with God's new laws of gravity, we are all of us blessed with the opportunity to rediscover how we are bound to one another, to God, and to all creation.

JIM KELSEY, Bishop of Northern Michigan,
homily given on 30th January 2005

Sing Alleluia and keep on walking.

ST AUGUSTINE OF HIPPO

The future of the East London work

By 2004 the funding had finally come close to its end. I think we were the only project which the Christendom Trust had funded for so long, and we were immensely grateful to them for enabling this work to happen. But the crucial issue was: what is the future? The future of the work, and my own future, were intertwined, but needed to be separated if clear decisions were to be made. When I began this project, I had some clear ideas about its role and direction. By 2004 I was not so clear. Many questions had arisen which I did not envisage at the beginning. My own thinking had changed, and, while I am still the same person, there had been major shifts in how I see God, the world, the Church, theology and myself. For example, I have become more aware of other currents within Christianity than I was in 1990. I have learned much from work with Bangladeshi people which has made me rethink many of my assumptions about 'inter-faith dialogue'. If I look back over the forty and more years since my ordination, the changes have been dramatic, often traumatic, and really important. Yet, in the context of this piece of work, 2004 was a *kairos* time, a time of rethinking, of self-examination, of reappraisal. I was encouraged by the words of my former tutor, the military historian Sir Michael Howard, quoted above. However, the changes were external and structural as well as internal and personal. The East End of 2004 was a different creature from that of 1990, even more so that of 1958 when I first arrived in the area.

During my time at St Botolph's, as is obvious even from reading the newspapers, the shape of the so-called 'City of London' and its relationship with the East End had changed. By the end of the 1990s the whole face of Aldgate in relation to the East End was different. St Botolph's Church is now dominated, geographically, culturally, commercially and, perhaps, theologically, by the financial district, the citadels of mammon.[1] The 'City' has been pushing relentlessly eastwards, and the East End now starts further east than it once did. It was time to rethink and reshape. The ending of the funding was the occasion, not the cause, of the need to rethink the work.

The property developers and estate agents had ceased to refer to my neighbourhood as 'the East End', preferring the gentrified term 'City Fringe'. This encouraged, and was encouraged by, the movement of 'yuppies' into the area, and, as property values soared, the squeezing out of ordinary people who were forced to seek accommodation further east or elsewhere. Most of the City and parts of the East End – parts of Spitalfields, Wapping and the Isle of Dogs in particular – were becoming 'ghettoes' of the super-rich and of highly paid professionals.

This was something which Ruth Glass had predicted years earlier. Earlier still she had introduced the term 'marginal men' into British urban sociology. The 'marginal', she warned, would increasingly figure on the edges of an increasingly affluent society. How right she was. At the 1991 Census, the Spitalfields Ward, where various millionaires live, came top in the list of most deprived wards in Greater London – not for the first time. The data were horrifying: 32.5 per cent unemployed, 29.8 per cent overcrowded, 81.9 per cent who did not own their home.[2]

The environment was constantly and swiftly changing. While I was away for three weeks, 'the gherkin' appeared. This is one of the more polite terms for Norman Foster's 40-storey edifice at 40 St Mary Axe in the City (though I note that the *Financial Times* of 30th June 2005 referred to it as 'the erotic gherkin'!). It dominated the view from my kitchen window in the final years. On 16th October 2004 it won the Stirling Prize, and on 9th December 2005 it was named the best new building on the planet by leading architects in *Building Design* magazine. Yet when I left, it was still half-empty and the owners were losing £35,000 per day in lost rent. What do we make of this kind of lunacy? Apparently not much, and the voices of any kind of prophetic church were remarkably silent. Soon the 217-metre Minerva Tower will put St Botolph's into the shade.

The gherkin and Minerva were only two of many high-rise buildings, each competing with the others for height. Until recently, the buildings have been offices, but, with the proposal for a 60-plus-storey tower south of Blackfriars Bridge, we are likely to see more high-rise dwellings for wealthy professionals. I think there are sound arguments for high-rise dwellings, though there are serious ethical and practical problems. The real issue is not about altitude: it is about inequality, and about the appalling, and growing, disparity between the ultra-rich and the rest of the people. In the past – not least in East London – high-rise dwellings were reserved for poor people, and there was often little concern for the structural safety of the property. Now we have a very different situation, and I hear few voices from the churches against this. As I look back, I blame myself very much for failing to respond adequately to these developments, and for focusing entirely on the needs of the East End at the expense of prophetic critique of the City itself.

There will be other major developments in East London in the coming years in preparation for the Olympics in 2012 in the Lower Lea Valley. What is called 'Thames Gateway' will be the biggest urban development in Europe. Although it is predicted that this will involve 120,000 new homes and 180,000 new jobs, it is not clear to what extent, if at all, the ordinary people of the area will benefit from the developments. Will this be Docklands all over again?

At the same time, there were shifts in the shape of the churches over these years. New voices were being heard in East End Christianity. One of the most interesting features has been the arrival of a number of young Baptist ministers who are strongly influenced by the Anabaptist tradition and have formed a network called Urban Expression. One of these is Karen Stallard who has founded a community church in Wapping. Karen has written that 'these voices are speaking the language needed for the church in the inner city today, a language which is straight-talking, peace-making and humble, a language which is active and alive, a language which speaks of love and suffering before all other things'. The emergence of Urban Expression is not unlike the New Monasticism movement in the USA.[3]

Increasingly I felt that it was important to withdraw from the East End. I had seen so much innovative work ruined by the fact that its founders stayed on, interfered and, 'with the best will in the world', breathed down the necks of their successors, making life impossible for them. Charles Landry and his colleagues pointed out in 1985 that those who set up projects 'find it hard to let go of the levers of control at a later stage', and regard the project as 'their baby'. If they do not withdraw, progress through the deadlock can often occur only through the 'ritual slaughter' of the founder. If this does not happen, the consequences for the project are usually decline and decay.[4] So even if the money had come rolling in, we would, I hope, have felt the need to rethink the whole idea. In 1990 it seemed sensible to base the project at St Botolph's, which, although technically in the City, was heavily involved with, and drew many people from, the East End. By the end of the 1990s this was no longer the case. There had been a gradual but clear withdrawal from the margins towards the more comfortable and 'safe space' of the City. We needed, therefore, to consider the future in the light of all the demographic, economic, political and religious shifts, as well as the changes of persons involved. It seemed to me that the way in which St Botolph's was developing had less and less obvious connection to the East End and to my work. While the people there were very kind and supportive, only a small number lived in the East End or had any connection with, or understanding of, the issues there. Though still technically 'outside the gate', it was, and remains, very much within it. The future of this work had to be elsewhere.

By 2003 the whole business of moving lots of books and papers to places where they would be most useful had become a nightmare. Many have now gone to St Katharine's Foundation in Butcher Row, while others are in libraries throughout the country. Many remain with me, and will take several years to sort and relocate. I am anxious that the material should be accessible to future generations concerned with urban work and ministry.

In order to move forward we had set up a working party to look at the options for the work after the Christendom Trust grant came to an end. These seemed to be three: that the work came to an end; that it continued in the present form, which would have involved major fund-raising again; and that it was absorbed into some other framework. The general view of the group was that we should seek to avert the first option, and should be wary of a too formalised structure in which what one member called the 'creative chaos' of the project might be lost. In our discussion we moved away from an earlier idea of a theological 'institute' in the conventional sense of a building with a college-type geographical base. Rather we favoured maintaining the work in its present form for a few years, but seeking to develop it more into a model of theological work which could, at the appropriate time, be offered to the wider community, including the Church, as a contribution to future work in the area. Indeed, it seemed that some of the fruits of the path followed were already evident in the working practices of people in various places. We wanted to emphasise a paradigm, a style, which perhaps needed to be loosely structured into a network, sufficiently detached from me as an individual that it could be disseminated and spread about.

The advantages of such a network would be that it would affirm and strengthen the corporate character of theological work; and that it would provide a base which would be independent of me, would survive my departure, senility or sudden death, and would help to move beyond any harmful indicators of personal idiosyncrasy or 'one-man band' ethos. The disadvantages would be that it might be yet another group for people who were already busy; that it could, unless we took careful precautions, become clerical, white, Anglican and Christian dominated, and so further disable people who did not fit those labels; and that it could lack resources, and therefore teeth, if it remained vague and amorphous. Nevertheless, the experience of other networks (such as the Community Research Networks in Tower Hamlets and Newham) suggested that it could work well.

Our proposal for a Contextual Theology Network for East London was publicised for some years before I left. The network would seek to be a facility for the Christian communities in the East End, and beyond them, building on and developing the work begun here. There were already similar groups in Birmingham, Manchester, Sheffield, Newcastle, West London, and elsewhere, and there were similar proposals in other places. They involve close links between local Christian communities, other local-based projects, universities, and other groups. In Manchester, for example, it has been said that 'led by Elaine Graham . . . Manchester is set to become, once again, the leading academy in Britain in Christian social thought and practice'.[5] This is very exciting, as I have discovered since moving to Manchester in 2004. There was even a gathering of Anglican contextual theologians in Cambridge, Massachusetts in May 2003. On 19th January 2004 a group of us met at the Royal Foundation of St Katharine to discuss the future in some detail. Soon after we heard that the Court of the Foundation had agreed that we could set up a Contextual Theology Network for East London there. The arrival of Fr Angus Ritchie at St Katharine's in January 2005, and the establishment there of the Contextual Theology Centre under his direction, is a good omen for the future. The appointment of Fr David Paton, a priest with considerable East End experience, as the new Master from 2006 is also a welcome development.

The future of the Church

A key issue for the Church of England, as for many parts of the Church, is the fact that, in many places, the Church has become a 'clerical reservation'. The laity has disappeared, except as consumers of sacramental and verbal ministrations, as customers and volunteers within the institution. This may seem an outrageous claim in the light of the immense involvement of lay people in church life, and of the clear increase in theological education involving what the Vatican once quaintly referred to as 'the non-ordained faithful'. There have been movements for, and books about, 'the liberation of the laity' for many years. My experience, however, is that lay people remain second-class citizens, devalued, not least within church congregations. They are seen as important and indispensable aids to the running of the business of the Church, which is basically controlled by clergy.

Yet 'the laity', the *laos*, *is* the people of God, and, if they disappear, the Church disappears.[6] The use of the terms 'lay' and 'laity' bring out, and focus, the central issue: what is the Church? In popular discourse, laity means inferior, second-rate, untrained. Even Rowan Williams recently described William Stringfellow as a 'lay theologian' as if that were some peculiar kind of theologian, while John Habgood, former

Archbishop of York, used the same term about Baron Von Hügel. Others write of 'lay theology'.[7] This kind of language suggests that 'normal' theology is done by clerics, while 'lay theology' is some radical, unusual innovation. I believe that the exact opposite is the case: most theology is done by 'lay' people, much academic theology is now written by 'lay' people, and ordained persons perform an important, though statistically minor, role in this activity. The use of 'lay' as a euphemism for inferior continues to trouble me. One recent handbook for people seeking ordained ministry spoke about the need for the Church – that is, the clergy – to 'mobilise lay people',[8] although the Church, for the most part, *is* lay people.

My experience in the Diocese of Northern Michigan is important here. This diocese is one of the largest and poorest in the USA. Indeed, many people in the USA seem unaware that Northern Michigan, or, as it is usually known, the Upper Peninsula, exists at all. They think Michigan ends at Detroit. But beyond Detroit, going up to the Canadian border, is a vast area, mostly rural, where the church has faced, and responded to, enormous problems. We have much to learn from them.

When I first went to speak in Northern Michigan, two things hit me. The first was that, in spite of the enormous geographical distances – fifty to a hundred miles between one parish and another – most of the people seemed to know one another. This seemed to be a community which was accustomed to co-operative work. The second was that I could not tell who were the clergy and who were the laity. When I mentioned this, and congratulated the people on it, an elderly woman stood up, and said, 'In this diocese we have abolished the word ' "laity" '. Although they knew it was a biblical word, they felt that it was now so tarnished, so damaged, that, for the foreseeable future, it was unusable. It meant inferior, second-rate, untrained, and so on. So they only spoke of 'the Church' and of 'the people of God'. In Northern Michigan, there has been a real recovery of what is called 'total ministry', the ministry of all the baptised. Baptism is seen as more important than ordination, and this has led to a church in which all minister on a basis of equality. When I visited the diocese last, the number of paid clergy, including the bishop and archdeacon, numbered nine. What began as an economic necessity – the survival of the church – quickly became a theological renewal, a transforming rediscovery of the nature of the Body of Christ.[9]

The future of contextual theology

Northern Michigan is not alone. Local-based theological work goes on in all sorts of places. I visited All Saints, Pasadena, California, where they ran a reflection programme on their various projects entitled 'What in God's name are we doing?' The Education for Ministry (EFM) programme, which emanates from Sewanee, Tennessee, has been enormously successful in rooting theology in local communities. There are many examples in Britain also. I believe that our little experiment in Whitechapel has contributed to the essential work of local theology. This is not, and must never become, a special type of theology. It is rather Christian theology as it engages with the specific character and needs of local communities. If theology fails to do this, it withers and decays as a discipline.

The future of the world

I began this book with the theme of movement. The movement into the future is, literally, of critical importance. In the year 2000 there was a great flurry of interest in what was called 'the Millennium'. Much of it was confused, and at times absurd, and little is now left of it apart from the ill-fated 'dome' in Greenwich and other relics. In a largely non-Christian culture, it was hardly surprising that there was confusion. Churches, particularly those of the evangelical brand, displayed – and many still display – posters announcing that the year 2000 was the anniversary of the 'birthday of Christ'. What kind of theology was involved here is unclear, but, whatever it was, it made little impact on the mass of the people, and reinforced the idea that churches lived in a kind of backwater of ideas. The Jubilee Group and others tried to treat the issue of millennial hope seriously, and for us it raised the question of the place of the future in the activity and thinking of the present. This concern was at the heart of our thinking about the future of theology in the East End, but it seemed vital to locate it within the context of the future of humanity, the world and the universe.

Eschatology, the doctrine of the 'end', is often dismissed by Christians and others as the preserve of fanatics and of those who have abandoned any hope for this world. I want to argue that it is of the greatest importance to any creative theological work. Christians are called to be 'a people of the last times, the people of the new age'.[10] The future of theology, in East London and elsewhere, can only be discussed within the context of the theology of the future. As Daniel Jenkins once put it, 'it is the world to come which writes the agenda for the Church'.[11]

References

Introduction

1. On these themes see my books listed in the bibliography below as well as *The Social God* (Sheldon Press 1981; reprinted by Wipf Stock 2003); *Spirituality and Pastoral Care* (Sheldon Press 1986: Cambridge MA, Cowley Press 1989); *True God* (Sheldon Press 1985: entitled *Experiencing God* in the USA, Eugene, Oregon, Wipf Stock 2002); *True Prayer* (Sheldon Press 1980, Harrisburg PA, Morehouse 1995).

Chapter one

1. Alasdair MacIntyre, *Whose Justice? Which Rationality?*, Duckworth 1988, pp. 357, 396.
2. Kenneth Leech, *Care and Conflict: leaves from a pastoral notebook*, Darton, Longman & Todd 1990.
3. The phrase comes from Ruth Musgrave (ed.), *Theology in the Making*, Birmingham, National Centre for Christian Communities Network, July 1982, p. 2.
4. Howard W. Stone and James O. Duke, *How to Think Theologically*, Minneapolis, Fortress Press 1996, p. 2.
5. See Judith Thompson and Stephen Pattison, 'Reflecting on reflection: problems and prospects for theological reflection', *Contact* 146 (2005), pp. 8–15.
6. V. A. Demant, *An Interpretation of the Aims of the Christendom Trust*, Christendom Trust, undated.
7. Gustavo Gutiérrez, *We Drink from Our Own Wells: the spiritual journey of a people*, ET, Orbis 1984.
8. Sara Maitland and Wendy Mulford, *Virtuous Magic: women saints and their meaning*, Mowbray 1998, p. 2.
9. I am grateful to my friend Greg Smith for this approach to 'biblical roads'.
10. *Letter to Diognetus* 5–6.
11. Richard Sennett, *The Conscience of the Eye: the design and social life of cities*, Faber 1993.
12. Joseph O'Leary cited in Rowan Williams, *On Christian Theology*, Blackwell 2000, p. 15.
13. Maurice Wiles, 'Theology in the 21st century', *Theology* (November–December 2000), pp. 403–411; Jeffrey Stout, *The Flight from Authority*, University of Notre Dame Press 1981, p. 148.
14. Wes Seeliger, *Western Theology*, Atlanta, Forum House 1973.
15. Elisabeth Schüssler-Fiorenza, *Jesus: Miriam's child, Sophia's prophet*, SCM Press 1995, p. 10.
16. See Gavin D'Costa, 'The end of systematic theology', *Theology* (September–October

1992), pp. 324–334; Nicholas Lash, *Theology on the Way to Emmaus,* SCM Press 1986, p. x. Peter McGeary, in an address to the Tower Hamlets Clergy Conference at Ely on 24th June 2003, called for a 'theology of mess'.

17. Luigi Zoja, *Cultivating the Soul,* Free Association Books 2005, p. 76.

18. Kenneth Leech, *Through Our Long Exile: contextual theology and the urban experience,* Darton, Longman & Todd 2001.

19. Langdon Gilkey, 'Dissolution and reconstruction in theology', *The Christian Century,* 3rd February 1965, reprinted in Dean Pearman (ed.), *Frontline Theology,* Richmond VA, John Knox Press 1967, p. 29.

20. Stanley G. Evans, *The Faith We Teach,* Church Literature Association 1975.

Chapter two

1. Orlando E. Costas, *Christ Outside the Gate,* Orbis 1982; Brian Castle, *Unofficial God: voices from beyond the walls,* SPCK 2004; Malcom Johnson, *Outside the Gate: St Botolph's and Aldgate 950–1994,* Stepney Books 1994.

2. See Irene Monroe, 'Taking theology to the streets', *The Witness* (July–August 2001), pp. 9–11.

3. J. B. Metz, *Faith in History and Society,* Burns Oates 1980, pp. 58–59.

4. J. A. Dodd, 'Trouble in a City parish under the Protectorate', *English Historical Review,* January 1895.

5. Michael De-la-Noy, *The Church of England: a portrait,* Simon & Schuster 1993, p. 146. For another highly sympathetic account of the ministry at St Botolph's, see Sister Catherine SLG, 'Faith (and hope and love) in the city', *Fairacres Chronicle* 28:2 (Summer 1995), pp. 27–32.

6. Cornel West, Inaugural Aims of Religion Address, 13th April 1994, Divinity School, University of Chicago, in *Criterion* (Spring–Summer 1994), pp. 16–25.

7. For accounts of some of this history see my *The Sky Is Red: discerning the signs of the times,* Darton, Longman & Todd 1997, pp. 91–97.

8. For more detailed discussion of drug abuse see my books *Pastoral Care and the Drug Scene,* SPCK 1970, and *Drugs and Pastoral Care,* Darton, Longman & Todd 1998.

9. Mary Beasley, *Mission on the Margins,* Lutterworth 1997.

10. The Revd John Ansell, personal communication, 13th May 2002.

11. Jennifer Phillips, 'Same sex unions', *The Witness* (December 1994), pp. 28–29.

12. Melissa M. Wright in Jean Comaroff and John L. Comaroff (eds.), *Millennial Capitalism and the Culture of Neoliberalism,* Durham NC, Duke University Press 2001, pp. 127, 139.

13. [Paula Skidmore] *Report of the Working Party on Prostitution and Commercial Sex Work in London E1,* Providence Row Charity and Toynbee Hall, April 2003. Paula had done her work well, though I was a little alarmed at what seemed to be a well-intentioned oversimplifying of history. Like many writers, she saw the Street Offences Act of 1959 as bringing about a major change. I was living at the heart of the 'red light district' of the East End – in a former brothel in fact – in August 1959 when that Act was passed. As I recall, it made virtually no difference to the street activity, and the soliciting continued below my window at 84 Cable Street. Nor am I sure that it is correct to claim, as Paula does, that 'the vice trade moved more decisively to Soho' (where I lived and worked for some years after 1967). However, it was good that three

organisations, one of them national, were concerned with this question which had
been of growing concern to us for some years.

For earlier writing on East End prostitution see David Downes, *The Delinquent
Solution*, Routledge 1965; Kenneth Leech, 'Human casualties in a crisis district', *East
London Papers* 11:1 (Summer 1968), pp. 3–19, and 'The end of the Dolling era? Joe
Williamson in Stepney' in Kenneth Leech, *The Anglo-Catholic Social Conscience: two
critical essays*, Croydon, Jubilee Group 1991, pp. 13–23; C. H. Rolph, *Women of the
Streets: a sociological study of the common prostitute*, Secker and Warburg for the
British Social Biology Council 1955; and Joseph Williamson, *Father Joe*, Hodder &
Stoughton 1963.

14. Robert J. Schreiter, *The New Catholicity*, Orbis 1997, p. 59. It has been claimed that
marginalisation is 'the greatest single problem facing the world in the Third Millennium' (D. Landes, *The Wealth and Poverty of Nations*, New York, Little, Brown &
Company 1998, p. xx).

15. Michel de Certeau, *The Practice of Everyday Life*, ET, Berkeley, University of California Press 1984, p. xvii. On marginality see H. F. Dickie-Clark, *The Marginal
Situation*, Routledge & Kegan Paul 1966; Arthur W. Frank III, 'Marginal man', *Ency-
clopaedia of Sociology*, Guilford CT, Dushkin 1974, p. 165; Thomas Ford Hoult in
Dictionary of Modern Sociology, Totowa NJ, Littlefield, Adams & Co. 1972; Janice E.
Perlman, *The Myth of Marginality: urban poverty and politics in Rio de Janiero*, Berkeley, University of California Press 1976, pp. 93–96.

16. See Jung Young Lee, *Marginality: the key to multicultural theology*, Minneapolis,
Fortress Press 1995; D. C. Duling, *Matthew and Marginality*, SBL 1993 Seminar
Papers, Atlanta, Scholars Press 1993, pp. 642–671; Gill Goulding IBVM, 'Celebrating
grace in and through the sacrament of their own lives – listening to the urban mar-
ginalised', *New Blackfriars*, January 1996, pp. 10–20; Carol Nelson et al., *Border
Crossings: resources of hope in community work with women in Greater Manchester*, MS
undated; Hannah Ward and Jennifer Wild, *Guard the Chaos*, Darton, Longman &
Todd 1995.

17. Christine D. Pohl, *Making Room: recovering hospitality as a Christian tradition*, Grand
Rapids, Eerdmans 1999.

18. Walter Brueggemann, *Interpretation and Obedience*, Minneapolis, Fortress Press
1991, p. 199.

19. Jan Berry, 'Rocking the boat or walking on water?', *Foundations* (Autumn 1999), p. 28.

20. Stuart Murray and Anne Wilkinson-Hayes, *Hope from the Margins: new ways of being
church*, Cambridge, Grove Booklets 2000, p. 3. See also Stuart Murray, 'Living on the
margins', *Anabaptism Today* (Autumn 2000), pp. 4–10.

21. Reginald Fuller, foreword to J. M. Barnett, *The Diaconate: a full and equal order*, New
York, Seabury Press 1981, p. xi.

22. John M. Collins, *Diakonia: reinterpreting the ancient sources*, Oxford University Press
1990, especially Chapter One 'The latter-day Servant Church' (pp. 5–45).

23. See, for example, Bennet J. Sims, *Servanthood: leadership for the third millennium*,
Boston, Cowley Press 1997. Sims sees servanthood as an 'attitude of the soul' (p. 29).
For warnings about the dangers in the use of 'servant' language see L. William
Countryman, *Living on the Border of the Holy: renewing the priesthood of all*, Harris-
burg, Morehouse 1999, p. 99. Some of the literature on the 'servant church' is very

lacking in rigour. For example, Don May and Margaret Simey, *The Servant Church in Granby* (University of Liverpool, Centre for Urban Studies 1989) ignores the servant idea altogether, and uses the word 'serve' once!

24. Richard Holloway, *Let God Arise,* Mowbray 1972, p. 21.
25. Ann Morisy, *Beyond the Good Samaritan*, Mowbray 1997.
26. Evelyn Underhill, *An Anthology of the Love of God,* Mowbray 1953, p. 123 f.
27. English and Welsh Roman Catholic Bishops, *The Permanent Diaconate*, 1987, p. 7.
28. Stanley G. Evans, *The Church in the Back Streets*, Mowbray 1962, pp. 5, 13.
29. John L. Jackson Jr, *Harlem World: doing race and class in contemporary black America,* University of Chicago Press 2001, p. x.
30. David Brandon, *Dharma and Homelessness*, MS, undated.

Chapter three

1. Aidan Kavanaugh OSB, 'Response: primary theology and liturgical act', *Worship* 57 (1983), pp. 321–334; and *Elements of Rite,* Collegeville, Liturgical Press 1990, p. 21. Frank Senn has said that today's congregations have often turned into 'an audience to be entertained rather than nurtured as a holy people with gifts to be exercised' (Frank C. Senn, 'What has become of the liturgical movement?', *Pro Ecclesia* 6:3 (Summer 1997), pp. 319–332. Joseph Gelineau referred to 'clergy managers' and 'lay consumers' (Joseph Gelineau, *The Liturgy Today and Tomorrow,* Darton, Longman & Todd 1978, p. 67).
2. Urban T. Holmes III, *Turning to Christ*, New York, Seabury Press 1981, p. 88.
3. According to Martin Buber, the religion of Israel begins with 'abiding astonishment' (*Moses*, Atlantic Highlands NJ, Humanities Press International 1946, pp. 75–76). See Walter Brueggemann, *Abiding Astonishment*, Louisville, Westminster John Knox Press 1991.
4. Arthur Vogel, *Is the Last Supper Finished?,* New York 1968, p. 64.
5. Catherine Madsen, 'Kitsch and liturgy', *Tikkun* 16:2 (March–April 2001), pp. 41–46. Cf. Ulrich Simon's complaint that modern liturgies offer no glory, no dread, no exultation and no weeping (*Theology*, May 1971, pp. 201–204).
6. Augustine, Sermon 1 on Psalm 32, used as the reading for St Cecilia's Day in the Liturgy of the Hours. The theme of the 'new song' is a common one biblically. See, for example, Ps. 33:3; 96:1; 144:9; Isa. 42:10; Rev. 5:9; 14:3. Cf. Thomas Merton: 'The Psalms are the new song, the *canticum novum*, the song of those who have been reborn in the new creation' (cited in George Woodcock, *Thomas Merton, Monk and Poet: a critical study,* Edinburgh, Canongate 1978, p. 53). See also Gareth Moore OP, 'Singing a new song: music and justice in the Bible', *Theology* (May–June 2004), pp. 159–168.
7. Walter Brueggemann, 'The daily voice of faith: the covenanted self', *Sewanee Theological Review* 37:2 (Easter 1994), pp. 123–143.
8. Stanley G. Evans, *The Church in the Back Streets*, Mowbray 1962, p. 28.
9. See Sanjeev Khagram, *Dams and Developments: transnational struggles for water and power*, Cornell University Press 2005; and Veronica Strang, *The Meaning of Water*, Oxford, Berg 2004.
10. Irenaeus, *Adv. Haer.* 5:2.2–3.

11. *Orate Fratres* 9 (1934–35), p. 545; R. Hovda, 'The Mass and its social consequences', *Liturgy* 80, 13:5 (June–July 1982), p. 6.

12. Kenneth Leech, *The Social God*, Sheldon Press 1980 and Wipf & Stock 2003.

Chapter four

1. James W. McClendon, *Systematic Theology: ethics*, Nashville, Abingdon Press 1986, p. 33.

2. Oliver O'Donovan, *The Desire of the Nations: rediscovering the roots of political theology*, Cambridge University Press 1996, p. 3.

3. Enoch H. Oglesby, *Born in the Fire*, New York, Pilgrim Press 1990, p. ix.

4. See Donald Nicholl, 'Is there a *locus classicus* for theology?', *Tantur Yearbook* 1981–82, pp. 137–149.

5. Rowan Williams, 'Rediscovering Augustine', *Church of England Newspaper*, 19th November 1999; Karl Barth, *Romans*, ET, Oxford University Press 1960 edn, p. 430.

6. Maggie Hewitt in *Rising East* 2:2 (1999), pp. 159–163.

7. See Juan Luis Segundo, *A Theology for Artisans of a New Humanity*, Orbis, 5 Volumes, 1968–74.

8. I am grateful to the Revd Sue Faulkner for permission to reprint this document. I hope it will inspire others to use the biblical texts in a similar way.

9. See Michael Herzfeld, *The Social Production of Indifference: exploring the symbolic roots of western bureaucracy*, Oxford, Berg 1992.

10. Fernando Coronil in Jean Comaroff and John L Comaroff (eds.), *Millennial Capitalism and the Culture of Neoliberalism*, Durham NC, Duke University Press 2001, pp. 63, 64.

11. Ched Myers in *Sojourners,* December 1987, p. 34.

12. Thomas Merton, *The Asian Journal of Thomas Merton*, Sheldon Press 1974, p. 306.

13. Peter Rose, *Reflections on Sailing and Spirituality*, privately published 2005, p. 19; R. D. Laing, *The Politics of Experience and the Bird of Paradise,* Penguin 1967, p. 108.

14. On trial see Ulrich Simon, *The Trial of Man*, Mowbray 1973.

15. Andrew Shanks, '*What Is Truth?' Towards a theological poetics*, Routledge 2001, pp. 13–24 on 'the pathos of shakenness'; Alan Ecclestone, letter in *Industrial Christian Fellowship Quarterly* (October 1977), p. 14.

16. Ched Myers, *Who Will Roll Away the Stone?,* Maryknoll, Orbis 1994; Peter McGeary, talk at the Tower Hamlets Clergy Conference, Ely, 24th June 2003; Nicholas Lash, *Theology on the Way to Emmaus*, SCM Press 1986, p. x.; Peter Medawar, *Pluto's Republic*, Oxford University Press 1984, p. 46.

17. See Robert Beckford, *God of the Rahtid: redeeming rage*, Darton, Longman & Todd 2001. For more on anger see Audre Lorde, 'The uses of anger: women responding to racism' in *Sister Outsider*, Trumansburg NY, The Crossing Press 1984, pp. 124–133.

18. Caroline Cox and Rachel Tingle, 'The new barbarians', *Salisbury Review* (October 1986), pp. 22–27.

19. J. L. Houlden, *Kenneth Leech as Community Theologian at St Botolph's, Aldgate,* 1998; Peter Sedgwick in David F. Ford (ed.), *The Modern Theologians,* Blackwell 1997, pp. 298–300; Steve Latham, *New Life in Paddington: a theological examination of urban regeneration*, Jubilee Group Discussion Paper 140, May 2001.

20. Kenneth Leech, 'Civil war in the East End', *East London Advertiser*, 9th September 1993.
21. Sue Mayo and Nic Holtam, *Learning from the Conflict,* Croydon, Jubilee Group 1994.
22. Ted Johns, cited in Caroline Adams and Gilli Salvat, *Once Upon a Time in Docklands*, Docklands Forum 1994, p. 5.
23. Kenneth Leech, *Brick Lane* 1978: *the events and their significance,* revised edition, Stepney Books 1993; *Struggle in Babylon*, Sheldon Press 1988, *Through Our Long Exile*, Darton, Longman & Todd 2001, and *Race*, SPCK 2005; and *Political Speech and Race Relations in a Liberal Democracy*, Report to Paddy Ashdown, December 1988.
24. See Kenneth Leech, *The Sky Is Red: discerning the signs of the times,* Darton, Longman & Todd 1997, Chapter Three, 'Fear and Fascism' (pp. 63–86).

Chapter five

1. See Kenneth Leech, *Youthquake: the growth of a counter culture through two decades,* Sheldon Press 1973.
2. Tim Gorringe, *Church Action Against Racism*, Christian Action for Justice in Immigration Law 1998. A good example of the notion that the Church should be concerned with 'spiritual' matters, leaving 'politics' to the professionals occurred in the advice given by former Home Secretary David Blunkett to the new Archbishop of Canterbury, Rowan Williams. 'Teach me about theology and spiritualism [*sic*]. Let me teach you about politics' (*Any Questions*, BBC Radio 4, 28th February 2003).
3. On culture and its complexities, see John W. O'Malley, *Four Cultures of the West,* Harvard University Press 2005.
4. H. Richard Niebuhr, *Christ and Culture,* New York, Harper & Row 1951.
5. See Cornel West, *Race Matters*, New York, Vintage Press 1994, pp. 18, 19, 29; and *Democracy Matters*, New York, Penguin Press 2004, especially Chapter Two, 'Nihilism in America' (pp. 25–62).
6. David Nicholls, *A Great Mystery,* Jubilee Group 1978.
7. Conrad Noel, *Jesus the Heretic,* Religious Book Club 1939, p. 27.
8. This did not please Mr Kensit of the Protestant Truth Society. When a friend of mine phoned him in 1959 to ask if he could recommend a 'sound church' in the East End, he described it as 'a barren part of the Lord's vineyard', and said that Christ Church was no longer sound! He recommended St James the Less, Bethnal Green, though, after the arrival of Ted Roberts, a very socially conscious evangelical, he changed his mind!
9. For the background of recent evangelical social thought see Kenneth Leech, *The Social God,* Sheldon Press 1981, especially Chapter One, 'Christian Social Action: its theological basis' (pp. 1–14).
10. *Soul Friend* was published by Sheldon Press in 1977, and reissued in a revised edition by Darton, Longman & Todd in 1994.
11. Richard Buck, 'Still losing our bearings', *SPIDIR Newsletter* 60, Autumn 2003.
12. John MacMurray cited in Jim Cotter (ed.), *Firing the Clay: occasional writings of Alan Ecclestone*, Sheffield, Cairns Publications 1999, p. 14.
13. The revised edition of *The Sky Is Red* appeared in 2003 with a new foreword by Rowan Williams based on his review in the *Church Times* on 7th November 1997. He

began by referring to an essay on Saunders Lewis which described him as a 'Necessary Figure'. He went on to say: 'I suspect that Ken Leech has become for many of us a Necessary Figure in much this sense.' I well recall the first person who rang me that Friday and asked to speak to 'the Necessary Figure'. He ended: 'The plain truth is that no one else writes with such authority about the pastoral (and prophetic) task in our church at the moment. Every chapter challenges – a Necessary Book.' That was very kind if a bit embarrassing.

14. Bruce Kenrick, *Come Out The Wilderness*, Fontana 1962, p. 155. I have discussed this in greater detail in my chapter 'On being a prophet and a theologian: reflections on Stringfellow and the East Harlem Protestant Parish' in Anthony Dancer (ed.), *William Stringfellow in Anglo-American Perspective,* Ashgate 2005, pp. 105–113, on which the material here is based. For more on Stringfellow see Robert Boak Slocum (ed.), *Prophet of Justice, Prophet of Life: essays on William Stringfellow,* New York, Church Publishing 1997.
15. William Stringfellow, *My People Is the Enemy,* New York, Holt, Rinehart & Winston 1964, p. 88.
16. J. Miguez-Bonino in Rex Ambler and David Haslam (eds.), *Agenda for Prophets,* Bowerdean Press 1980, p. 104.
17. A. M. Ramsey, *From Gore to Temple: the development of Anglican theology between* Lux Mundi *and the Second World War* 1889–1939, Longmans 1960, p. 14.
18. E. R. Norman, *The Victorian Christian Socialists*, Cambridge University Press 1987, p. 173; William Temple, *Christianity and the State*, Macmillan 1929, and *Citizen and Churchman*, Eyre & Spottiswoode 1941; David Nicholls, 'William Temple and the welfare state', *Crucible* (October–December 1984), pp. 161–168.
19. David Nicholls and Rowan Williams, *Politics and Theological Identity,* London, Jubilee Group 1984, p. 20.
20. George Orwell, *Inside the Whale and Other Essays,* Penguin 1979 edn, p. 35; *Daily Worker,* 23rd August 1932.
21. A. M. Ramsey, *The Gospel and the Catholic Church*, Longmans Green & Co. 1936, p. 38.
22. John A. T. Robinson, *On Being the Church in the World*, SCM Press 1963, p. 70; John Davies in Kenneth Leech and Rowan Williams (eds.), *Essays Catholic and Radical*, Bowerdean Press 1983, pp. 188–189.
23. Stewart Headlam, *The Laws of Eternal Life,* Frederick Verinder 1888, p. 52.
24. Frederic Hastings Smyth, *Discerning the Lord's Body,* Louisville, Cloister Press 1946, pp. 84–85.
25. S. A. Skinner, *Tractarians and the 'Condition of England': the social and political thought of the Oxford Movement*, Oxford, Clarendon Press 2004.
26. James Adderley, 'Christian socialism past and present', *The Commonwealth*, December 1926.
27. J. M. Winter and D. M. Joslin (eds.), *R. H. Tawney's Commonplace Book,* Economic History Review Supplement 5, Cambridge University Press 1972, p. 51.
28. This section is taken from a longer article, published in *Sewanee Theological Review* (Easter 2006), and also draws on material in my book *The Eye of the Storm: spiritual resources for the pursuit of justice,* Darton, Longman & Todd 1992, pp. 122–132.
29. Elaine Graham, Heather Walton and Frances Ward, *Theological Reflection: Methods*,

SCM Press 2005; Frances Ward, *Lifelong Learning; theological education and supervision*, SCM Press 2005. See also Stephen Pattison et al., 'Theological reflection for the real world: time to think again', *British Journal of Theological Education* 13:2 (2003), pp. 119–131.

30. See Imre Lakatos, *The Methodology of Scientific Research Programmes,* Cambridge University Press 1978; and Nancey Murphy, *Theology in the Age of Scientific Reasoning*, Ithaca, Cornell University Press 1990. Sir Peter Medawar, *Pluto's Republic*, Oxford University Press 1984, p. 46 argues that all advances in scientific understanding begin with 'an imaginative preconception of what might be true' and that scientific work involves a dialogue between the imaginative and the critical. See, for an earlier account of scientific reasoning, Karl Popper, *The Logic of Scientific Discovery*, Hutchinson 1959.

Chapter six

1. Dietrich Bonhoeffer, *Gesammelte Schriften*, ed. E. Bethge, Chr Kaiser Verlag, Munich, Vol. 2, pp. 284ff.

2. St Cyril of Alexandria, *Com. on John* Book 10, *PG* 74:434.

3. Vladimir Lossky, *The Mystical Theology of the Eastern Church,* James Clarke 1957. During my regular visits to Chicago over twenty-five years, one of my fondest memories is of a Russian Orthodox woman who attended almost all ecumenical gatherings of theologians in the University of Chicago area. At a certain point in every meeting, she would remind us that, in the Eastern Orthodox tradition, there were only three theologians – St John the Evangelist, St Gregory Nazianzen, and St Symeon the New Theologian. (She frequently forgot the third, and a Lutheran or Anglican would have to remind her.) On one occasion Rowan Williams gave a paper on modern Russian ecclesiology, focusing on the work of Fedotov, Solovyev and Bulgakov. The lady looked somewhat baffled by this display of learning, but she eventually exploded. 'Professor Williams, this has been a very learned paper. You have only made one mistake. You are quite wrong to call these worthy gentlemen theologians. There are only three theologians in Orthodox tradition.'

4. See M. A. McIntosh, *Mystical Theology: the integration of spirituality and theology,* Blackwell 1998; Maggie Ross, *The Fountain and the Furnace*, Paulist Press 1987, p. 196; and all the works of the other writers.

5. Bernice Martin, *A Sociology of Contemporary Cultural Change,* Blackwell 1981, p. 189.

6. Jeremy Seabrook, 'Poverty as metaphor: or why both Peter and Paul feel robbed', *New Society*, 28th February 1980, pp. 439–441.

7. Cheryl Costa, cited in *The Times,* 21st October 1991.

8. D. W. Hardy, *Finding the Church*, SCM Press 2000, p. 95.

9. Maggie Ross, op. cit., p. 196.

10. Ann and Barry Ulanov, *Primary Speech: a psychology of prayer*, Atlanta, John Knox Press 1982.

11. Alan Ecclestone, 'On Praying', originally published in 1968, and reprinted in Jim Cotter, *Firing the Clay: articles and addresses by Alan Ecclestone*, Sheffield, Cairns Publications 1999, p. 60; Alan Ecclestone, *The Scaffolding of Spirit*, Darton, Longman & Todd 1987.

12. St Gregory of Sinai, *Alia capita* 113, *PG* 150:1280A.

13. Julian of Norwich, *Revelations of Divine Love*. The claim that 'God is closer to us than we are to ourselves' also occurs in Eckhart. See M. O. C. Walshe, *Meister Eckhart: Sermons and Treatises*, Watkins 1979, p. 165.

14. *The Ascetical Homilies of Isaac the Syrian*, ET, Boston MA, Holy Transfiguration Monastery 1994.

15. The reading in the Office of Readings in the Roman Liturgy of the Hours for 4th November.

16. St Gregory of Nyssa, *Sermon 5 on the Lord's Prayer*.

17. Walter Wink, 'Prayer and the powers', *Sojourners*, October 1990, pp. 10–14.

18. Gustavo Gutiérrez, *We Drink from Our Own Wells: the spiritual journey of a people*, Orbis 1983, p. xx.

19. St Symeon the New Theologian, *Catecheses* 5:122–141; 6:153–161.

20. Audre Lorde, *Sister Outsider*, op. cit., p. 142.

21. E. L. Mascall, *Theology and the Gospel of Christ*, SPCK 1977, p. 35.

22. Andrew Louth, *The Origins of the Christian Mystical Tradition*, Oxford, Clarendon Press 1981, p. xi.

23. Alan Ecclestone, *A Staircase for Silence*, Darton, Longman & Todd 1977, p. 5. On prayer as protest see Gordon Mursell, *Out of the Deep: prayer as protest*, Darton, Longman & Todd 1989.

Chapter seven

1. Alasdair MacIntyre, *Marxism: an interpretation*, SCM Press 1953; and 'A society without a metaphysics', *The Listener*, 13th September 1956, pp. 375–376.

2. E. L. Mascall, *Via Media: an essay in theological synthesis*, Longmans 1957.

3. T. S. Eliot, *The Idea of a Christian Society*, Faber 1939; *A Kind of Believing*, General Synod Board of Education 1977.

   The notion of 'post-Christian' seems to have antedated most of the other 'posts' by several decades. It was used by J. V. Langmead Casserley, *The Retreat from Christianity in the Modern World* (Longmans 1952), p. 65. Casserley warned that the coming danger was not irreligion but bad religion. Thomas Merton used the phrase in *New Seeds of Contemplation*, New York, New Directions 1961, p. 123. Jacques Elllul's book *The New Demons* (Mowbray 1975) had a chapter entitled 'The post-Christian era and secularization' (pp. 18–47), though, interestingly, the chapter headings read 'Post-Christendom and secularization'. In 2001 Rowan Williams, in *Writing in the Dust: reflections on 11th September and its aftermath* (Hodder & Stoughton 2001, p. 4) said that 'postmodernism blossoms on post-Christian soil'. Around the same time, one Douglas Daft, head of Coca Cola, said that they were becoming 'post-global'!

4. Bruce Anderson, 'As a post-religious society, England has forgotten how to cope with religious fervour', *Independent*, 18th July 2005.

5. Anthony King, 'Britons' belief in God vanishing as religion is replaced by apathy', *Daily Telegraph*, 27th December 2004.

6. Callum Brown, *The Death of Christian Britain*, Routledge 2001, p. 1.

7. This study produced contrasting headlines on 21st September 1978 with 'School age faith in rapid decline' (*The Times*) and 'Teenagers reveal belief in God' (*Guardian*).

8. Madeleine Bunting, *Guardian*, 28th March 2005.

9. I was criticised by a colleague for using the term 'Roman Church' in an earlier book,

rather than 'Catholic Church'. He regarded this usage as insulting and abusive. I intend no insult or abuse, and use it for three reasons. First, I believe that the Catholic Church, of which I am a member, is wider than the community of those in communion with the See of Rome. To use the title 'Catholic Church' exclusively in relation to *Roman* Catholics would indeed be insulting to thousands of Orthodox, Anglican and other Christians. Secondly, it is an accurate description of those Catholic Christians who accept the universal ordinary jurisdiction of the Bishop of Rome. Thirdly, it is a term used by Roman Catholics themselves, and within the last few days before writing these words, I note that Pope Benedict XVI has referred to 'the Roman Church' in his speeches.

10. See various writings by Greg Smith, particularly 'Believing and Belonging in Newham', paper at the Marchant Seminar, 6th June 1995; *Religious Organisations in Newham in* 1998–9, Aston Charities 1989; The Christ of the Barking Road, on the internet; and 'The unsecular city: the revival of religion in East London' in Tim Butler and Michael Rustin (eds), *Rising in the East? The regeneration of East London*, Lawrence & Wishart 1996, pp. 123–145.

11. *Social Trends* 23, HMSO 1993.

12. Diana L. Eck, *A New Religious America*, HarperSanFrancisco 2001, p. 4; *National Catholic Reporter*, 19th April 1991.

13. Roger Haight SJ, *Jesus Symbol of God*, Orbis 1999, p. 456.

14. David Tracy, *Dialogue with the Other*, Peeters Press 1990.

Chapter eight

1. Ruth Glass and John Westergaard, *London's Housing Needs*, Centre for Urban Studies 1965.

2. See R. John Elford, *The Pastoral Nature of Theology*, Cassell 1999; Frances Ward, *Lifelong Learning: theological education and supervision*, SCM Press 2005.

3. Letter from me published in *The Listener*, 18th January 1990.

4. John Eade and Christopher Mele, *Understanding the City*, Blackwell 2002; Christopher R. Mele, *Selling the Lower East Side: culture, real estate and resistance in New York City*, University of Minnesota Press 2000.

5. Saskia Sassen, *The Global City*, Princeton University Press 1991.

6. Christopher Jencks, *The Homeless*, Harvard University Press 1994, Chapter 4, 'The crack epidemic' (pp. 41–48).

7. Carolyn Ye-Myint, *Who's Hiding*, No Fixed Abode 1992; Nina Bernstein, *New York Times*, 25th March 2001.

8. Frank Prochaska, *Christianity and Social Service in Modern Britain: the disinherited spirit*, Oxford University Press 2006.

9. *Oratio* 14 *De Pauperum Amore*, PG 35:907–910.

10. Marianne Sawicki, *Seeing the Lord: resurrection and early Christian practice*, Minneapolis, Fortress Press 1994, pp. 89–91.

11. Christine Allen and Barbara D'Arcy (eds), *The Trampled Vineyard: worship resources on housing and homelessness*, Catholic Housing Aid Society and UNLEASH 1992.

12. Phil Barker, obituary of David Brandon, *Guardian*, 13th December 2001.

Chapter nine

1. Kathryn Tanner, 'Incarnation, cross and sacrifice: a feminist-inspired reappraisal', *Anglican Theological Review* 86:1 (Winter 2004), pp. 35–56.
2. Sharon G. Thornton, *Broken Yet Beloved: a pastoral theology of the Cross*, St Louis MO, Chalice Press 2002.
3. Sheila Cassidy in *The Tablet*, 10th–17th April 1993, p. 456.
4. Donald Nicholl, *The Testing of Hearts*, Lamp Press 1989, p. 304.
5. Colin Gunton, *Yesterday and Today: a study of continuities in Christology*, Darton, Longman & Todd 1983, p. 196.
6. For the term 'cruciform church' see Douglas John Hall, 'Responses to the humiliation of the church', *Sewanee Theological Review* 36:4 (Michaelmas 1993), pp. 482–492.
7. *We Preach Christ Crucified* was published in the UK by Darton, Longman & Todd, and in the USA by Cowley Press. The revised edition appeared from Church Publishing Inc. in the USA in 2005 and from Darton, Longman & Todd in the UK in 2006.
8. Beverley Barr, *Stations of the Cross at Christ Church, Eastbourne*, privately published. The stations can be viewed on www.xpeastbourne.org.
9. John Behr, 'The paschal foundations of Christian theology', *St Vladimir's Theological Quarterly* 45:2 (2001), pp. 115–136.

Chapter ten

1. Joerg Rieger, *Theology and the Excluded*, Minneapolis, Fortress Press 2001, p. 4.
2. Ronald J. Sider, *The Scandal of the Evangelical Conscience*, Grand Rapids, Baker Books 2005.
3. Laurie Green, *Let's Do Theology*, Mowbray 1990, p. 125; Margaret Kane, *Theology in an Industrial Society*, SCM Press 1975; Ann Morisy, *Journeying Out: a new approach to Christian mission*, Continuum 2004.
4. Nigel Wright, 'Church without walls', *Baptist Times*, 24th June 1993.
5. Stuart Murray, *Biblical Interpretation in the Anabaptist Tradition*, Waterloo, Pandora Press 2000.
6. Gareth Jones, 'After Kant: the Liverpool Statement', *Reviews in Religion and Theology* (August 1998), pp. 85–91.
7. Ann Morisy, *Journeying Out*, op. cit., pp. 128–129; Anthony Harvey, *By What Authority?*, SCM Press 2001, p. 11.
8. Elaine L. Graham, *Transforming Practice: pastoral theology in an age of uncertainty*, Mowbray 1996; Mark McIntosh, *Mystical Theology: the integrity of spirituality and theology*, Blackwell 1998, p. 22. Cf. Lynne Price, 'Maggots in the luggage: facing contextuality' in Simon Barrow and Graeme Smith (eds), *Christian Mission in Western Society*, Churches Together in Britain and Ireland 2001, pp. 92–105.
9. On context see Roy Dilley (ed.), *The Problem of Context*, New York and Oxford, Berghahn Books 1999; Douglas John Hall, 'The meaning of contextuality in Christian thought' in *Thinking the Faith: Christian theology in a North American context*, Philadelphia, Fortress Press 1991, pp. 69–144.
10. Bertrand Russell, *The Analysis of Mind*, Allen & Unwin 1921, p. 101.
11. See, for example, Chris Baker and Hannah Skinner, *Telling the Stories: how churches are contributing to social capital*, Manchester, William Temple Foundation 2005; Steve

Chalke, *Faithworks: actions speak louder than words,* Eastbourne, Kingsway 2001; *Enterprising Faith: faith in the social economy,* Churches Regional Commission for Yorkshire and the Humber 2004; Jonathan Evens, *Faith in Work: faith communities, employment and vocational training,* North Thames Ministerial Training Course, September 2001; Richard Farnell et al., *Engaging Faith Communities in Urban Regeneration,* Joseph Rowntree Foundation/Policy Press 2003; Robert Furbey and Marie Macey, 'Religion and urban regeneration: a place for faith?', *Policy and Politics* 33:1 (2005), pp. 95–116; Elaine Graham and Chris Baker, *Religious Capital in Regenerating Communities,* Manchester, William Temple Foundation 2004; Anna Greenberg, 'The church and the revitalisation of politics and community', *Political Science Quarterly* 115:3 (Fall 2000), pp. 377–394; *Faith, Hope and Participation: celebrating faith groups' role in neighbourhood renewal,* New Economics Foundation and Church Urban Fund 2001; *More than Happy: the role of faith in wellbeing,* Churches Regional Commission for Yorkshire and the Humber 2004; Sandra C. Newton, *BandAid and Beyond: a study of church involvement in community outreach and vocational training in Urban Priority Areas in Great Britain and the USA,* New York, The Commonwealth Fund 1992; Greg Smith, *Faith-based Groups in Partnership with the State,* MS, University of East London, 26th April 2001.

12. Ruth Glass in David Donnison and David Eversley (eds), *London: urban patterns, problems and policies,* Heinemann 1973, p. 426.

13. Richard Rogers, *Cities for a Small Planet,* Faber 1997, p. 19.

14. See Richard G. Wilkinson, *The Impact of Inequality: how to make sick societies healthy,* Routledge 2005.

15. Kenneth Leech, 'How low can they go?', *East London Advertiser,* 6th January 1994.

16. See Chris Phillipson et al., *Women in Transition: a study of the experience of Bangladeshi women living in Tower Hamlets,* Bristol, Policy Press 2003. On the Bangladeshi community in general see John Eade et al., 'The Bangladeshis: the encapsulated community' in Ceri Peach (ed.), *Ethnicity in the 1991 Census,* Vol. 2, Office of National Statistics 1996, pp. 150–160.

17. See Muhammad Yunus and Alan Jolis, *Banker to the Poor: the autobiography of Muhammad Yunus, founder of the Grameen Bank,* Aurum Books 1998; Muhammad Yunus, 'The Grameen Bank', *Scientific American* (November 1999), pp. 114–119.

18. Nick Cohen and Mark Gould, 'The East End's forgotten people', *Independent on Sunday,* 23rd August 1992.

19. *East London Advertiser,* 11th September 1992.

20. On khat see Kieran Conlon, *Khat in East London Research Dossier,* East London and City Health Promotion, March 1995; A. S. Elmi, 'The chewing of khat in Somalia', *Journal of Ethnopharmacology* 8 (1983), pp. 163–176; Ezekiel Gebissa, *Leaf of Allah: khat and agricultural transformation,* Oxford, Clarendon Press 2005; *Khat Use in the Somali, Ethiopian and Yemeni Communities: issues and solutions,* Home Office and Turning Point 2005; P. McLaren, 'Khat psychosis', *British Journal of Psychiatry* 150 (1987), pp. 712–713.

21. On the issue of female genital mutilation see Shamis Dirir, 'The female eunuchs', *Time Out,* 7th–14th April 1999, pp. 12–13; Efura Dorkenoo and Scilla Elworthy, *Female Genital Mutilation: proposals for change,* Minorities Rights Group 1992; Julie Flint, 'The first cut', *Guardian,* 25th April 1994; Audrey Gillan, 'The worst cut', *Guardian,*

21st December 2000; Ellen Gruenbaum, *The Female Circumcision Controversy: an anthropological perspective*, University of Pennsylvanuia Press 2001; Esther K. Hicks, *Infibulation: female mutilation in Islamic North Eastern Africa*, New Brunswick, Transaction Books 1993; Donu Kogbara, 'The damaged women of Africa', *Independent*, 1st March 1997; Brigid McConville, 'A bloody tradition', *Nursing Times*, 21st January 1998, pp. 34–36; Alice Walker, *Possessing the Secret of Joy*, Jonathan Cape 1992. The most important recent presentation of the issue is in Ousmane Sembene's film 'Moolaade', based in Burkina Faso.

22. On wider Somali issues see Dooniya Banya, *The Somali Community in Tower Hamlets: a demographic survey*, Wapping Neighbourhood, 26th February 1992; Lee V. Cassanelli, *The Shaping of Somali Society*, Philadelphia, University of Pennsylvania Press 1982; Nuruddin Farah, *Yesterday, Tomorrow: voices from the Somali diaspora*, Cassell 2000; Camillia Fawzi El-Solh, 'Somalis in London's East End: a community striving for recognition', *Immigrants and Minorities* 12:1 (March 1993), pp. 21–46; Rhoda Ibrahim, 'The changing lives of Somali women' in Tina Wallace (ed.), *Changing Perspectives: writings on gender and development*, OXFAM 1991; I. M. Lewis, *A Pastoral Democracy*, Oxford University Press 1961 and *A Modern History of Somalia*, New York, Westview Press 1988; Rima Berns McGown, *Muslims in the Diaspora*, University of Toronto Press 1999; Marion Monteno, *A Shield of Coolest Air*, Shola Books 1992; Said S. Samatar, *Somalia: a nation in turmoil,* Minorities Rights Group 1991.

23. Ruth Miskin, *Superphonics,* Hodder 2000, 5 vols. There was an article about this in the *Daily Telegraph* of 19th July 2000, one of a number which dealt with the school's approach to literacy. See my *Through Our Long Exile* (Darton, Longman & Todd 2001), pp. 146–149, for more on the school.

24. See Stephen K. Roberts, 'The centenary of the WEA', *History Today* (February 2003), pp. 26–28.

25. See *The Sky Is Red*, op. cit., pp. 144–147, and *Through Our Long Exile,* op. cit., pp. 105 f, 115 f.

26. Alan Ecclestone, *Gather the Fragments*, ed. Jim Cotter, Sheffield, Cairns 1993, p. 54.

27. On MacMurray see his *The Philosophy of Communism,* Faber 1933; *Reason and Emotion,* Faber 1935; *Creative Society,* SCM Press 1935; *Conditions of Freedom,* Faber 1956; *The Self as Agent*, Faber 1957; *Persons in Relation*, Faber 1957; *The Search for Reality in Religion*, Allen & Unwin 1965, and 'The community of mankind', *The Listener,* 24th December 1941. See also Samuel Brittan, 'Tony Blair's real guru', *New Statesman*, 7th February 1997, pp. 18–20; Philip Cornford (ed.), *The Personal World of John MacMurray,* Floris Books 1997; Michael Fielding, 'The point of politics: friendship and community in the work of John MacMurray', *Renewal* 6:1 (Winter 19998), pp. 55–64.

28. On Blair and community see Mark D. Chapman, *Blair's Britain: A Christian critique,* Darton, Longman & Todd 2005.

Blair turned up unexpectedly at my flat on 14th January 1997 for a meeting of the East London Jubilee Group which was being addressed by Fiona Macleod on 'Living on benefits' and by his friend Peter Thompson on 'Community'. We assumed that it was a private meeting (from his point of view) and were surprised to find it written up in the 'News from Nowhere' column of the *New Statesman* on 24th January, and by Martin Wroe in the *Observer* under the title 'Hot pursuit of the pious' on 23rd

February. The former article claimed that Blair 'apparently had them [the Jubilee Group] eating out of his hand within minutes'. In fact all the people who spoke disagreed with his position. See the replies from myself and Fr Paul Butler in the *New Statesman* of 31st January 1997.

29. David Cesarani, 'Between a dock and a hard place', *Guardian*, 21st September 1993.
30. On Alinsky and community organising see Saul D. Alinsky, *Reveille for Radicals,* New York, Random House 1946; *Broad Based Organising on Merseyside: a Working Party Report,* Merseyside Churches Urban Institute, April 1991; Ian Davies and Dave Wiles, *Community Organising in the UK?*, Bristol, Children's Society, February 1987; P. David Finks, *The Radical Vision of Saul Alinsky,* New York, Paulist Press 1984; Sanford D. Horwitt, *Let Them Call Me Rebel; Saul Alinsky, his life and legacy,* New York, Knopf 1989; Neil Jameson (ed.) *Organising for a Change, Christian Action Journal* (Autumn 1988); and Jay Macleod, *Community Organising: a practical and theological appraisal*, Christian Action 1993.
31. David Clark, *Breaking the Mould of Christendom*, Epworth Press 2005, writes of 'community or chaos' (pp. 3–12) and of 'the choice between community and chaos' (p. 57). I want to raise questions about this way of seeing it in what is in many respects an excellent book.

Chapter eleven

1. Philip J. Lee, *Against the Protestant Gnostics,* Oxford University Press 1987, p. 3.
2. John A. T. Robinson, *The Body*, SCM Press 1961 edn.
3. Peter Sedgwick in David F. Ford (ed.), *The Modern Theologians,* Blackwell 1997, pp. 298–300.
4. Elaine L. Graham, *Transforming Practice: pastoral theology in an age of uncertainty,* Mowbray 1996, p. 24; Ian Fraser in Ruth Musgrave (ed.), *Theology in the Making*, Birmingham, National Centre for Christian Communities Network, July 1982, p. 7.
5. The Instruction was printed in *The Tablet*, 30th June 1990, pp. 838–841.
6. Stanley Hauerwas in Garrett Green (ed.), *Scriptural Authority and Narrative Interpretation,* Philadelphia, Fortress Press 1987, pp. 179–198.
7. Kenneth Leech (ed.), *Setting the Church of England Free,* Jubilee Group 2002; C. B. Moss, *Anglo-Catholicism at the Cross Roads,* Faith Press 1933, p. 3: state control of the church is 'an issue of life or death, not only for Anglo-Catholicism but for spiritual religion of every kind'.
8. Ellen Clark-King, *Theology by Heart: women, the church and God,* Epworth Press 2004, especially pp. 135, 157 and 186.
9. Robin Greenwood, 'Mission, community and the local church', *Crucible* (July-September 2001), pp. 155–167.
10. Alan Ecclestone, cited in Tim Gorringe, *Alan Ecclestone: priest as revolutionary,* Sheffield, Cairns Publications 1994, p. 103.
11. Robert Gallagher, *Staying in the City,* Cincinnati, Forward Movement 1981, p. 13.
12. Simon Jenkins, *Accountable to None: the Tory nationalisation of Britain*, Hamish Hamilton 1996.
13. See Liam Walsh's excellent articles 'How to ruin a voluntary organisation', *MDU Bulletin* 2 and 5 (1985), Management Development Unit of the National Council of

Voluntary Organisations, where such delaying tactics are seen as part of an overall strategy!

14. Fredrica Harris Thompsett, *We Are Theologians,* Boston, Cowley Press 1989, p. 2; and 'Authority begins at baptism', *The Witness* (March 2000), p. 15.

15. Andrew Henderson, *Staffing Review,* MS 1998, paras 1.6; 2.3; 3.1.4.

16. See Martin Thornton, *Pastoral Theology: a reorientation*, SPCK 1956, and *Essays in Pastoral Reconstruction*, SPCK 1960.

Chapter twelve

1. Belden C. Lane, *The Solace of Fierce Landscapes: exploring desert and mountain spirituality,* Oxford University Press 1998, pp. 4f and passim; Alan Ecclestone, *The Night Sky of the Lord*, Darton, Longman & Todd 1980, p. 39.

2. Linda Schierse Leonard, *Witness to the Fire: creativity and the veil of addiction,* Shaftesbury, Shambala 1989, p. 225.

3. Karol Wojtyla, *Faith According to St John of the Cross,* ET, San Francisco, Ignatius Press 1981, pp. 142–144.

4. Jan van Ruysbroeck, *The Adornment of the Spiritual Marriage* 2.

5. Nicola Slee, *Praying Like a Woman*, SPCK 2004, p. 42. See the whole of Chapter Four, 'Under the brooding breast: silence, darkness, unknowing', pp. 41–57.

6. Constance Fitzgerald, 'Impasse and the dark night' in Joann Wolski Conn (ed.), *Women's Spirituality: resources for Christian development,* Paulist Press 1986, pp. 287–288; Austin Smith CP, 'The church and powerlessness', *The Way* 23:3 (July 1983), pp. 207–208.

    On the dark night see Joann Wolski Conn, 'Psychological depression and spiritual darkness' in *Spirituality and Personal Maturity*, Paulist Press 1989, Chapter Six, pp. 128–167; Michael Fordham, 'The dark night of the soul' in *The Objective Psyche*, Routledge & Kegan Paul 1958, Chapter Nine, pp. 130–148; Linda Schierse Leonard, *Witness to the Fire: creativity and the veil of addiction,* Shaftesbury, Shambala 1989, Chapter 13, 'The dark night of the soul', pp. 227–242; Andrew Louth, *The Origins of the Christian Mystical Tradition*, Oxford, Clarendon Press 1981, 'Divine Darkness and Dark Night', pp. 181–190; Eileen Lyddon, *Door through Darkness: St John of the Cross and mysticism in everyday life,* New City 1994. On social and political dimensions see Daniel Berrigan, *The Dark Night of Resistance,* New York, Bantam Books 1972.

7. Herbert McCabe OP, cited by Columba Ryan OP, 'Homily at Herbert McCabe's funeral', *New Blackfriars* (July–August 2001), pp. 308–312. See, for example, Augustine, *De Trinitate* 15:50, Aquinas, *De Div Nominibus* 1:2; and Joseph Pieper, *The Silence of St Thomas,* Chicago, Henry Regnery Company 1965.

8. Rowan Williams, *The Wound of Knowledge*, Darton, Longman & Todd 1979, pp. 169, 180, and 'Theological integrity', *Cross Currents* 45:3 (Fall 1995), pp. 312–325 (320).

9. Jim Garrison, *The Darkness of God: theology after Hiroshima*, SCM Press 1982; Nicholas Lash in *The Tablet*, 26th February 2000, p. 272; Vladimir Lossky, *The Mystical Theology of the Eastern Church,* James Clarke 1957, p. 26, and Chapter Two, 'The Divine Darkness', pp. 23–43. See also his *In the Image and Likeness of God,* Mowbray 1975, Chapter One, 'Apophasis and Trinitarian Theology', pp. 13–29.

10. Hans Urs von Balthasar, *The Glory of the Lord,* Volume 3, San Francisco, Ignatius

Press 1986, p. 134. See also Denys Turner, *The Darkness of God: negativity in Christian mysticism,* Cambridge University Press 1995.

11. Sharon G. Thornton, *Broken Yet Beloved: a pastoral theology of the Cross,* St Louis MO, Chalice Press 2002, p. 10.

12. Margaret Spufford, *Celebration,* Fount 1989, p. 18.

13. See Morton Schatzman's obituary of Mary Barnes in the *Independent,* 11th July 2001; and R. D. Laing, *The Divided Self,* Penguin 1965, and *The Politics of Experience and the Bird of Paradise,* Penguin 1967. See also Kay Redfield Jamison, *Touched with Fire: manic-depressive illness and the artistic temperament,* New York, Free Press 1993, and 'Manic depressive illness and creativity', *Scientific American* (February 1995), pp. 46–51. On psychological 'emergency' as spiritual 'emergence' see Christina and Stanislav Grof, *The Stormy Search for the Self,* Mandala 1991, and Stanislav Grof, *Beyond the Brain: birth, death and transformation in psychotherapy,* State University of New York Press 1985.

14. Peter Rose, *Reflections on Sailing and Spirituality,* privately published 2005, p. 23.

15. J. J. Vincent, *Here I Stand; the faith of a radical,* Epworth Press 1983, p. 59; Mary C. Grey, *Prophecy and Mysticism: the heart of the postmodern church,* Edinburgh, T. & T. Clark 1997, Chapter Three, 'The "Dark Night of the Church" as liberation of community?' (pp. 43–60). See also Daniel Berrigan, *The Dark Night of Resistance,* New York, Bantam 1972. For earlier references to a corporate dark night see Eric Hayman, *Disciplines of the Spiritual Life,* SPCK 1957, pp. 54–59, and Gilbert Shaw, *Christian Prayer: a way of progress,* Oxford, SLG Press 1970, p. 20. Shaw died in 1967 and, in one of his papers, he referred to 'the night that has come upon the Church', seeing it as having a purifying purpose. Richard Buck spoke of a collective dark night of the Church' at a conference of spiritual directors at Glenmazaran, Scotland 15th–18th July 1974.

16. John McCausland in *Anglican Theological Review* 76:1 (Winter 1994), p. 7; Donald B. Cozzens, 'Priesthood emerges from a dark night', *America,* 20th March 1999, p. 24. On the theme of a new 'Dark Age' see L. S. Stavrianos, *The Promise of the Coming Dark Age,* San Francisco, W. H. Freeman & Co 1976.

17. See Denise Levertov, 'On the edge of darkness: what is political poetry?', *Light Up the Cave,* New York, New Directions 1981 edn, pp. 115–129.

Chapter thirteen

1. Gresham Kirkby, 'Kingdom come: the Catholic faith and millennial hopes' in Kenneth Leech and Rowan Williams (eds), *Essays Catholic and Radical,* Bowerdean Press 1983, pp. 52–69. The article is also available on the website www.anglocatholic socialism.org. Father Kirkby died on 10th August 2006, a few hours before his 90th birthday. See my obituaries of him in the *Church Times,* 18th August 2006 and the *Guardian,* 22nd August 2006.

2. P. E. T. Widdrington, 'The return of the Kingdom of God' in *The Return of Christendom,* Allen & Unwin 1922, p. 102. Walter Rauschenbusch, a key figure in the early American 'social gospel' movement, saw the Kingdom of God as 'the first and most essential dogma of the Christian faith', the unifying principle of the gospel. However, he does seem to have shared something in common with Christendom ideas, referring to 'the lost social ideal of Christendom'. See Walter Rauschenbusch,

Christianising the Social Order, New York, 1919 edn, p. 49.

For other uses of the idea of a 'new reformation', Philip Jenkins sees the current changes in the Church as being as 'epochal' as the first Reformation ('The next Christianity', *Atlantic Monthly* (October 2002), pp. 53–68).

3. Diairmuid O'Murchu, *Reclaiming Spirituality*, New York, Crossroads 1999, especially Chapter Ten, 'Spirituality and the Kingdom of God' (pp. 157–169); Peter Selby, *Jesus and Salvation Today*, SPCK 1997; Andrew Shanks, '*What Is Truth?*' *Towards a theological poetics,* Routledge 2001; Sharon D. Welch, A *Feminist Ethic of Risk,* Minneapolis, Fortress Press 1990, pp. 160–161.

4. Norman Perrin, *Jesus and the Language of the Kingdom,* SCM Press 1976, pp. 5–6.

5. James D. G. Dunn et al., *The Kingdom of God in North-East England,* SCM Press 1986, p. 16.

6. Stanley G. Evans in *Religion and the People*, January 1957.

7. W. Pannenberg, *Theology and the Kingdom of God*, Philadelphia, Westminster Press 1977, p. 51; Charles L. Kammer, *The Kingdom Revisited,* University Press of America 1981, p. 48; Marcus Borg, 'Jesus and the Kingdom of God', *Christian Century*, 22nd April 1987, pp. 378–380.

8. R. M. Hiers, 'Eschatology and methodology', *Journal of Biblical Literature* 85 (1966), p. 183.

9. Stanley J. Grenz, *Revisioning Evangelical Theology*, Downers Grove, Intervarsity Press 1993, p. 180; G. E. Ladd, *The Gospel of the Kingdom*, Paternoster 1977; *Jesus and the Kingdom*, SPCK 1966; *Crucial Questions About the Kingdom of God*, Eerdmans 1977; and *The Presence of the Future*, SPCK 1980.

10. John A. T. Robinson, 'Kingdom, church and ministry' in K. M. Carey (ed.), *The Historic Episcopate*, Dacre 1954, pp. 11–22. Leonardo Boff makes a similar comment in his *Church, Charism and Power*, SCM Press 1985, p. 2.

11. Norman Perrin, *Jesus and the Language of the Kingdom*, SCM Press 1976, p. 5. For other material on the Kingdom of God see Bruce Chilton, *The Kingdom of God in the Teaching of Jesus*, SPCK 1984 and *Pure Kingdom: Jesus' vision of God*, SPCK 1996; Bruce Chilton and J. I. H. McDonald, *Jesus and the Ethics of the Kingdom*, Grand Rapids, Eerdmans; Norman Perrin, *The Kingdom of God in the Teaching of Jesus*, SCM Press 1963.

12. A. E. Harvey, *Jesus and the Constraints of History*, Duckworth 1982, p. 86.

13. J. P. Meier, *A Marginal Jew: rethinking the historical Jesus,* New York, Doubleday 1994, Vol. 2, p. 10.

14. Tom Cullinan OSB, *The Passion of Political Love*, Sheed & Ward 1987, pp. 123–124; *Human Rights in the Catholic Church,* 10th December 1998, p. 2. Recent research has shown that Pope John Paul was using the phrase 'building God's Kingdom' as early as the 1950s, long before he became Pope. See Jonathan Luxmoore and Jolanta Babiuch, 'John Paul's debt to Marxism', *The Tablet*, 14th December 2006, pp. 4–5.

15. *Didache* 9:4, 10:5.

16. Augustine, *City of God,* trans. Marcus Dods, New York, Modern Library 1950, pp. 725–726; R. C. Moberly, *Ministerial Priesthood*, SPCK [1869] 1969 edn, p. 40. The identification of the Kingdom of God with the Church occasionally appeared among Christian socialists. Thus Lewis Donaldson, a key figure in the Church Socialist League, said, in a sermon of 1916, that the Church was 'the Kingdom of God on earth'.

See Barbara J. Butler, *Frederic Lewis Donaldson and the Christian socialist movement*, MPhil dissertation, Leeds University 1970, p. 72.

17. Stanley Hauerwas, *The Peaceable Kingdom*, University of Notre Dame Press 1983, p. 97; Karl Rahner cited by J. B. Medz in *New Theology* 5, New York, Macmillan 1968, p. 137; *For the Sake of the Kingdom: God's Church and the new creation,* Report of the Inter-Anglican Theological and Doctrinal Commission, Cincinnati, Forward Movement Publications 1986.

18. Albert F. Gedraitis, *Worship and Politics,* Toronto, Wedge Publishing Foundation 1972, p. 21.

19. Jim Wallis, *The Call to Conversion*, Tring, Lion Publishing 1982; Steve Latham, '69 theses on the doctrine of urban regeneration', *Crucible* (July–September 2004), pp. 37–48. Walter Brueggemann sees the Kingdom as 'the core metaphor for a new social imagination'. See Walter Brueggemann, *Hope within History,* Atlanta, John Knox Press 1987, p. 22.

20. R. H. Preston, *Religion and the Persistence of Capitalism*, SCM Press 1980, p. 46; and *Religion and the Ambiguities of Capitalism*, SCM Press 1991, p. 41. See also Denys L. Munby, *God and the Rich Society*, Oxford University Press 1961, p. 2. Both Preston and Munby were economists. By contrast, the biblical scholar John Howard Yoder insisted that the Kingdom *is* a social order (*The Politics of Jesus*, Eerdmans 1975, p. 108).

21. Walter Brueggemann, *Hope within History*, Atlanta, John Knox Press 1987, p. 22; Stanley M. Hauerwas and William H. Willimon, 'Your Kingdom come', *Sojourners* (May–June 1996), pp. 30–31.

22. For example, see John Gladwin, 'The Kingdom of God and human society' in H. W. Montefiore et al., *Theology and Social Concern*, Board for Social Responsibility 1986, pp. 6–8. Gladwin argues that the doctrine of the Kingdom has 'profound social implications'.

Chapter fourteen

1. I place 'City' in inverted commas to indicate the absurdity of speaking of one small, largely non-residential, part of London as 'the city', when most countries would use the word to describe the whole area.

2. Office of Population Censuses and Surveys, *Census of Population.* I have also drawn on work done by the Department of Geography at the University of Aberystwyth, some of which appeared in C. Philo (ed.), *Off the Map: the social geography of poverty in the UK,* Child Poverty Action Group 1995.

3. Karen Stallard, 'Releasing the radical back into the church: inner city church planting and Anabaptism', *Anabaptism Today* 35 (February 2004), pp. 2–6. For further on the Anabaptist revival see Noel Moules, 'Anabaptism tomorrow', *Anabaptism Today* 6 (June 1994), pp. 2–6.

4. Charles Landry et al., *What A Way to Run a Railroad: an analysis of radical failure*, Comedia Publishing Group 1985, p. 65. See also S. Eisenstadt, 'Charisma and institution building: Max Weber and modern sociology' in S. Eisenstadt (ed.), *Max Weber on Charisma and Institution Building*, University of Chicago Press 1968, pp. ix–lvi.

5. John Atherton, *Marginalisation*, SCM Press 2003, p. xii.

6. Fredrica Harris Thompsett, 'Authority begins at baptism', *The Witness* (March 2000), p. 15. Thompsett urges the abandonment of the word 'lay'.

7. For the use of 'lay theologian' see Rowan Williams in *Church Times*, 26th August 2005, and John Habgood in Douglas Dales et al., *Glory Descending: Michael Ramsey and his writings*, Norwich, Canterbury Press 2005, p. 140. John Atherton refers to R. H. Tawney as a 'lay theologian' in his contribution to Elaine Graham and Anna Rowlands (eds), *Pathways to the Public Square: practical theology in an age of pluralism*, Münster, Lit Verlag 2005, p. 68. For 'lay theology' see John B. Cobb, *Lay Theology*, St Louis, Chalice Press 1994, and Robert Brizee, 'Lay theology: an idea whose hour has come', *Creative Transformation* 10:2 (Winter 2001), pp. 5–8.

8. Gordon Kuhrt, *An Introduction to Christian Ministry: following your vocation in the Church of England*, Church House Publishing 2000, p. 79.

9. Thomas K. Ray, 'The small church, radical reformation and renewal of ministry', *Anglican Theological Review* 78:4 (Fall 1996), pp. 615–627. Also on Northern Michigan see Marianne Arbogast, 'Liberating the baptised: shared ministry in Northern Michigan', *The Witness* (August–September 1994), pp. 8–10.

10. Stanley Hauerwas, *The Peaceable Kingdom*, University of Notre Dame Press 1983, p. 85.

11. Daniel Jenkins in Charles Elliot et al., *Christian Faith and Political Hopes*, Epworth Press 1979, p. 72.

Appendices

Appendix 1
The Community Theology Project: members of the support, management and advisory groups

Support group

Kinsi Abdulleh, Somali artist

Dr Sadia Ahmed, Somali anthropologist

Tassaduq Ahmed MBE, pioneer of Bangladeshi independence, and former owner of The Ganges Restaurant in Soho (died in 2001)

Councillor Bodrul Alom, local councillor and activist on health and related issues

Terry Drummond, at the time urban missioner, Croydon Episcopal Area

Andria Efthimiou-Mordaunt, activist in the drug users' movement

Professor W. J. (Bill) Fishman, Jewish historian and anarchist

Jackie Gooding, teacher at Tower Hamlets College and active urban evangelical

Savi Hensman, worker in the voluntary sector, a founder of the Black Lesbian and Gay Centre, and activist in the Jubilee Group

The Revd Dr Jenny King, priest-dentist, lecturer in the Department of Medical Ethics, London Hospital Medical College

The Revd Dr David Nicholls, representing the Christendom Trust (died in 1996)

Bill Risebero, architect and university lecturer in urban regeneration issues

Petra Salva, at the time outreach worker with homeless people at St Botolph's Project

The Revd Ron Swan, Master of the Royal Foundation of St Katharine

The Revd William Taylor, at the time Chaplain of the London Metropolitan University

The Revd John Webber, at the time inter-faith advisor, Stepney Episcopal Area

Management committee

John Downie, at the time Director of St Botolph's Project

Terry Drummond (see above)

The Revd Malcolm Johnson (1990–93) and the Revd Brian Lee (1993–2004), Rectors of St Botolph's Church

Tim Mills, Lecturer in Law, London Metropolitan University, and member of St Botolph's congregation

Marybel Moore, member of St Botolph's congregation
Sarah Mussington, member of St Botolph's congregation (died in 1998)

Advisory panel

[This group, by design and intention, never met, but consisted of people whom I would consult, often by telephone.]

Janet Batsleer, Senior Lecturer in Youth and Community Work, Manchester Metropolitan University
Harriet Crabtree, Assistant Director, Inter-Faith Network
Elizabeth Frazer, Fellow and Tutor in Politics, New College, Oxford
Elaine Graham, Professor of Social and Pastoral Theology, University of Manchester
Sara Maitland, writer and feminist activist
John Milbank, at the time Professor of Philosophical Theology, University of Virginia
Robert Moore, at the time Eleanor Rathbone Professor of Sociology, University of Liverpool
Christopher Rowland, Dean Ireland Professor of Exegesis of Holy Scripture, Oxford University
Hilary Russell, Research Fellow, Centre for European Urban Studies, Liverpool John Moores University, and Director, Merseyside Churches Urban Institute
Robert Schreiter CPPS, Professor of Dogmatic Theology, Catholic Theological Union, Chicago
Susan J. Smith, at the time Professor of Geography, University of Edinburgh
David Tracy, Professor of Theology, University of Chicago
Angela West, writer and long-term activist in the peace movement
Rowan Williams, now Archbishop of Canterbury

Appendix 2
Deaths during the period of the project

I have listed below some of the deaths of people closely associated with the work, or, more generally, with the life of the East End. I have said more about some of them in earlier pages, but I owe a debt to every one of them. They are all people who mattered and matter to me, and from whom I learned much. But they are also important figures in the history of the second half of the twentieth century whose final years roughly coincided with the period of my project.

Ruth Glass died on 7th March 1990. She was the pioneer of urban sociology in Britain, founder and director of the Centre for Urban Studies, University College, London. References to Ruth's work in urban sociology, housing and related issues are scattered throughout most of my books.

On 3rd May 1991 **Donald Chesworth's** funeral took place at St Botolph's. He had been an LCC (London County Council) councillor for North Kensington in the late 1950s when Perec Rachman was active as a landlord. Chesworth played an important role in exposing

Rachman and in work for equality in housing. More recently he had been Warden of Toynbee Hall, the university settlement close to St Botolph's, where he built up much of its work with the Bengali community.

On 17th September 1991 I heard the news of the death of **Canon Edward Charles**. Edward was a key figure in the Christian Left from the 1930s to the 1960s, and continued to write and speak in his retirement after 1976. Most of his ministry was in Hertfordshire. He had joined the Labour Party in 1937, and was Vice President of the British Soviet Friendship Society. I preached at his funeral in St Albans Abbey. He was one of the kindest people I ever met. Once, when he phoned me in Bethnal Green, and was told that I was ill, he immediately asked whether it would help if he travelled from Hitchin to take the services!

The death of **David Widgery**, a local doctor and political activist, on 26th October 1992, was a tragedy. He had died from asphyxiation, and evidence was found that he had taken alcohol, barbiturates and pethidine. David had written a good deal on health-care issues, not least in the East End, and had been a leading campaigner for improved conditions in hospitals.

Ian Mikardo died on 6th May 1993. He was MP for Bethnal Green for many years, and a close colleague in anti-racist work. 'Mik', as he was always known, belonged to the tradition of 'Old Labour' at its best. We could do with him now.

Fr Kenneth Loveless died on 19th March 1995. He had been my first vicar in Hoxton (1964–67). He was Squire of the Morris Ring of England, a folk singer, and the world authority on the anglo-concertina, as well as a devoted parish priest. In many ways a 'simple soul', he was intensely emotional, utterly dedicated to people, one of the last of the ritualist East London parish priests.

Kathleen Wrsama died on 9th February 1996. She was my next-door neighbour in Cable Street (1958–62), of Ethiopian origin, married to a Somali. A key figure in East London, she spoke with a Yorkshire accent. She pioneered anti-racist work in the 1950s, founded the Stepney Coloured People's Association in the late 1950s, and, for many years, never locked her front door as a sign of hospitality and welcome. I remember her as a symbol of patience, rationality and conviction through the worst years of the violence and exploitation of women in Cable Street.

Sarah Mussington died on 23rd February 1998. Sarah arrived in the East End from the West Indies in 1958 as I arrived from Manchester. We were planning a joint 40th anniversary celebration when she died. She was gentle, perceptive and wise, prayerful and utterly reliable. For her funeral she requested that, on this occasion, all women should wear hats.

David Nicholls died in June 1996: priest, political theorist, expert on Haiti and the Caribbean. He represented the Christendom Trust on my support group. He was one of the most astute, yet often neglected, theological and political thinkers in the Church of England. David's sudden death was a terrible shock to many people. I have said more about his work and thought in Chapter 5 and elsewhere.

David Randall died on 13th August 1996. He was a priest who had developed much youth and community work from St Botolph's, and generally in the East End, before moving to Notting Dale where he pioneered ministry to people with HIV and AIDS. I have written about David in earlier books.

Valerie Pitt, who died on 4th January 1999, was a socialist academic, a leading campaigner for the disestablishment of the Church of England, and an entertaining and formidable writer. She was a frequent contributor to Jubilee Group papers and meetings.

Daphne Jones died on 11th June 1999 while making a pot of tea: a nurse, midwife and parish worker in Poplar and Stepney from 1942 until her death, she, with Nora Neal and Fr Joe Williamson, built up a major work with prostitutes in the old 'red-light' district in Cable Street.

Marie Lewis died on 3rd September 1999: community-relations worker in East London, and a key figure in building resource and advice centres for asylum seekers. Marie was a real pioneer, quiet, firm and dedicated.

Peter Rose died on 30th May 2001. Peter was a former student of mine. He exercised a remarkable ministry of personal care and direction, often in the midst of his own severe depression. He also exercised a dedicated and relentless ministry of personal correspondence, some of it with prisoners on 'death row' in the USA. His correspondence with, and personal spiritual guidance of, David Spence, is documented in a remarkable pamphlet *And Yet Not All Is Darkness*, published by the Corrymeela Community. David was put to death in Easter Week 1997, and Peter had ministered to him in Huntsville Prison, Texas, during Holy Week. He wrote, with his usual, profound, yet almost Bede-like abruptness: 'Last Thursday, April 3, at about 6pm local time, the State of Texas killed our friend.' I learned so much from Peter about personal ministry, about doubt and depression, and about the need for consistency and constancy. I have referred to him in Chapters 4 and 12.

I had just returned from Peter's funeral when I heard of the death of **Caroline Adams**. Caroline was a close colleague and was the first youth worker in Britain to work mainly with Bangladeshi young people. She had been working in Calcutta at the time of the war of independence, and, returning to Britain, trained many young people for youth and community work in the East End. She was a close colleague for many years.

Dorothy Howell-Thomas died on 12th July 2001 while I was at a conference in Norwich to celebrate the fiftieth anniversary of the Malvern Conference of 1941 in which she was closely involved. Dorothy united in herself different periods of history – the 1930s and the struggle against fascism and unemployment, the 1960s, and her 'retirement' from the 1970s until a few weeks before her death. She was William Temple's private secretary and, in 1941, typed his book *Christianity and Social Order*. (She always corrected people who referred to it as 'Christianity and *the* Social Order'.) In her retirement, she wrote a book called *Socialism in West Sussex* (1983) – worth buying just for the title. (It was in fact a history of Chichester Labour Party.)

David Brandon died on 26th November 2001. He was the only academic, to my knowledge, who was involved with the study of, and response to, homelessness for forty years. There are references to David throughout the book.

A leading Bengali intellectual, **Tassaduq Ahmed** died towards the end of 2001, after a stroke in 1998. He had not spoken any words in English, though a few in Bengali, since then.

Betty Care, who died on 5th September 2002, had been a Salvation Army officer, and, in retirement, lived in Brick Lane and worshipped at St Botolph's. She often said that Anglicanism ministered to her head and Salvationism to her heart.

Doris Boyd, the longest-serving volunteer at St Botolph's Project, died on 10th March 2003, after many years of service with homeless people.

Alan Shadwick, former deputy editor of the *Church Times* and a regular member of St Botolph's congregation, died on 14th April 2003. He had lived in the East End since the 1950s.

Appendix 3
Bibliography on the Urban Church, Urban Society, Urban Theology and East London

Books

Paul Ballard and John Pritchard, *Practical Theology in Action,* SPCK 1996

Mary Beasley, *Mission on the Margins,* Lutterworth Press 1997

Eric Blakebrough (ed.), *Church for the City*, Darton, Longman & Todd 1995

Murray Bookchin, *Urbanisation without Cities*, Montreal, Black Rose Books 1992

Ellen Clark-King, *Theology by Heart: women, the Church and God,* Epworth Press 2004

Darrel Crilley et al., *New Migrants in London's Docklands*, Dept of Geography, Queen Mary Westfield College, 1991

Andrew Davey, *Urban Christianity and Global Order*, SPCK 2001, and Peabody MA, Hendrickson 2001

Geoff Dench, Kate Gavron and Michael Young, *The New East Enders*, Profile 2006

Ian K. Duffield (ed.), *Urban Christ: responses to John Vincent*, Sheffield, Urban Theology Unit 1997

Michael Eastman and Steve Latham (ed.), *Urban Church: a practitioner's resource book,* SPCK 2004

Stanley G. Evans, *The Church in the Back Streets,* Mowbray 1962

Nuruddin Farah, *Yesterday, Tomorrow: voices from the Somali diaspora,* Cassell 2000

Michael Fielding, *Homelessness and the Church: a personal view of church action in London and New York*, Lambeth Mission 1992

William J. Fishman, *East End 1888*, Duckworth 1988

Marjorie Frisbie, *An Alley in Chicago*, Kansas City, Sheed & Ward 1991.

Herbert J. Gans, *People, Plans and Policies*, New York, Columbia UP 1993

Katy Gardner, *Global Migrants, Local Lives,* Oxford, Clarendon Press 1995

Jeremy Gavron, *An Acre of Barren Ground: or the history of everyone who ever lived in Brick Lane*, Scribners 2005

Ruth Glass, *Clichés of Urban Doom,* Oxford UK and Cambridge MA, Blackwell 1989

Ed Glinert, *East End Chronicles,* Allen Lane 2005

Tim Gorringe, *Alan Ecclestone, Priest as Revolutionary*, Sheffield, Cairns Publications 1994

Laurie Green, *Let's Do Theology*, Mowbray 1990

John W. de Gruchy and Charles Villa Vicencio (ed.), *Doing Theology in Context: South African perspectives*, Maryknoll, Orbis 1994

Tarquin Hall, *Salaam Brick Lane*, John Murray 2005

Nicholas Holtam and Sue Mayo, *Learning from the Conflict: reflections on the struggle against the BNP on the Isle of Dogs* 1993–4, Jubilee Group 1994

Patrick Hutt et al., *Confronting an Ill Society: David Widgery, general practice, idealism and the case for change*, Radcliffe 2005

Kenneth Leech, *Brick Lane* 1978: *the events and their significance*, Stepney Books 1993

Kenneth Leech, *Care and Conflict: leaves from a pastoral notebook*, Darton, Longman & Todd 1990

Kenneth Leech, *The Eye of the Storm*, Darton, Longman & Todd 1993; USA edn, HarperSanFrancisco 1993

Kenneth Leech, *The Sky Is Red: discerning the signs of the times*, Darton, Longman & Todd 1997

Kenneth Leech, *Subversive Orthodoxy*, Toronto, Anglican Book Centre 1992

Kenneth Leech, *Through Our Long Exile: contextual theology and the urban experience*, Darton, Longman & Todd 2001

Robert C. Linthicum, *City of God, City of Satan*, Zondervan 1992

Pat Logan, *A Life to Be Lived: homelessness and pastoral care*, Darton, Longman & Todd 1989

Eleanor Scott Meyers (ed.), *Envisioning the New City*, Louisville, Westminster/John Knox Press 1992

Michael Northcott (ed.), *Urban Theology: a reader*, Cassell 1998

Chris Phillipson et al., *Women in Transition: a study of the experiences of Bangladeshi women living in Tower Hamlets*, Bristol, Policy Press 2003

John Reader, *Local Theology*, SPCK 1994

Chris Rowland and John Vincent (ed.), *Gospel from the City*, Sheffield, Urban Theology Unit 1997

Hilary Russell, *Poverty Close to Home*, Mowbray 1995

Sukhdev Sandhu, *London Calling: how black and Asian writers imagined a city*, HarperCollins 2003

Robert J. Schreiter, *Constructing Local Theologies*, Orbis 1993

Peter Sedgwick (ed.), *God in the City*, Mowbray 1995

Staying in the City, Church House Publishing 1995

John Wilkinson, *Church in Black and White*, Edinburgh, St Andrew Press 1993

Gibson Winter, *The Suburban Captivity of the Churches*, Garden City, Doubleday 1961

Articles

Tim Brindley, 'Community roles in urban regeneration: new partnerships on London's South Bank', *City* 4:3 (November 2000), pp. 363–376

Andy Delmege, 'Putting down roots', *Movement* (Summer 1992) [on working at St Botolph's]

Michael Fielding (1992), *Homelessness and the Church: a personal view of church action in London and New York*, Lambeth Mission

Liz Ellis, 'Communities of interest, sites of significance', *Feminist Arts News* 3:9 (1991)

Katy Gardner, 'Identity, age and masculinity among Bengali elders in East London' in Anne Kershen (ed.), *A Question of Identity*, Aldershot, Avebury 1997, pp. 160−178

Derek Grasby, 'Thinking theologically', *Epworth Review* 20:1 (January 1993), pp. 9−16

T. Groome, 'Theology at our feet: revisionist pedagogy for healing the gap between academia and ecclesia' in L. Mudge and J. Poling (eds), *Formation and Reflection*, Philadelphia, Fortress Press 1987, pp. 55−78

Kenneth Leech, 'From East End to City Fringe: reflections on doing theology under and against late capitalism', *Crucible* (July−September 2004), pp. 31−36

Kenneth Leech, 'The decay of Spitalfields', *East London Papers* 7 (1964), pp. 57−62

Kenneth Leech, 'The East London drug traffic', *Social Work* 24 (1966), pp. 23−27

Kenneth Leech, 'The history of a trouble zone' [on Brick Lane], *New Society*, 21, 18 December 1978, pp. 687−690

Kenneth Leech, 'Housing and immigration: crisis in London', *Race* 8 (1967), pp. 329−343

Kenneth Leech, 'Human casualties in a crisis district', *East London Papers* 11 (1968), pp. 3−19

Kenneth Leech, 'Regeneration und Versohnung: Reflektionem aus Ost-London' in Engelbert Kerkhof et al., *CityKirchenArbeit: Grundlagen, Modelle und Impulse zur sozialen und kirchlichen Arbeit*, Munchengladbach, Hochschule Niederrhein, Fachbereich Socialwesen 2004, pp. 111−121

Kenneth Leech, 'The role of immigration in recent East London history', *East London Papers* 10 (1967), pp. 3−18

J. E. Thomas, 'The inheritance and the future of learning in the East End of London', *Rising East* 4:2 (2001), pp. 70−79

Unpublished Material

Lindsey Ellin, Placement Report, MS privately circulated, 1992

James Francis, Social Policy and Purpose, MS privately circulated, 1992

Katy Gardner, Migrants to Citizens: changing orientations among Bangladeshis in Tower Hamlets, University of London PhD 1997

Martin Jarrett-Kerr CR, History of Twenty Years of the Christendom Trust, MS 1990

Studies arising from the work in London

Valerie Dawn Davis, *Moral and Ascetical Components in the Ascetical Theologies of F. P. Harton and Kenneth Leech,* MA thesis, General Theological Seminary, New York, April 1982

Joe Driskill, *The Psychological and Theological Anthropologies of Seward Hiltner and Kenneth Leech: towards a synthesis suitable for pastoral counselling and spiritual direction*, PhD thesis, Graduate Theological Union, Berkeley CA, 1996

Derek Grasby, *A reflection on the Christian Social Tradition as Focused in the Ministries of Henry Scott Holland and Kenneth Leech,* MPhil thesis, University of Manchester 1997

Nia Wyn Jones, *Holiness and Humanness: a dialogue in liberation spirituality. A study of contemporary spirituality with special reference to the writings of Kenneth Leech,* MA thesis, Anglia Polytechnic University, November 1999

Philip Seadon, *Critically appraise the contribution to contemporary perspectives on pastoral theology by Kenneth Leech,* long essay, Dept of Pastoral Studies, University of Birmingham May 1999

Andrew Taylor, *The Social Dimensions of Christian Spirituality in the Thought of Kenneth Leech,* MA thesis, McGill University 1985

Index

In this index, the names of individuals have only been included if there has been some extended reference to them in the text.